CONFESSIONS OF A
FAKE SHEIK

CONFESSIONS OF A FAKE SHEIK

"THE KING OF THE STING REVEALS ALL"

MAZHER MAHMOOD

HarperCollins*Publishers*

HarperCollins*Publishers*
77–85 Fulham Palace Road,
Hammersmith, London W6 8JB

www.harpercollins.co.uk

First published by HarperCollins*Publishers* in 2008

2

A catalogue record for this book
is available from the British Library

ISBN 13 978-0-00-728809-0 (hardback)
ISBN 10 0-00-728809-3 (hardback)
ISBN 13 978-0-00-728810-6 (paperback)
ISBN 10 0-00-728810-7 (paperback)

Printed and bound in Great Britain by
Clays Ltd, St Ives plc

Mixed Sources
Product group from well-managed
forests and other controlled sources
www.fsc.org Cert no. SW-COC-1806
© 1996 Forest Stewardship Council

FSC is a non-profit international organisation established to promote the
responsible management of the world's forests. Products carrying the FSC
label are independently certified to assure consumers that they come
from forests that are managed to meet the social, economic and
ecological needs of present and future generations.

Find out more about HarperCollins and the environment at
www.harpercollins.co.uk/green

CONTENTS

To my dad Sultan and mum Shamim who led me
by the hand down the road of journalism.

And to my son Danyal who brings innocence,
immense laughter and a sense of reality
to my extraordinary life.

With my love and apologies.

ACKNOWLEDGEMENTS

 As an Asian kid from Birmingham, to make it in Fleet Street was nothing but a dream. I would like to thank the people who helped make my dream a reality; my mentors Laurie Manifold (formerly of the *Sunday People*), Robin Morgan (of the *Sunday Times*), and Bob Warren (of the *News of the World*) who all gave me a break and helped mould my career.

During the last 17 years at the *News of the World* I have had the honour of working with some of the most talented reporters and photographers in the world, who think nothing of putting their lives at risk to bring villains to book. My own life has often been in the safe hands of my team including, Alex D'Souza, Mahmood 'Jaws' Qureshi, Alan Smith, Naresh 'Harry' Kumar, and Conrad Brown, who I have dragged into drug dens, bondage parties, and near-death experiences with the Albanian mafia and the Taliban.

I would also like to thank *News of the World* editor Colin Myler, who I first met on the *Sunday People* when I was an 18-year-old aspiring reporter, for his continued guidance and support. Also Stuart Kuttner, our managing editor, for his constant backing over the years, and Tom Crone, News International's legal manager with whom I have shared endless trials and tribulations – literally!

Investigative journalism is all about teamwork, and everyone from reference library staff, sub-editors, and the art desk plays a vital role in getting stories into the paper and I thank them all. Top of the long list of unsung heroes are the editor's PA Belinda Sharrier, newsdesk assistant Frances Carman, contributions co-ordinator James Morgan, the

Managing Editor's PA, Bev Stokes, and very importantly all the staff at BCD Travel.

Then there are the friends who over the years have not only stood by me but have regularly volunteered to assist on stories too. I thank Robert Cole, senior producer at Sky TV, solicitor Dr Akbar Ali Malik, and Aseem Kazi.

As for my family they have endured a great deal of stress, hostility, and even violence because of my work. I couldn't have wished for more supportive parents who have been a rock for me. My father's last words before he died, proudly uttered to a nurse were: 'Please call my son, Mazher Mahmood, you must have heard of him. He does all the big exposés for the *News of the World*. I'm his father!'

For helping make this book come to life I must thank Mr Rupert Murdoch's PA, Karen Colognese, and at HarperCollins, CEO Victoria Barnsley, publishing director Jonathan Taylor, and the book doctor Humphrey Price for expertly piecing together my acres of text.

CHAPTER 1
READY TO
SHEIK THE
WORLD

At the back of an Islamic bookshop in Coventry Road, Birmingham, I flicked through the Arab robes hanging on a small clothing rail, crammed between Arabic books and a pile of prayer mats.

'Them come with the headscarf and rings them do. It's all included for £9.99 and they're all one size bruvver,' said the Asian shopkeeper. The heavy Brummie accent jarred with the long black beard, lace prayer cap and traditional Pakistani outfit – it made him appear almost comical. 'I can do you some beads as well if you want. Twelve quid for the lot!'

It was a good deal. I bought the outfit and ran to the car, where my colleague Roger Insall was parked outside. We were both freelance journalists working for the *Sunday People* and had been despatched by our boss, Laurie Manifold, to expose a vice ring operating at the Metropole hotel next to the National Exhibition Centre. The NEC was playing host to the annual Motor Show, and a story about hookers amid the flash cars would make a traditional saucy exposé for the paper. Laurie had received a tip that the elderly doorman at the hotel, like most concierges around the world, would readily lay on girls for VIP guests.

Roger thought that a good cover story for our sting would be for me to pose as a wealthy young Arab seeking to buy a Ferrari at the Motor Show, with him as my minder. It was 1984, and rivers of crude oil gushing from the Middle East had turned desert dwellers into some of the world's wealthiest men. The Arab *nouveau riche* were buying up properties in Mayfair and Park Lane as if they were playing Monopoly. The very word 'Arab' became synonymous with wealth, as they cruised around in flash cars and flaunted their riches in casinos, hotels, and on high-class call girls.

But as a 21-year-old with a Brummie accent myself, I'd be rumbled in seconds as a second-generation Pakistani lad from the backstreets of Birmingham. The only way I could pose as a young Arab would be if I donned robes and spoke with a broken English accent. Later that day, I strolled into the Metropole twirling my worry beads, feeling very self-conscious, with Roger walking behind me carrying my bags. But the robes created an amazing impression on hotel staff and other guests, as I was virtually transformed into royalty. The hotel manager personally checked me in, bypassing the queue of guests waiting at reception. A bellboy and deputy head porter Eric Fisher rushed to escort the young Sheik to his room at the plush hotel.

Eric was keen to please the Sheik; he ushered a succession of high-class hookers to my suite, helping Roger and myself to smash the vice ring operating at the hotel. Complete with glamorous photos of the 'sporty attractions' on offer at the Motor Show and details of the 'optional extras' available to visitors, it made a great tabloid read. The Fake Sheik had claimed his first scalp. As I threw the Arab outfit into a drawer at home, I couldn't have imagined that the cheap cotton robes would become the most famous disguise in the history of invest-igative journalism.

Back at the office Laurie Manifold, a bearded man with half-moon glasses and a pipe clamped permanently to his mouth, looked up over his old typewriter and told me: 'That Arab caper you and Roger pulled was fantastic. You can claim for the outfit on expenses, and hang onto it. It'll come in useful again.' They were prophetic words.

The Arab caper had been good but my biggest blag had been gate-crashing into Fleet Street in the first place. I came into journalism at a time when reporters had to undergo apprenticeships on local papers, gain Union membership, sit tough National Council for the Training of Journalists (NCTJ) exams, then struggle for years before getting a whiff of work on a national newspaper. I was turned down two years in a row at the end of the Seventies for unpaid work experience at the

Birmingham *Evening Mail*. It was hugely disappointing and I felt that my ethnicity was working against me. But rejection was the best thing that could have happened to me.

Just a few months later I was writing stories for the *Daily Mail*, *Sunday People*, *Daily Star*, *News of the World*, and the *Sunday Times*. There are few things more important to news editors than THE STORY, a simple fact that paved my way to Fleet Street. As a 17-year-old desperate to forge a career in journalism, I rang the *News of the World* news desk offering an exclusive about a gang involved in manufacturing pirate videos of the latest film releases. The year was 1980, when VHS videos had recently arrived on the scene – and inside information on how films were being stolen from cinemas, copied onto VHS and then circulated up and down the country, would make a good investigation. Ray Chapman, a veteran investigative reporter, discussed details of the story and then immediately invited me to travel from Birmingham to London at the paper's expense. He even laid on a hotel room at the Royal Scot Hotel in King's Cross.

Neither Chapman nor news editor Robert Warren seemed to care that I had just finished my O-levels and had absolutely no experience; all that mattered was getting the story to work. I spent an adventurous week working alongside Chapman, visiting video shops in Soho, wired up with a covert recording device. Being an Asian kid, none of the dealers batted an eyelid as they reached under the counter to hand me the illegal tapes. After all, I could hardly be a policeman – or a reporter.

The exciting week in London marked the start of my long and eventful relationship with Fleet Street. It also gave me my first insight into the downside of investigative journalism. One of the men I had exposed was a family friend, the son of a respected GP. I had got the inside information about the video piracy ring over dinner at our home. The man had been bragging about bribing projectionists at the local cinema to copy the reels of film onto VHS. My father was furious, and threatened to throw me out of the house, as my mother struggled to calm him down. I was surprised by my father's reaction;

as a journalist himself, one who'd pioneered the first Urdu-language newspaper in Britain, he had always wanted his two sons to follow him into journalism. While other Asian kids were choosing traditional careers as doctors and engineers, my father pushed us towards a career in the media.

But he claimed my work at the *News of the World* had 'blackened the family name', 'shamed the community' and that I would be seen as a 'traitor'. He was right. Later in life I would face endless *fatwas*, death threats, and even a curse from an African witch. But the backlash only served to fuel my rebellious streak and strengthened my resolve to expose villains.

My career was catapulted by the Handsworth riots, full-blown violent protests night after night where cars and shops were burned down. With hardly any Asian reporters working in Fleet Street, I was headhunted by news editors who knew that I could speak to rioters in their own language and provide a unique insight into the troubles. With my foot in the door, there was no turning back. I was now an established freelance journalist.

> ‘You can claim for the outfit on expenses and hang onto it. It'll come in useful again.’

At the age of 22, I got my first staff job – as a reporter working for the *Sunday Times*. A three-year stint at TV-am, working as a producer on the David Frost programme followed. I joined the *News of the World* in December 1991, where my first investigation involved being smuggled into Britain in the back of a lorry from Belgium, alongside a hoard of Turkish illegal immigrants.

It was time to dust off the old Arab robes; my first job as the Sheik for the paper, inevitably, involved hookers. Today, I have a store room containing a dozen Arab outfits which I've learned to call *jalabia*; most are traditional white robes called *agal*, accompanied by a variety of headscarves and head rings called *ghatra*. I also have a black and gold embroidered robe, the kind worn by Middle Eastern royalty. But pride of place in my wardrobe is the lucky robe I bought from a Dubai souk when I was on holiday, for just £10.

Next to the Arab outfits is a startling range of ultra-loud Versace jackets, bright shirts, and a white suit, which only an Arab would dare to wear. To go with the outfits, I have a range of expensive designer shoes, a flashy £5,000 Rolex watch (a real one that I'd had to buy myself, as the Sheik's targets would recognize a fake ... sometimes), and a jewellery box full of Sheik bling including fake diamond rings.

There is a whole team of people, including three stand-in Sheiks, security staff, assistants and drivers, who make up the Sheik's impressive entourage. Over the years, we have perfected our cover stories so that we don't contradict each other on small details, like the number of wives and children the Sheik has, or where his mansions are dotted around the world.

The improvised script has been perfected after a series of near misses. There was the time when I went to the toilet and my assistant Alex D'Souza told a top model that I was in Britain to watch the polo and wanted to sponsor the Guards Polo Club. Unfortunately the model had been dating a member of the England polo team and played polo herself; I'd never witnessed a live chukka in my life and knew nothing about polo, so was left struggling to get off the topic quickly. Or there was the time when another colleague claimed that I spent most of my life in my palatial home in a suburb of Singapore, while I had only been there on holiday once. The only problem was that the high-powered businessman we were trying to expose had grown up in Singapore and knew every backstreet.

At the beginning of every Fake Sheik assignment, I pick the team from my squad that I feel would be appropriate to provide the most convincing scenario for the subject of the investigation. For example, if I were visiting a Royal, my minder would have to be a respectable ex-Army officer or ex-police officer rather than one of my big and mean-looking bodyguards, Harry or Jaws, who I would take along when seeing a pop star. Similarly, if there is a chance that the Sheik's guest might speak Arabic, I have to call in a second Sheik, Marwan – a Palestinian plumber from east London, who scrubs up nicely (once he's cleaned his fingernails properly) to pose as my relative. Or I can also ask Akbar Ali Malik, whose quick thinking has saved the day on many occasions.

In a *GQ* survey, following my Countess of Wessex sting, the Fake Sheik was listed as the 45th most powerful man in Britain. Prince Charles, the future King, was ranked at number 69. But the life of the Fake Sheik is not all five-star hotels, limos, yachts, and lavish dinners with the rich and famous. I am more likely to be found in a crack den exposing drug dealers or exposing arms dealers, paedophiles, corrupt politicians, and people traffickers. To date I have been responsible for more than 230 successful criminal prosecutions. Success, though, in the world of investigative journalism, comes at a price. I have had guns pointed at me on a few occasions, have received numerous death threats and have a price on my head. I've even been threatened by the Czech intelligence services.

Conrad, Jaws, and I were arrested as we were about to leave the country after completing an illegal immigration story. Handcuffed, strip-searched, and interrogated, we were thrown into separate cells. A senior official from the secret service told me that we would be charged for being in possession of forged Czech documents and would be jailed for ten years; however, all charges would be dropped and we'd be on the next plane home, as long as I agreed to sign up to work as a spy for the Czech secret service. It was an easy decision to take.

When I got home I changed my mind, and I was warned by an intimidating Eastern European voice on the phone that I would 'suffer the consequences'. In an unprecedented move, the Czech intelligence service issued a press release revealing that they had arrested me several months earlier. They claimed that they were already onto the gang of forgers that we exposed and that the *News of the World* had failed to highlight the good work of the Czech officers. They also issued a global notice linking me to the Czech secret service, which has resulted in me being held and questioned for hours at various airports around the world.

My undercover work has also had serious repercussions for my family. In one terrifying incident a gang I exposed for a massive credit card cloning scam broke into my parents' home. They smashed the front door off its hinges and used a machete to hack apart the entire contents of the lounge, before leaving a warning note for me. It took a letter from the editor Phil Hall to the Home Secretary before local cops took the matter seriously.

My father's words of wisdom proved spot on. Besides the understandable anger of the people who end up behind bars, there is often a massive backlash from the Asian community, who regard me as a traitor for exposing my own people. There have been several demonstrations outside the *News of the World* offices by Muslim and left-wing groups condemning my exposés. It is this hush-hush mentality that led to the birth of Britain's first homegrown suicide bomber, Shehzad Tanweer. Without members of the Muslim community willing to shop their own, and without investigative journalists joining the fight against terrorism, the world will be a less safe place.

Subterfuge is a legitimate and basic tool of investigative journalism, and the Fake Sheik is just one of a whole range of personas that I adopt to infiltrate targets; I am just as likely to turn up as an asylum seeker, a taxi driver, or worker from a building site. By the gift of my birth, I am unlikely to be seen as a policeman, customs officer, or immigration official, thanks to the prevailing stereotypes of Asian men. Without going undercover my colleagues and I would have no hope of exposing drug dealers, paedophiles and the like. After all, nobody would offer to sell me drugs or weapons if I proudly announced I am a reporter from the *News of the World*.

Undercover reporting is enshrined in the Press Complaints Commission (PCC) code and is justified where we can show that it is in the public interest and that the material cannot be obtained by other means. The 'public interest' includes 'detecting or exposing crime or serious impropriety' and 'preventing the public from being misled by an action or statement of an individual or organization'. Sometimes the story comes about because of an insider supplying me with the information, and in those circumstances – when they are going to be paid – that too is covered by the PCC code.

Fellow journalists, media commentators who sit in their armchairs and pontificate on our investigations, also subject the *News of the World* and my work to regular assaults. While condemning tabloid journalism, broadsheets steal our stories and fill column inches with details of our exposés for their own readers. It is a dog-eat-dog world. The life of any tabloid journalist on a personal level is tough too; the long hours and unpredictable nature of the work puts an incredible strain on any reporter's relationships. For investigative journalists it's twice as hard, as it means living a life in the shadows. You cannot attend parties and social events where there is a likelihood of being recognized and subjected to verbal or physical attacks by people you have exposed or their sympathisers, and you have to choose your friends very carefully. Besides high-tech security cameras and safety devices at my home, I have two bodyguards permanently at my beck and call to watch my back. My small team of minders, assistants, and drivers has become part of my extended family.

For me, though, the rewards far outweigh the disadvantages. One 13-year-old girl I rescued from the clutches of an evil paedophile wrote me a letter saying: 'Thank you for rescuing me and saving my life. You are like Superman! You are my hero. You saved me from this evil man.'

No baubles or gongs could match that honour.

And despite the small group of people who want to de-robe the Fake Sheik, I can assure them that the robes will not be handed in to Oxfam anytime soon.

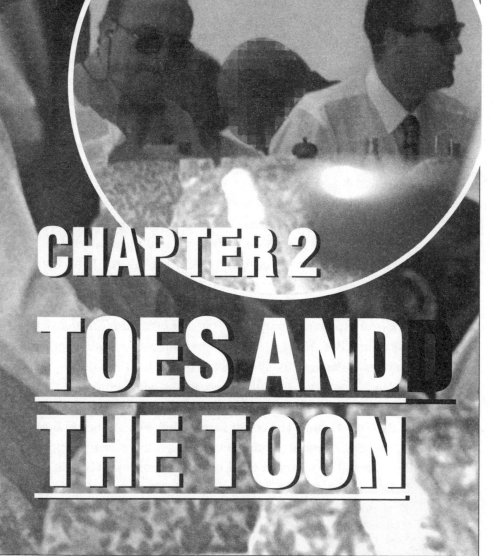

CHAPTER 2
TOES AND
THE TOON

Two of my escapades with the *News of the World* taught me a lot about the business of being an undercover reporter – and the pleasure that donning the Fake Sheik's robes can bring to the reporter in me. Both of these stories remain among the most famous I've ever been involved in, but one nearly didn't happen – and the other almost slipped through my fingers when I didn't realize just how big it was going to be.

'I've got the editor for you,' announced PA Vicky Bubb in her cut-glass English accent. This was the first time Patsy Chapman had phoned me since she gave me my job at the *News of the World* – but my excitement quickly evaporated as the normally soft-spoken Patsy shouted, 'Maz, get your bloody cameras and bugs out of that flat straight away. We've got to be really careful with this guy. If this ever got out we'd all be in serious trouble. Do it *right now.*'

A few seconds after Patsy – a founder member of the Press Complaints Commission – hung up, the phone rang again. This time it was news editor Bob Warren, a grey-haired mild-mannered gentleman who you would more likely expect to find at the helm of *The Times* than the *News of the World.* He seemed equally nervous. 'I think it would be wise if you could remove all your electronic gadgetry from that flat immediately. The editor is really quite concerned about this one,' said Bob. I sensed the urgency in Bob's voice, even if he appeared calm – after all, he was on holiday, calling me from a golf course in Suffolk. Bob, the longest serving news editor in the history of Fleet Street with twenty years under his belt, continued, 'This really could have very serious implications for the media as a whole. We have got to play it totally by the book.'

I understood their shared concerns. And just in case I hadn't understood, deputy news editor Alex Marunchak weighed in with yet another call along similar lines.

Why the fuss? Maybe it was because the man I was about to expose was the Secretary of State for National Heritage, and had threatened to muzzle the free press. At the time he was heading government deliberations on proposals to introduce a Privacy Law to protect the private lives of public figures. In a speech that sent shivers down the spines of reporters all over the country, the minister had warned that controls of press freedom were necessary, that self-regulation wasn't working and, famously, that the press were 'drinking in the Last Chance Saloon'. The Secretary of State was the Rt. Hon. David Mellor MP.

I raced into the second-floor flat in Finborough Road, Earls Court, and grabbed the covert cameras cunningly secreted in a hi-fi system and potted plant, as well as the recording devices scattered throughout the property. I quickly bundled everything into a black bin liner and ran down the steps out of the flat. I had to be quick as Mellor – branded the 'Minister of Fun' because of his arts, culture, and sports portfolio, and regarded as Prime Minister Major's right-hand man – was due any minute.

I knew that because I had just recorded a telephone conversation between his secret mistress and her friend, Nick Philp, who owned the flat where she was living. Antonia de Sancha had confided to Philp about her clandestine affair, and, over a period of two weeks, several of her conversations with Philp in which she spoke intimately about her relationship with Mellor had been tape recorded by myself.

It was heart breaking removing the recording equipment from the premises. I would have been able to watch and record all the action live, from the comfort of our surveillance van parked down the road. I knew that it was neither illegal, nor were we contravening the PCC code of conduct by installing devices in the flat. I had Philp's consent; it was his futon that de Sancha and Mellor were romping about upon.

The young businessman stood to pocket a huge amount of money for the story. As for justification, Mellor was guilty of adultery, incompetence, and above all unashamed hypocrisy. The MP for Putney had always presented himself as a family man, happily living with his wife of eighteen years, Judith, and their two children.

William Somerset Maugham, in his novel *Cakes And Ale* published in 1930, wrote: 'Hypocrisy is the most difficult and nerve-racking vice that any man can pursue; it needs an unceasing vigilance and a rare detachment of spirit. It cannot, like adultery or gluttony, be practised at spare moments. It is a wholetime job.'

From the back of our van I watched as first Antonia, and then Mellor, arrived and went into the flat. A short while later they emerged together and headed to the La Famiglia Italian restaurant off the Fulham Road, where they dined.

I went into the restaurant as well and sat nervously at a table a few yards away. I was worried that Mellor might recognize me, as, before joining the *News of the World,* I had worked as a producer on David Frost's Sunday programme at TV-am. Mellor, a charismatic man, was a regular guest on the programme and I had shared coffee and croissants with him on many occasions.

Fortunately, I wasn't spotted either in the restaurant or later when I followed him as he strolled with Antonia back to the nearby flat.

I spent the time waiting for Mellor to emerge again in the back of the van, drinking cans of Red Bull. Alongside me was freelance photographer Les Chudziki, who had met Philp through a mutual friend and brought the story to me. 'Cheeky Chudziki' was a loveable rogue who could easily have used his charm and cunning to make a fortune selling timeshares on the Costa del Sol. He bragged how he had made over £25,000 from a single photograph of Princess Diana handing a trophy to her lover James Hewitt at a polo tournament. Chudziki hadn't even taken the picture; he'd bought it off a punter in his local for £100.

'It's one of my better deals,' Chudziki said proudly. 'And it's still *kerching, kerching, kerching* thanks to that wanker Hewitt!' Whenever scumbag Hewitt was back in the news for taking drugs or sleeping with hookers, it meant the photo was sure to be used and more money would come rolling into Chudziki's pockets.

Mellor finally emerged from the flat in the early hours of the following morning and hailed a cab.

Philp met Chudziki and me at the flat later that day when Antonia had left; I was hoping to find evidence of what may have taken place the night before. As I desperately scoured the flat on my hands and knees, I managed to find a tape recorder hidden under a bookshelf in the lounge, near the futon. Rather absent-mindedly I'd forgotten to remove the device in a mad rush to clear the flat of all the bugs. I listened to the tape and in between the soothing notes of classical music playing in the background, Mellor could clearly be heard bonking Antonia.

'Fucking brilliant, I love you, you sly bastard!' declared Chudziki as he planted a big grisly kiss on my cheek. After hearing the tape I gave it to him as a gift. 'This is the best present I've had since my fucking wooden leg was fitted,' proclaimed Chudziki; the one-legged Polish photographer had lost a limb to polio as a child.

It was clear that Antonia, the daughter of a Swedish model and a Spanish writer, was a woman who was easily seduced by men of power and wealth, so I asked Philp to call Antonia to she if she would be interested in meeting the Sheik. Philp told her that the wealthy Arab had asked him to arrange a £1,000-a-night call girl. Antonia jumped at the chance of making easy money by bedding the Sheik herself.

'I'll go, I'll go. For £1,000 I'll do it,' she told him in the taped call. When told that she would have to have sex with the Sheik, Antonia replied: 'I don't care!'

As the investigation progressed I spoke to one of Antonia's close pals, a fellow actress called Victoria Harwood. She told me how Antonia, an out-of-work actress who had trained at RADA with her, was using Mellor to help boost her career. Antonia had discussed the idea of sleeping with somebody famous, then selling the story; and had mentioned her relationship with Mellor.

I suspected that either Antonia was secretly working hand-in-hand with Philp to sell the story, or she was feeding him details of her affair in the knowledge that he would surely betray her trust and sell the story, which would bring her instant fame.

In any event, with all the evidence I had collated I knew I had a major scoop. I carefully transcribed the phone conversations between Philp and Antonia and wrote my story, which I believed would make headlines all over the world. But a few hours after filing the story to the news desk, Alex Marunchak called me. 'Forget the Mellor story, Patsy won't run it. It's far too sensitive and she doesn't think it's worth the risk of upsetting him,' he said bluntly. 'Get rid of any tapes you've got – I don't believe for a second that you didn't tape him shagging.'

I was devastated as Chudziki was on his way to the office expecting to be handed a £40,000 contract for the story. I'd even booked a table that evening at Mellor's favourite La Famiglia restaurant for a celebratory dinner with Chudziki and Philp. Chudziki was probably more disappointed than me when I broke the news; we had both worked very hard to get the evidence, and it's not everyday you get the chance to expose a government minister. Before he left the office, I handed Chudziki all the tapes of the phone calls that his pal Philp had made on my instructions and I wished him luck.

> **‘We can fly off to Marbella and have some fun … Do you mind if my partner in crime Freddie Shepherd comes too?’**

Chudziki and Philp drove straight to the offices of the *Sunday People* with their haul. The *Sunday People* welcomed them with open arms and put their own team on the case to gather further incriminating photographic and audio evidence. But my role in the Mellor affair wasn't over. A few days later when I wandered into the office on a Saturday morning as usual, I found myself ushered immediately into Alex's office again.

'The *People* are splashing on the Mellor affair,' he whispered to me with a huge grin. 'Dig out your copy and let's nail the bastard!' Information had been leaked to us that the *People* were about to break the story; deputy editor Paul Connew had put in a call to Mellor's people, alerting him to the story and invited him to come clean and confess all to us. Not surprisingly he declined.

We weren't about to let a rival newspaper, which had only a fraction of the sales of the *News of the World*, steal our thunder. Our front page, already prepared with a photograph of Lady Helen Windsor's wedding, was quickly replaced by photos of Mellor, John Major and Antonia de Sancha. My story – *Minister Of Fun And The Actress* – sent sales soaring and the government reeling into crisis.

Mellor had not got away with it and it was drinks all round on me at the Last Chance Saloon. It was the most lurid political scandal since the Profumo affair, and in the days that followed acres of newsprint were dedicated to cringe-inducing details of the Mellor affair. Every skeleton was dragged out of the cupboards of both Mellor and Antonia.

I was dispatched to Antigua where I lay on the beach on a sun lounger beside Antonia who had fled there to seek refuge from the press. Again we were one step ahead of all our rivals. I spent a couple of days posing as a tourist, sunbathing next to Antonia, pretending I didn't know who she was; we had several conversations as fellow tourists, we even ate dinner together. I was also privy to her chats with her friend as they lay on the beach. I eventually revealed my true identity and asked her for an interview; she rang controversial publicist Max Clifford and was told not to talk to me.

With the Max spin applied, the Mellor story took on a whole new dimension as Antonia now claimed to have spanked Mellor and sucked his toes. At first it looked as if Mellor's political career would survive the scandal, but then details of how he had allowed Mona Bauwens, the daughter of a senior Palestinian Liberation Organization leader, to pay for his holiday led to another media onslaught. His position became untenable and Mellor had to resign. The *Sun* splashed on the news with the memorable headline, *From Toe Job To No Job*.

But the one element of the Mellor affair, which passed immediately into folk-law, was the allegation that he made love to Antonia while wearing nothing but his prized Chelsea football shirt. Years later Antonia confessed that the spanking, toe-sucking, and the memorable image of the Chelsea shirt, were all made up. Which goes to show that somebody somewhere wanted more out of the story than it originally promised.

Just as David Mellor will always be synonymous with the Chelsea shirt, ex-Newcastle United boss Freddie Shepherd will always be remembered for branding as 'ugly dogs' *all* Geordie lasses. But his drunken utterances in a Marbella brothel were no spin; they were captured for posterity on my tape recorder.

My exposé of Newcastle chairman Freddie Shepherd and vice-chairman Doug Hall sent shockwaves throughout the world of soccer from the terraces upwards, and made the Fake Sheik a household name on the Tyne. It also won me the prestigious Reporter of the Year award presented by my colleagues at a glittering ceremony at London's Park Lane Hilton. Given it was the simplest sting I'd ever done, it was all the more surprising that – not being a football fan – I had never heard of either man beforehand.

Freelance journalist Nigel Bowden, who lived and worked on the Costa del Sol, had been banging on to me about Douglas Hall for weeks. He told me that Hall's dad, Sir John Hall, had a villa in Marbella that Doug would regularly fly to for nights of drunken debauchery with local hookers. Nigel had spoken to a girl, an attractive barmaid, to whom Hall had offered money to sleep with him. She was furious and wanted him exposed.

It was a quiet week and I quite fancied sharing tapas in Marbella with Nigel while keeping watch on the wayward football boss. I casually asked my minder John Miller to put in a call to Newcastle United on behalf of the Sheik to see if Hall would be interested in meeting him the next time he was in Spain. Miller spoke to Hall's PA, and told her the Sheik was interested in developing a football team in the Middle East. By making the call we would at least find out when Hall would be at his dad's villa, so we could set up a straightforward surveillance operation. But within an hour, Hall rang Miller back himself from the St James's Park ground to invite the Sheik to watch the home match that weekend.

'We can fly off in my plane to Marbella and have some fun,' he invited. 'Do you mind if my partner in crime Freddie Shepherd comes too? He wants to get in on the action. I'm a tax exile, I can go anywhere. If you can't make the game on Sunday, I'll fly over to Marbella straight after and meet you.'

The fact that Hall was so keen to meet me and that the meeting had been fixed up with such ease, made me think that he was small fry; nevertheless, I had to get the expenses past the news desk as I'd need them to sanction a suitable suite in Marbella, as well as flights and hotel rooms for the Sheik's crew. Trying to appear casual, I mentioned the story to news editor Greg Miskiw. 'I'll try and keep the costs down, and luckily Hall will be staying at his dad's place. The only problem is the tosser wants to bring his mate Freddie Shepherd along as well. It'll only mean an extra meal and a few drinks, I suppose,' I said, trying to convince him it would be a low-budget production.

Miskiw thought I was joking. 'What? You've got Doug Hall and Freddie Shepherd wanting to meet you in Marbella this weekend? Fucking hell, fucking hell, what a fucking coup!' said Miskiw as he stubbed his cigarette out in the bin beneath his desk.

Greg walked straight over to editor Phil Hall's office and an impromptu meeting was called, the door of the office firmly closed behind us. They were both very excited by the potential of the story and discussed all possible angles; Greg made notes on a pad jotting down names of players, managers, and details of recent transfer deals that he felt I should talk to them about.

I still had no idea how big Hall and Shepherd were in the world of football but didn't want to look a fool in front of the editor so I pretended I had understood the magnitude of the story from the start. As soon as I got out of the editor's office, I ordered cuttings on the pair and read up on them. I didn't take long to realize that football is a religion on the Tyne, which made Hall and Shepherd nothing short of gods. That made it all the more baffling that the mere mention of a Sheik had been enough to gain instant access to the Newcastle United chiefs. Nobody had asked for any company details and the only number they had was a mobile for my part-time minder, but then the popular prejudice of a wealthy Arab, with a hedonistic streak beneath his flowing robes, had worked wonders in the past.

Once, while dressed in my robes, I was seeing off a well-known supermodel after a meeting at the Dorchester hotel in London's Park Lane. It's a tough job, but somebody's got to do it. As I stood in the lobby with my support team, Sylvester Stallone walked in with his equally impressive entourage. Sly spotted me and was so curious that he sent one of his bodyguards over to talk to my driver, Alan Smith, to ask who I was. Alan said I was a Sheik from Saudi Arabia who was a fan, so Sly walked over to introduce himself. I shook hands and we chatted briefly in my broken English about his Rocky films; he was pleased to learn that he was such a big star among the Sheiks of Jeddah.

Sly told the Sheik how he was in London because he was getting married to Jennifer Flavin in a private ceremony on the roof terrace of his hotel suite the following day. My ears immediate pricked up under my headscarf; as soon as Sly disappeared, I asked my minder to extend my suite for another night and to ask reception to move me to a room that overlooked Sly's lavish £2,000-a-night Oliver Messel suite. I ordered a huge bouquet of flowers to be sent from the Sheik to my new Hollywood star friend.

The following day our photographers got exclusive pictures of the roof-top wedding ceremony, attended by just ten guests, from the comfort of my room, while I got all the inside information from his bodyguard who had befriended my driver Smithy. It included the detail that Sly had bought several pots of £90 anti-wrinkle cream, which he slapped on to keep his fresh look for his beautiful bride.

The power of the Sheik's robes was to be proved again, ten times over, in Spain. The Fake Sheik and his crew – Akbar Ali Malik, John Miller, Steve Burton, Conrad Brown (a vital part of our team) – settled into our impressive villa in the Marbella Club; everything was going smoothly, and when Hall had called at about 11.30pm from Sir John Hall's villa, announcing that he and Shepherd had arrived – 'We're here and ready to celebrate. Have you got any girls there?' – we prepared the recording devices and my colleague Ali Malik and I put on our robes. They were going to get two Sheiks tonight.

Then disaster struck. The sheesha pipe wouldn't light, as the tobacco was wet. This wouldn't look very convincing, a Sheik who couldn't light his pipe. I huffed and puffed, at one point sucking so hard on the red and gold snaked pipe that I swallowed some of the vile tobacco, but nothing was happening. Thankfully Miller came to my aid, smashing open a disposable cigarette lighter and pouring the lighter fuel onto the coals while I spluttered and coughed in the corner. A three-foot flame shot up from the pipe, threatening to set the villa on fire. Frantically we damped the flames down and managed to get the tobacco going, so when Hall and Shepherd arrived, along with their splendidly named minder Brian Tough, they had to fight their way through billowing clouds of smoke to be greeted by myself and Ali dressed in our Arab outfits.

The pair were already half pissed. They had flown over in their private Learjet after watching Newcastle beat Barnsley 3–1 and had been celebrating throughout the two and a half hour flight. Conrad had installed two covert video cameras in the suite and photographer Steve Burton was hiding in the dark garden outside snapping pictures though the window.

Tough, who was a surveillance expert, did not spot any of our covert recording devices. He happily chatted to Miller while his bosses chatted to the Sheiks. The conversation that followed, once published, rocked the Geordie nation and the football world alike, as the tycoons showed themselves to be worthy of every derogatory tabloid adjective I could sling at them – 'depraved', 'sex-crazed', 'conniving', 'greedy', 'perverts lost in a mire of sleaze'. It was an extraordinary evening and I had to do almost nothing except listen as they condemned themselves out of their own mouths.

The Premiership bosses started off by explaining how they had sacked Tyneside legend, manager Kevin Keegan: at the time it had been reported that the former England captain had gone so the club's £150 million stock market flotation could move ahead smoothly. 'We sacked him because we gave him £60 million to spend and we won nothing,' explained Shepherd. Hall added, 'We had to say to Kevin, "Your style isn't working. We need a manager to win something." When we got rid of Kevin we tried to get Alex Ferguson. We offered him a lot of money but he was happy where he was. We ended up with Kenny Dalglish.'

As the pair downed champagne and brandies, they turned on England star and Newcastle hero Alan Shearer. 'Shearer is boring, we call him Mary Poppins. He never gets into trouble,' said Shepherd. 'We're not like him though. He needs to make £3 million a year, we've already made our money,' added Hall smugly.

The pair also revealed how they had sold star striker Andy Cole to Manchester United for £7 million, knowing that he was due to have an operation that could end his career. 'It was a serious operation, he had a 50–50 chance of recovery,' said Shepherd. 'We knew but we didn't tell Cole and we certainly didn't tell Manchester.' Cole was out for six months because of the operation shortly after joining the Old Trafford club.

Hall and Shepherd, however, hadn't flown to Marbella to sit around chatting in the Sheik's luxury suite; they wanted action. The duo invited me to join them at a club down the road called MiLady Palace. In my broken English, I inquired if it was a cabaret club with entertainment. Hall described the venue succinctly: 'There's no entertainment. It's a brothel. All the places here are like that.' The Sheik would go along with this until the moment came for me to look a little uncomfortable and say I'd rather see the girl in private at my hotel – that way, I not only avoided the tricky moment, I also got the girl's number to follow up on my story later.

Together with our minders, both Sheiks joined the party heading in two flash limousines to the seedy brothel. Inside the dimly lit club, the walls were covered with red flock paper and the place was littered with gilt couches and erotic statues. Hall and Shepherd immediately ordered beers at the bar and started leering at the dozens of scantily clad girls. They discussed the attractions on offer as if they were in a catalogue: 'I prefer a beautiful face first, long legs, and I like a nice tight bum,' grinned Hall, who was married to Tonia with two sons. Shepherd added: 'I like blondes, big bust, good legs. I don't like coloured girls. I want a lesbian show with handcuffs.'

As the pair bragged how they had travelled the world bedding some of the most beautiful women in the world, I thought in a way the pair were living the lifestyle that many men would aspire to – jetting round the globe in their Learjet, staying at luxury hotels, dining in the best restaurants, guzzling the finest Cristal champagne, and bedding a string of stunning girls. The only problem with this chauvinistic fantasy was that these men were married – and the stunning girls were all paid hookers.

In between eyeing up the girls the drooling bosses spoke about their other love – football. 'Keegan has a halo like a saint, no vices like us,' said Shepherd as he told how he had tried unsuccessfully to drag the Newcastle manager to an Amsterdam brothel. 'We used to call Keegan "Shirley Temple".' It was hard to imagine that this pair – who as the evening wore on began increasingly to resemble Laurel and Hardy – were in charge of a multi-million-pound football club.

The drunken duo then stooped even lower and delivered an amazing slur on their fans, based on the fans' affection for their star winger, Keith Gillespie. 'Our fans like people like Gillespie, because they relate to people that behave like them, have a drink and get into trouble,' said Hall, as the irony of his comments went sailing right past him. 'Gillespie is 23, earns £1.5 million a year and drinks too much. When he drinks he has a fight. You can't control young boys that don't have a sensible head.' Or old boys, I thought. Then it was time for the Sheik to watch as the pair fondled a string of girls, before negotiating a deal for a lesbian show with two attractive Spanish hookers. When they had finished their session in a private room at MiLady Palace, the multi-millionaires took me to another even seedier joint – the Crescendo strip club in Puerto Banus.

There, as the men downed more pints and repeatedly took strippers to the back of the club for one-on-one groping sessions, Shepherd delivered his memorable attack on Geordie women. 'Newcastle girls are all dogs. England is full of them. The girls are ugly and they're dogs,' snarled Shepherd, a married man with a grown-up daughter. 'We've had *Penthouse* Pets, the fucking lot. The best in the world!'

Hall and Shepherd claimed to have bedded twelve girls at a *Penthouse* party in New York, and Hall boasted that he had slept with girls of every nationality except Icelandic. Hall, whose family fortune was listed as £220 million, said, 'English girls are crazy. They do it for nothing. I've got six hundred, seven hundred mistresses.' The boozy brothel crawl finally ended at around 5am. Fortunately the Sheik doesn't touch alcohol so at least I wouldn't have a crashing hangover the following day: John Miller would ask me, loudly enough for those around to hear, 'A Bacardi and Coke, Sir?' to which I'd nod my head; he would return with a Diet Coke in ice. As my guests were always happy to spend my money, no one else ever tried to buy me a drink.

As arranged, I met Shepherd and Hall for lunch at a seafood restaurant in Puerto Banus harbour. To further their blossoming friendship with the Sheik, they announced that they had arranged a special present for me – a hooker called Maria who they were flying in from Greece. Minder Tough had made the call and she was trying to get on a flight from Athens. 'She is the best, the dirtiest. She's a Greek,' explained Hall. 'You can have her as a present.' I politely declined their offer; I knew if the tart turned up and reported that the Sheik had not had sex with her, my cover would be blown instantly. I told them that I had been invited to dinner at a villa near Puerto Banus; the Saudi King has a huge villa and mosque there, marked by a large Arabian sword made up of lights on the lawn, a popular landmark in the area, and I let them assume that's where I was going.

Over lunch, the sleazebags continued to sneer at the very fans that made their disgraceful lifestyles possible. They told how they cashed in by selling football shirts for £50 each – that cost just £5 to make; and how they liked to see their fans getting drunk at home matches, 'because we own the bars where they drink, so we can't complain too much about drunken behaviour,' said Hall.

Hall and Shepherd explained why they both travelled the world paying for sex. 'We have to watch the British papers,' confided Shepherd. 'I'm the Chairman of Newcastle United. In the UK we can't play, we'd be sacked!' They were prophetic words.

The duo headed back to London, this time on a scheduled flight from Malaga airport; by coincidence, I was booked on the same flight, so I hid with my crew in the airport lounge as Hall and Shepherd boarded, with Brian Tough in tow. Luckily – for me – they were in first class, so I could sneak on board to take my seat at the back of the plane. If they had spotted me wearing faded denim jeans, carrying my own bags into the economy cabin, they would have quickly realized that they had been the targets of a Fake Sheik sting.

Vice Girls Shame Of Top Soccer Bosses was published across nine pages of the paper and caused a sensation; the loyal Toon Army, especially the female legion, were furious. Despite a pathetic apology to their fans, as the pair sat in the Directors' box at the next match they faced angry chants of 'Judas!' and 'Get Out Of Toon!' from the terraces. Football, besides being our national sport, is also one of Britain's most successful businesses. Following publication of the story – which led TV news bulletins and was copied by every paper in the land – shares in the Premiership club tumbled, wiping £6.5 million off the club's value.

Even the Prime Minister, Tony Blair, a Newcastle United fan, expressed concern about the situation at the club during a House of Commons meeting.

Hall and Shepherd knew that further revelations would be made the following weekend, and in a ludicrous attempt to stop publication they went to the High Court arguing that their privacy had been invaded. Hall even issued a bizarre statement denying that he had ever taken drugs, something we had no intention of accusing him of doing. The pair failed in their bid to gag the *News of the World*. Mr Justice Lindsay said, 'Shepherd and Hall made a long series of boastful, lewd statements bragging about the way they whored their way around the world. If they were in and out of brothels in all the places mentioned, can they expect behaviour of that scale or of that type to remain in confidence? Anyone who behaves like this surely bears the risk that it will come to light. I see nothing relating to business confidentiality.'

Our legal manager Tom Crone who led the courtroom battle was jubilant. A bottle of champagne was cracked open in Phil Hall's office – orange juice for me – and we quietly toasted our success.

We published the entire Toongate tapes, heaping yet more shame on the soccer bosses. Disgraced Hall and Shepherd were forced to resign and Sir John Hall came out of retirement to steady the ship. It would be a long time before the pair managed to return to their former positions at the club.

Eight years after the original Newcastle United exposé, Brian Tough, their loyal henchman and guardian of the Filofax packed with numbers for their favourite prostitutes, approached me. He'd fallen out with Doug Hall over a pub they opened together in Gibraltar called 'Toon On The Rock'; he felt that Hall had betrayed him. Tough opened the black book and provided more sleazy details of Hall's sexual antics, which had continued after Hall had been exposed by the paper years before.

Tough also confessed how he had been ordered to carry out illegal phone taps and sabotage operations for Newcastle United. The surveillance expert, who was on £40,000 a year plus cash bungs, revealed how he had secretly filmed Alan Shearer in a meeting to use against him if he left the club. Tough also admitted he had been involved in bugging Kevin Keegan's phone to see if he was planning to quit as manager, as well as rival Sunderland manager Bob Murray to find out about their plans for a new stadium. In a confession which could have landed him behind bars, Tough told me: 'At times I felt really bad about it, especially when I spied on our own players and senior staff. The players and fans would have gone mad if they'd found out what I had been up to.'

I rang Shepherd to ask him if he had ever been made aware of the bugging allegations made by Tough. Not surprisingly, Shepherd remembered me well. He admitted, 'Tough did make me aware of what he had done but I did not condone it; I couldn't control what he did, he didn't work for me. I had nothing to do with bugging anybody.' During the phone call, Shepherd said that he might seek legal advice before speaking to me, at which I reminded him of our last courtroom battle. He agreed it wasn't worth the bother. It looked like he'd learned a lesson from his brush with the *News of the World*.

The Toongate exposé taught me a couple of lessons too: never to underestimate the power of football – and to take my pal Nigel a little bit more seriously if he rang in from Spain with a tip.

CHAPTER 3

THE PORN STARS, THE TV HOST, AND THE HITMAN

It seemed straightforward – film the guy with the girls, get some interviews, pick up some duty-frees at the airport on the way home – but it wasn't to be. Over the years I have learned that the jobs that seem straightforward never are, and when it came to the Executive Plaza hotel in Chicago, I was proved right.

On the day, I found myself crouched on some concrete steps in the stairwell of the hotel, next to technician Conrad Brown, and wearing a bright blue boiler suit that was a size too small. We'd picked up the outfits at the local Wal-Mart for $9.99 each an hour earlier. We needed them for our undercover mission posing as engineers while we gathered evidence on TV chat show host Jerry Springer, who was about to have sex with a guest due to appear on his TV show – *and* her stepmother!

It was a classic *News of the World* story that ticked all the boxes. We had a TV celebrity, a former politician, and a man who liked to expose oddballs and perverts on his programmes and then give his own moral sermon at the end of every show. Besides which he was very wealthy, earning hundreds of thousands of dollars for every show. With a threesome starring a mother and daughter (both porno queens) due to appear on his show the following day, it was perfect for our readers.

As a maid walked past us carrying a tray, I puffed on a cigarette and coughed to make sure Conrad slammed shut the box as it had a TV monitor concealed inside, secretly recording video of the antics taking place around the corridor. I said 'Hola' in my best Hispanic accent, so that the maid would think we were nothing more than hotel engineers skiving off for a cigarette break. In fact our camera was concealed in the hotel bedroom and we had to be close enough to pick up the signal it was transmitting.

Even though it was three years before 9/11, if we'd been caught dressed as workmen with our box of tricks we'd have had some serious explaining to do down at the local sheriff's office. Luckily we got away with it, and as the tape rolled I pictured the headline: 'TV Chat King Romps With A Porn Star'.

The story had come from a British journalist, Peter Bond, who ran a news agency in California called Headline News. He had given me a brief summary of the story and told me to meet two porno models called Kendra Jade (star of *Anal Unlimited*, *Hot Ass Babes* and *Strap-On Queen* among many, many others) and her stepmother Kelly at Chicago's O'Hare airport. 'How will I recognize them?' I asked. 'You'll spot them, no problem!' He laughed down the phone at me.

So Conrad and I scanned all the passengers that got off the flight, cursing Bond. The airport was crammed full with stunning women, their faces plastered with make-up and fake boobs pushed outwards. We could have spent the whole day approaching potential porn queens asking if they were Kendra Jade. But good old Bond was spot on.

It was almost like a dreamy film sequence. The crowd suddenly parted disappearing into the background and almost as if in slow motion a girl that could only be described in the paper as a 'blonde bombshell' emerged. The curvy girl with her boobs bursting out of her yellow skimpy top, bright red lipstick and the micro denim-skirt could be no one else but Kendra Jade. Alongside her was Kelly, a stunning brunette complete with huge designer sunglasses, an enormous Gucci handbag and tanned body.

The sounds of their stilettos pounding on the floor echoed in our ears as they walked towards us and greeted us with a kiss and hug as if we were intimate old friends. 'You're really cute,' Kendra told me as I turned to Conrad with a huge grin. But then she added, '... for a reporter!'

So I quickly wiped the lipstick from my face and we all headed in a cab to the bar of the Executive Plaza hotel where they had been booked to stay by the Springer team.

There, over cocktails, 28-year-old Kelly from Massachusetts told us how she had married Kendra's dad and so became stepmother to his daughter when Kendra was ten years old. 'I used to take her to school. As she grew older she became a dancer and got involved in porn, and now I act as her manager,' said brunette Kelly matter-of-factly. She explained how they had met Jerry Springer when she appeared on a show titled 'Unfit Mothers' alongside Kendra's real mum. 'We met Jerry in the Green Room after the programme and we were all having a great time. He couldn't take his eyes off me and Kendra.'

A few weeks later the pair were invited back on Springer's programme, this time so that Kendra could shock her real mother by showing her clips from her hit movies – a typical Springer show. After the recording Springer had chatted to the girls again. 'He couldn't keep his hands off me,' explained Kendra. 'He kept touching me and then led me along a corridor to the make-up room where we started kissing, cuddling, and groping.' An apparently nervous Springer told Kendra, 'I shouldn't be doing this,' but carried on anyway. Meanwhile Kelly performed her motherly duties by standing outside the door of the make-up room keeping watch in case her daughter was disturbed while she gave Springer a blowjob.

Later he took them to his spacious office where he closed the blinds and enjoyed steamy action, with both mother and stepdaughter taking it in turns to perform oral sex with him. Although I knew that his political career as a councillor in Cincinnati had ended when, at the age of 27, he was caught with a $30 hooker because he'd been dumb enough to pay her by cheque, I had to admit I was pretty impressed with Springer's sexual prowess for taking on the two porn queens at the same time.

But these two had clearly put a spring back into Springer's step. He kept making dirty late night phone calls to Kendra and said he was masturbating while she talked dirty to him. Kendra's sultry tones were so effective that even hearing her whinge about the weather in Chicago in her husky voice was mildly arousing.

As with all informants, I wanted to know why she felt the urge to come to us with her story. Was it on moral grounds? Was it to expose his sheer hypocrisy? Or was she seeking publicity to increase her profile? 'I just want to get some money to be able to buy a new pair of tits. I need them to be bigger,' she explained. 'I want them real real big!'

It all made perfect sense.

Springer had invited Kendra Jade back on the programme yet again; this time she would be on the show to discuss her record attempt along with five other porno stars to sleep with 350 men in a day. Springer arranged to put her and Kelly up in the hotel the night before the recording, and said that he'd slip into her room for sex with the two of them.

> **❛I had to admit I was pretty impressed with Springer's sexual prowess for taking on two porn queens at the same time.❜**

Just before we left the bar to head to the bedroom to position our covert cameras, Kendra received a phone call. 'Oh, I must take this,' she breathed, 'it's my agent.' After a moment, Kendra said, 'He wants to speak to you,' and handed me her pink diamante-studded mobile phone. The deep voice that came over the phone was, bizarrely, a mix of broad Lancashire laced with an American twang. While I was grappling with that, the agent asked me what format our covert recordings would be, 'analogue video tape or digital?' I asked why. 'The deal is that my girls will do the business, you write your story and you hand over the tapes to me,' he said firmly, claiming that he had thrashed out this agreement with Bond. I asked him who he was and he said, 'I'm the John T Bone, and these are my girls.' He was a bit disappointed that I didn't know who the hell he was.

He announced that he was on his way to join us in Chicago because he too was to be on the Springer show the following day, in his capacity as the organizer of the gang-bang. Hastily I said that it would be foolish for him to show his face at the hotel before Springer arrived, in case he spotted him and got worried; so instead he insisted that we call him straight after Springer had left and show him the tapes. I told him that I was unaware of any deal he may have struck but we could sort it all out once he arrived in town. His motives were as clear to me as Kendra's and became even clearer as I quickly rang the newspaper's library in London and did a cuttings check on him.

John Gilbert Bowen had moved to the US from his hometown of Blackpool and had started his career as a porn star. Now he'd worked his way up in the industry and was a top pornographer, producing and directing films. The five-times married man, now in his fifties, was obviously intending to make our videoed evidence his next money-spinning porn release. It was something that we would never allow to happen, but it meant a lot of diplomacy would be needed for us to get the job done.

Firstly, though, I had to brief Kendra Jade. I wanted her to talk to Springer to provide me with proof that he had instigated the meeting that was about to take place as I wanted to be sure that he wasn't just being set up by a pornographer trying to make some money. I also wanted her to get him to talk about the show, whether he knew some of the guests were fake and to describe his guests' wild antics. But briefing Kendra wasn't easy as both she and her mum stood in the room stark naked, asking Conrad and myself to choose what lingerie they should wear.

Kendra's phone rang and it was Springer, who told her that he would turn up shortly after midnight; he was a bit concerned about being recognized. He wanted to know if there were any people milling around who might spot him and then suggested that it might be safer for him to pick up the girls in his limo. 'Maybe we could go round in the limo for a bit,' he said, planning his threesome on wheels. I stood next to Kendra and listened in; I could almost hear his male hormones racing as I whispered into her ear to tell him she wasn't on for sex in a stretch limo. He definitely didn't want to miss the opportunity and I wasn't surprised when he said he would be in the hotel in ten minutes.

Conrad and I waited for the events to unfold. While the girls had sprayed on clouds of perfume and slipped into their seductive attire, we had trampled on our new overalls to make them look worn. I had written the words 'Love' and 'Hate' on my knuckles with a biro to add authenticity to my role as the workman. It worked: Springer walked straight past me as he sneaked into the hotel room casually dressed in a brown jacket, green sweatshirt, and jeans.

Feeling safe in the comfort of the hotel room, Springer immediately threw off his jacket, hugged the girls and sat beside Kendra on the bed. Kendra was wearing skimpy black lingerie and Springer started to stroke her long peroxide blonde hair. Kendra hadn't forgotten her lines. She discussed the show with him. Springer told her: 'It works partly because I'm separated from the chaos on the stage.'

Kelly, who was lying beside her stepdaughter, asked him if he knew the guests on the show were fake. He replied, 'I never talk to the guests beforehand.' He didn't realize it but he was gifting me quotes and justification for exposing him – how could he say that when he was in a room trying to bed a couple of his guests?

Springer then asked the girls, 'What's tomorrow's show about?' Recording ten shows a week he had no idea what the topics would be. Kelly reminded him the show was about the 350-man gang-bang; Springer, keen to get in before the other 349, asked Kendra for a massage. First she took off his trousers, he peeled off her underwear and they started to grope each other.

Once we'd checked the action was being recorded on the set in the toolbox, Conrad pulled out sandwiches and cans of Coke, as we hadn't eaten all day. So while Springer romped with Kendra as Kelly looked on, we calmly sat on the concrete steps and tucked into our chicken sandwiches. I had just started to take a bite of my chocolate bar when Conrad suggested another peep at the video. I opened the box to be faced with an image of Springer standing in the bathroom doorway masturbating in front of naked Kelly.

I slammed the lid shut and lost my appetite completely. Conrad commented, 'That's something you don't see everyday!'

Springer left within the hour, but the drama was just about to begin for us. No sooner had he left than in came 'The John T Bone', a portly man dripping in gold chains who looked more like a used car dealer from Blackpool than the head of a porn empire. After crunching my hand with his firm shake, he demanded we hand over the tapes immediately.

I told him that I was not aware of any deal to give him our tapes and we needed them to write the story, so he angrily rang Peter Bond, who sheepishly confirmed to me that he had promised the tapes to the porn master. Livid with Bond, I convinced the porn king that we needed to copy the tapes overnight to get the story past our lawyers. He said he would be round to join me for breakfast and to collect the originals. As soon as he left I was on the phone to Bond, who explained that he'd told deputy editor Bob Bird in London that he'd promised the tapes to the pornographer while I was flying across the Atlantic. Bird had responded by telling him that I would handle the situation. So I did: I ran. I checked out of the Executive Plaza hotel and checked into one next door, hanging onto a copy of the tapes to write the story while Conrad flew back to London with the originals to hand to our legal department.

The following morning I turned up at the NBC studios in North Columbus Drive, where the programme is recorded, at the invitation of Springer himself. I had approached him as a British journalist wishing to interview him about his popular show, which had a massive British audience. I told his PR team that Springer was even more relevant for our readers since he had been born in London (his family lived in north London after they fled the Holocaust, en-route to New York).

I was escorted around the set, introduced to the producers and researchers on the show, and sat in the gallery to watch as the programme was recorded. Springer basically helped me write my story by churning out a string of gems that would humiliate him as much as he was humiliating his guests. First he confronted John T Bone: 'Doesn't this perpetuate the myth that women are nothing but sex objects? If you had a daughter is this something you would want her to do?' asked Springer.

I sat there thinking, what a dirty two-faced toe-rag, as he turned to Kendra and began to question her about her morals. 'Three hundred and fifty men is not sex, that's assault! What do you say to the majority of people who say this is highly immoral?' he asked. Kendra did herself proud as she truthfully replied: 'I love sex!' Springer then continued his moral rant saying: 'Having sex with someone you're mad about is special, it's supposed to be something intimate, something personal.' In his trademark final thought, Springer continued: 'Our show is about the outrageous and I can't imagine anything more outrageous. Sex is to do with an emotional relationship with each other. When sex is involved make sure you have at least some feeling with the person with whom you are having sex!'

Straight after the show, I was invited into Springer's office to meet him. As he shook my hand I prayed to god that he had washed it thoroughly after having seen what else he'd used it for a few hours earlier.

I was planning to have a polite chat about his programme and then suddenly confront him; ask him where he had been last night and how he felt he was fit to moralize on TV. I realized that it would probably lead to me being thrown out of the studios by Springer's security, but that would only make for even better reading. I was readying myself for the kill when suddenly more journalists from London, a film crew from the *Richard & Judy* show, arrived.

Introductions were made and then one of the crew remarked: 'Aren't you the reporter that does all the undercover stings on celebrities?'

Springer almost bit his fat cigar in half. My heart sank as I had to confess that yes, that was me. I tried to pass it off by saying that I was in town on an immigration investigation and had been asked to do a small piece about Jerry, but I knew that I couldn't confront Springer in front of the British crew as they'd be straight on the phone to London and our exclusive would leak out. It was a shame as it was a showdown I was looking forward to.

As I left the studios, I caught a glimpse of John T Bone getting into a white limo. With my heart pounding, I quickly turned the other way, flagged down a yellow cab and raced back to the comfort of my hotel. There I transcribed my interviews with Kendra and Kelly, wrote the story and went to bed.

At around 3am I was rudely woken by a phone call from Bob Bird in London. He told me that John T Bone had gone mad since I had fled with the tapes, and had yelled at him about a local state law that made it illegal to film without the consent of all the parties. He had apparently tipped off the authorities and I was told to destroy the tapes before I got nicked.

I jumped out of bed, smashed up one of the three small plastic 8mm video tape cartridges and pulled out what seemed like a never-ending stream of tape. Still half asleep I decided to try and burn the tapes, so I stood in the hotel bathroom, put the first tape into the sink and set it alight. Within seconds clouds of dark black fumes billowed up as the tape melted and smouldered. I realized that the smoke alarms would soon go off and I had to find a plan B.

My heart jumped as a cop car raced past the hotel and a loud police siren sounded outside my window. I smashed open the rest of the plastic cases, pulled out the tape and decided to flush it down the toilet. But that was another failure; the tangled mass of tape wouldn't flush, there was just too much of it. I rang Conrad as our technical expert in desperation and he suggested that I cut the tape up before flushing it. It sounded like good advice but the problem was I didn't have any scissors, and requesting a pair from room service at 3am didn't seem a good idea. I quickly put my hand down the loo and pulled all the tape out, dried it on a towel and stuffed it into a laundry bag. I hastily packed my bags and left the hotel. Outside the hotel I slung the laundry bag into a trash can and flagged a cab to take me to the airport.

Sitting on the plane, I breathed a sigh of relief. I looked down; there on the backs of my hands, faded so that only I could see them still, were the words that I'd scrawled there: Love and Hate. Well I'd had my fill of 'Love' in America; it was time to catch up with 'Hate' back in my hometown.

After a lifetime of exposing villains and witnessing human nature at its worst, it's inevitable that I was hardened, so there were very few things that shocked me; this story did. I was told there was a general practitioner in Birmingham who wanted his mistress, a fellow GP, killed. What followed was a story that would have made great TV for Jerry Springer.

Dr Manohar Rangwani had already approached a local thug and paid him a few hundred quid to throw acid in the face of his ex-lover, but Rangwani became more and more impatient as time went by and her attractive features remained intact. He had decided to seek more professional help; Dr Rangwani contacted Paul Samrai. Samrai, who was based in the West Midlands, was a disgraced barrister who had served a prison stretch after being found guilty of running a multi-million pound passport racket. Sentencing him to three years imprisonment at Southwark Crown Court, Judge Butler said he was guilty of 'large-scale fraud and forgery of a sophisticated kind'. But unbeknown to Dr Rangwani, while Samrai had certainly made a few contacts inside prison, he wasn't using them to further his criminal career; instead he was trying to forge a career in the media as an investigative journalist. He was earning a living by working for *The Cook Report* and for TV investigator Donal McIntyre. Samrai also fed me with tips from time to time.

Samrai had telephoned me, casually asking if I would be interested in a story about a doctor who wanted to hire a hitman to kill his ex-lover, whom he alleged was blackmailing him. Of course I would; what a bizarre and horrible story. However I remained sceptical.

Larger-than-life character Samrai is a typical Punjabi, oozing charm but a little too carefree and prone to exaggeration. He once dragged me all the way to India to show me Mohan Singh, a man from Coventry who'd supposedly died and then reappeared in his home village where he had bought a huge farm with the insurance payout. It was looking good as I got the turbaned old man to stand next to a well on his farm to pose for a photo – I already had the caption 'Alive And Well' in my mind – but although Mohan Singh had the same name as the deceased and had recently returned home to the Punjab, he looked nothing like the photo of the dead man I was clutching in my hands. Samrai tried to convince me that the friendly man with the long white beard who could barely speak English might have undergone plastic surgery and was simply trying to con us. That was until good old Mohan produced paperwork to show that he had just retired after spending most of his life making tyres at the local Dunlop factory.

Nevertheless, when Samrai called that afternoon, despite my cynicism I couldn't take a risk. I told Samrai that if there was any imminent threat to life then we had to alert the police straight away. He reassured me that he knew the doctor personally and that he was a local general practitioner who trusted him; Rangwani wouldn't approach anybody else to carry out the hit. It made sense; after all, as a GP he would have limited sources to find himself a professional hitman.

I told Samrai to go and see Dr Rangwani straight away, to make sure that the acid-thrower was taken off the case immediately, and to tell him that he had found just the right man to carry out the contract killing. I got straight down to work carrying out background checks on the names and addresses I had been given by Samrai.

Dr Manohar Rangwani was a 62-year-old respected general practitioner who had qualified in Pakistan. He lived in a £300,000 house in Knowle, a posh Birmingham suburb with his wife, and ran a busy GP's practice called the Arran Medical Centre in Chelmsley Wood. The family man with two grown-up daughters was also a police surgeon, which meant he was in and out of local police stations examining prisoners and taking blood samples from drunk drivers. That he was an Asian doctor in my hometown made it all the easier for me to ring a few contacts and find out all about him.

His mistress was an attractive Asian woman called Dr Kumundini Khare, a GP from Minworth in Sutton Coldfield. The pair had met back in 1979 when she worked briefly at Dr Rangwani's surgery, at a time when his wife was the receptionist there. Dr Khare was also married at the time. The couples got on very well and set up the Grosvenor Lodge nursing home together in Brownhills in 1988. By then Dr Rangwani and Dr Khare were deep into their fourteen-year secret affair; she even had three children by him, unbeknown to her husband. They would meet in secret twice a week at her surgery, and, while her husband was away on business, at her home. But by 1995 the affair collapsed, along with the nursing home business. Dr Khare alleged that Dr Rangwani raped her, and a furious Dr Rangwani was hauled into his local police station for questioning.

Even though Dr Khare did not press charges, the doc had found it a bitter pill to swallow. And to rub salt in his wounds, Dr Khare had named him in a paternity suit so she could claim from him through the Child Support Agency for the three children he had fathered. He realized his long-suffering wife would finally find out about the affair and his reputation in the local Asian community would be in tatters: he was sent over the edge.

Dr Rangwani was ready to meet a would-be assassin at the Hyatt hotel in the centre of Birmingham. Like some French farce, we would all be undercover: Dr Rangwani came as a shopkeeper called 'Anwar', Samrai pretended I was a dangerous underworld character he'd dug up so he wanted to be referred to as 'Sammy' in my presence; and I, of course, brought my minder Jaws along so that I looked the part of a hitman. Oh, and a one-legged Polish man, Les Chudziki, to take photographs.

On a cold Friday evening, Dr Rangwani turned up with Samrai at the dimly lit hotel bar wearing a long dark coat and a flat cap; if he was trying not to attract attention he didn't do a good job. At the table opposite Les was secretly trying to take a picture; he'd concealed a small camera inside a box of cigarettes and was hoping to get the photo as he lit up a fag. I'd warned him to be ultra discreet, as many stories have been blown by over-zealous photographers trying to snap a picture before we've got the words.

Bespectacled Dr Rangwani nervously introduced himself as 'Anwar' and ordered a glass of whisky. He stared at my unshaven face for a few lingering seconds – which was good as I had a video camera concealed in the button of my denim jacket pointing at his face – then he turned his gaze towards crop-haired Jaws. His eyes caught sight of Jaws's full set of diamond-studded gold teeth crowning his muscular 6ft 2in frame. We looked exactly like a pair of hitmen.

'Jaws' was the name we gave Mahmood Qureshi, a second cousin of mine. Jaws was huge, and spent every day at the gym, so was a powerful looking man as well. He was from Bradford and had spent his early adult life committing a number of petty crimes in and around the area. He'd gone to see a fortune teller who told him that a long-lost relative would change his life, so he flew out to Pakistan and spent all his money trying to find a relative who'd do that, speaking in his Yorkshire accent as he went; but found no one to help so returned home. He saw my name in the paper and called me, and I did – change his life, that is. He joined me, working as my bodyguard, and with his size and those teeth he was an unforgettable sight. He was a great man to have standing next to you, intimidating – and forceful when needed.

'Anwar's' nervous smile indicated that he appeared satisfied that we were capable of carrying out his gruesome orders. Les lit his third cigarette in what couldn't have been more than five minutes, so I suggested we all head up in the lift to our room to plan the murder before he gave the game away. Upstairs, I urged Dr Rangwani to sit in the seat right in front of one of the two video cameras Conrad had concealed in the room.

The conversation that ensued took us all back. 'Anwar' straightaway said, 'You must kill this woman.' He then produced two photographs of Dr Khare; one showed her lying on a couch with her breasts exposed. 'These are the only pictures I could get hold of,' he explained. He said he wanted his mistress killed within the next 24 hours by having her drugged, then strangled, and her body dumped in a river. 'I had an affair with her. Now she has started demanding money from me. She is going to expose me to my family. She was also a business partner and lost me money.'

He outlined how we'd find her and what her movements were. 'She is a doctor, divorced. She works in a practice, drives a Mercedes and lives in a big house in the country,' he said. 'She is there with four of her children, nobody else. She has people there from time to time but nobody stops the night.' Her oldest child was at university, her youngest was only six years old.

He suggested places where we could abduct her. 'At her surgery there are no cameras, but outside her house I think there are,' he warned. 'Near the house after 7pm when she goes there, it's easy to pick her up. She arrives alone and it is deserted. The children will be in the house.'

The dark conversation then turned to the method of killing her. He suggested that Dr Khare should be drugged first to sedate her, then strangled. Then 'Anwar' turned to Sammy with a knowing smile and suggested they may be able to supply the drugs; he was clearly a resourceful shopkeeper. When I asked him if he wanted it to look like an accident he replied, 'You know what to do, I leave it entirely up to you. But make sure you do it properly – don't stab her because she might live. She is a noose around my neck and I want her out of my life.'

Dr Rangwani agreed to pay me £5,000 for the contract killing. 'I don't want to higgle-haggle over these things. I've given you my word,' he said. 'When the job is done you'll have the money in cash. You have to do it.' The cruel doctor told us that, once she was dead, he planned to post the topless photo of Dr Khare to members of her family back in India to cause them further grief.

After he'd left the room, we checked the tapes, which had clearly captured his murderous intent. It was hard to believe that this soft-spoken man nearing retirement age – and who'd taken the Hippocratic oath to help preserve life – was planning to rob five children of their mother.

We went along the next day to watch Dr Khare go to work, and snapped off some photos of her. There are rare occasions when as investigative journalists you feel that you are really making a change to someone's life, or contributing something to society. This was one of them; without us the woman whose photograph we'd just taken could easily be dead.

Dr Rangwani had arranged to meet us again to supply the tranquillizers needed to sedate Dr Khare. The meeting was to take place at a coffee shop above Birmingham's New Street railway station. This time I wouldn't have to worry about disguising my drink, so I took along another of my minders, Harry (someone I knew I could trust as I went to college with his brother: Harry is enormous, a 6ft 4in man weighing in at over 20 stones, an Asian version of that wrestler, Giant Haystacks). He stood guard next to Jaws while I waited for Dr Rangwani to arrive; when he did so, he was smartly dressed in a grey suit, with his balding head of dyed grey hair clearly on display. He looked just like your average trustworthy Asian GP.

He clocked us too and immediately rang Samrai, asking him to meet him alone on the station concourse. Dr Rangwani seemed pleased with my crew and was convinced that we would carry out his orders, telling Samrai that he thought the 'fat man' would be the one that would lift the body and throw it into the river.

The doctor had arranged for the drugs which would knock Dr Khare unconscious to be collected from a chemist near his surgery, we simply had to go there to pick them up. He even gave instructions on how to use the medicine: 'Fill the syringes, inject her in the leg or bottom. Two is more than enough to knock her out for six hours, three might kill her.'

We headed straight over to a chemist on the outskirts of Birmingham. There, the pharmacist, unaware of the doctor's deadly intent, handed over the drugs without asking for a prescription. The bag contained ten ampoules of Lygactil, a strong anti-psychotic drug known as 'liquid cosh'. In another brown envelope were a set of syringes and needles.

Dr Rangwani meant business and the evidence against him was piling up. I arranged to meet him again the following day to collect my deposit for the hit. We met outside a health centre in Fredrick Road, Five Ways, in central Birmingham. Conrad filmed the meeting from the back of his van. First I showed Dr Rangwani the photograph we had taken of Dr Khare so he could identify her as the target, to convince him that we were professionals who'd done our homework and were preparing to murder her.

Although I'd asked for £1,000 up front, he slipped me an envelope containing £200 in crisp notes and assured me that the rest of the money would be paid once the job was done. As we walked off and Dr Rangwani strolled back towards the health centre, he grinned and punched the air with joy. Conrad captured his unashamed excitement on video.

I still wanted to get a shot of Dr Rangwani with a stethoscope draped round his neck. I sent Conrad to see the doc, a video camera concealed in his rucksack, posing as a patient. After waiting for an hour to be seen as a temporary patient, Conrad made a frantic phone call to me, saying that his turn had come, but the receptionist had ushered him into a room to see a lady doc. I told Conrad to say that he had a rash on his testicles and was too shy to show it to a female doctor and insist on seeing Dr Rangwani. But after a lecture from the lady doc explaining how examining male genitals was an everyday part of her job and that Dr Rangwani had finished for the day, Conrad emerged from the surgery red-faced.

That evening Dr Rangwani rang Samrai to confirm that the hit was about to take place; 'So they're at it. So by tomorrow will she be done?' he asked. But it was too late for him; we'd already contacted the police and handed them our evidence. Initially the police were annoyed that we'd not come to them earlier and let them take over the investigation, but one of the officers on the case told me that I'd done a better job than they could have done because they had to follow strict legal guidelines to gain proof.

The story appeared across two pages, headlined 'Doctor In £5,000 Plot To Murder Mistress'. Under the sub-heading 'Prescription For Death' were pictures taken from our covert recordings showing Dr Rangwani handing over the deposit and the drugs.

Dr Rangwani was charged with soliciting a third party to murder. The case, though, didn't rush into court; the wheels of justice grind slowly, but in this case they came to a halt on several occasions because Dr Rangwani claimed he was ill. One court date had to be adjourned because Dr Rangwani was rushed to hospital suffering from chest pains.

It's hard to argue against a doctor on medical grounds. But despite being nailed bang to rights, as they say in our industry, Dr Rangwani refused to plead guilty. So the farce continued and the next scenes were played out at Birmingham Crown Court.

Courts are pure theatre and a case often hinges on whether the reporter can give a good performance before the jury. Over the years I have tried to hone my court skills so that I don't get angry at provocative questions hurled at me or riled by false allegations slung my way. It's a difficult balancing act, not to appear too cocky or over-confident, while not being intimidated or appearing unable to bat off the inevitable attacks on my work and character.

There is nothing more that defence barristers enjoy than courtroom jousting matches with tabloid journalists in the witness box; the cases are guaranteed to be high profile and normally mean that they get their names in the papers the following day by attacking us hacks. The briefs love to play on a jury's mistrust of the tabloid press. The more damning the evidence against their clients, the more they try to divert attention by slinging mud.

It's natural to be a little nervous before entering a courtroom, but in this case I was looking forward to it. It was only the regular phone calls from editor Phil Hall telling me that we had to win this case that piled on any pressure. If Dr Rangwani had got off it would have been terrible PR for the paper and all the usual accusations of the *News of the World* 'setting people up' would have been hurled at us from all the usual quarters.

But Phil had no reason to worry. Dr Rangwani's defence was suicidal. Members of the jury were just as amazed as I was as his barrister struggled to stand up the weak defence.

Dr Rangwani claimed he had never suggested to anyone that any harm should come to Dr Khare. He said Samrai had only contacted me to profit from the story, and had organized the meeting at Birmingham's Hyatt hotel with a group called the 'Asian Council', which would, he claimed, 'amicably' iron out any problems between him and Dr Khare.

Rangwani's explanation for the meeting at which he was filmed discussing details of the murder plot was breathtaking: 'I really do not have any recollection of going into the hotel room upstairs. I may be getting old but I have an excellent memory. I remember being offered another drink in the bar downstairs and I said I didn't want it but someone poured it anyway. I think I must have taken something that blocked my memory. I can only come to the conclusion that I was given some drugs.'

'I remember meeting two men in the public bar of the hotel but the next thing I remember was waking up at home the next day. The first time I heard of the conversations in the hotel bedroom was when I saw the video evidence,' he said.

Even the issue of the dangerous drugs he'd supplied to the 'hit team' had a plausible explanation – plausible, that is, if you were Dr Rangwani. The doctor told defence counsel Mr Richard Wakerley QC that he believed the drugs were for a female relative of mine.

When I had to give evidence, I asked the judge if I could be shown the entire covert video recordings that we had made to refresh my memory. It also meant that the jury could see once again how ludicrous his defence was. Some members of the jury smirked as I told the court how I had never heard of any 'Asian Council' and the videoed conversation in the room didn't sound like someone talking to the Muslim equivalent of the Samaritans.

As the court reporter filed his copy to our newsdesk, a very nervous Phil Hall rang me again, saying that it looked as if the doctor had seemingly credible explanation for his actions. As a witness I couldn't discuss my evidence with Phil, but I told him not to worry. I went back into the witness box with renewed determination, and told the court that Dr Rangwani might be able to put the first meeting with the 'Asian Council' down to a drug-induced memory loss, and he might be able to explain away the drugs as something for my relative, but how could he explain the handover of the cash deposit to me? Or for that matter the phone call asking if Dr Khare would be killed soon?

The jury went out and came back with their verdict within the hour: guilty. Now it was time for me to punch the air with joy. Sentencing Dr Rangwani to seven years imprisonment, Mr Justice Alliott told him: 'The jury has convicted you in my view on overwhelming evidence. You have shown no flicker of remorse and you have invented the most elaborate lies to account for the plain soliciting.' The judge went on to say that a 'peculiarly evil' aspect of the case was that Rangwani had contemplated sending 'unfortunate' topless photographs of Dr Khare to her relatives in India if the plot had succeeded.

But even from behind bars Dr Rangwani didn't give up the fight to save his career. He took the Birmingham Heartlands and Solihull NHS Trust who employed him to an industrial tribunal, claiming unfair dismissal; not surprisingly he lost that too and was struck off the medical register.

That wasn't the most bizarre twist to the tale. I walked into the office one morning to be handed a letter by executive editor Bob Warren. 'It's from Dr Khare, the woman whose life you saved,' he said. Call me naïve, but I thought it would be a nice thank you letter. How wrong I was; she'd put in a complaint about me to the Press Complaints Commission, arguing that I had intruded on her privacy by publishing her name and photograph. I thought bloody hell, I save your life and that's all the thanks I get!

After hours of writing tedious memos and providing justifications for the story, Dr Khare's complaint was dismissed by the PCC.

Why did Dr Rangwani plead not guilty, when there was such a large amount of damning material stacked against him? My father was a magistrate in Birmingham for over twenty-five years, and I remember him telling me that he had never come across any Asian defendant who would put his hands up and plead guilty before him, they always wanted to fight and take their chances. I've had the same experience; in all my years I have not come across a single Asian villain who has simply turned to me and said: 'It's a fair cop guv.' Even when faced with overwhelming videoed evidence, my Asian brethren try to either lie or talk their way out of it.

CHAPTER 4
DISHING UP THE EVIDENCE

It's not all glamour, you know, working for the *News of the World*, it's not all champagne launches and star-studded parties, it's not all plush overseas hotels. Sometimes it's life and death – not always mine, though I have come close; but life and death it is, all the same. Blood sports, for instance. As blood sports go, quail fighting is not the first that springs to mind, yet in illicit battles up and down the country, punters bet up to £40,000 on a single bird fight. The tiny starving birds, their beaks sharpened to a point with a razor blade, are forced to tear and claw at each other until one of them dies in agony.

In early 1999, thanks to Jaws, I penetrated the secret world of the bird butchers by gaining the trust of quail breeder Mohamed Taj Khan, known in the bird world as 'Tarzan'. Under Khan's guidance, I learned how helpless quail are tortured, deafened and even made drunk to goad them into fighting each other to the death. Jaws had heard about this vile activity in the unlikeliest of places; an Asian sweet shop in Great Horton Road, Bradford. A Pakistani milkman came in, celebrating a small windfall; Jaws overheard him and listened intently as the milkman bragged how he had won £250 the night before by betting on a quail fight. Immediately sensing a story, Jaws told him that he too fancied a flutter on the birds, so the milkman drove Jaws in his milk float round to Khan's home where he was welcomed into Khan's group of quail fighters.

After a few meetings to befriend Khan, Jaws claimed that his wealthy boss in London was interested in buying birds and investing in the sport, which paved the way for me to go in and nail the gang. I was invited to witness a tournament held in the dingy front room of Khan's run-down terrace home in Bradford, West Yorkshire. Khan had challenged a group of fellow breeders from Cardiff to take on his champion bird 'Hero', unbeaten in five fights. A white sheet was spread on the floor and a dozen carefully vetted spectators gathered round. Bets totalling £2,300 in cash were collected in a bucket before the birds took centre stage.

Khan, his arms covered with crudely etched homemade tattoos, pulled Hero from a cloth bag and screamed into its delicate ears, explaining that, 'this deafens the bird and it will be stunned. Just watch it go for the other bird. After I've driven it wild, it will fight all day. If you want to put some money down, you won't lose if you back my bird. Hero will tear the other to bits.' As music blared from a stereo to drown the noise of the crowd and the birds' squeals of pain, the dazed contestants were fed some alcohol-soaked seeds, and then brought face to face.

Cruel trainers spend hours squeezing the bird's tender bodies in their hands; this is supposed to encourage the development of powerful neck and breast muscles, sweat off surplus weight, and accustom the quail to pain. The contestants had also been partly plucked to 'streamline' them.

As soon as the maddened birds were released, they started pecking at each other's eyes and striking out with their claws. Each member of the crowd cheered on his fancy. Hero's hapless rival began bleeding, the Bradford contingent chanted 'Kill, kill, kill!', and five minutes later, the cruel spectacle was all over. The Cardiff bird lay twitching in its death throes on the blood-smeared sheet. The losing owner, named Razzak, picked up his mortally wounded bird and callously tossed it into a nearby plastic waste bin. Jubilant Khan kissed the exhausted Hero and punched the air with joy. I couldn't believe the vile spectacle I'd just witnessed, and more was to come, as a series of similar bouts continued throughout the evening, with punters betting on each fight.

Khan boasted of his success as a trainer: 'I've had fights with mobs from London, Luton, Birmingham, Oxford, and Leicester, everywhere.

They all know me in this trade and that I am one of the top men for fighting quail. I've been nicked six times, paid £7,000 in fines and had my birds taken away, but no one can stop me. I can breed and train top killer birds from scratch in a matter of weeks.' Khan thought I wanted to buy birds from him so that I too could train fighting birds. Jaws, with a camera concealed in a sports bag, managed to secretly video the evening, capturing the incriminating evidence. As one of his sidekicks sat squeezing a quail in his hands, Khan pointed to six mesh-bottomed bags hanging from the ceiling, with a young bird in each. He explained: 'I keep the birds in these special bags because it means they have to balance their little claws on the mesh bottoms. It builds their legs up so they will fight better. I have people come round here to learn from me about how to train quails. But I only see people a couple of times a week when my wife Anne is out of the way.'

> **'When I asked how the quail were, my Aunt replied, "They were very tasty, son. I cooked them and we all ate them yesterday."'**

Pulling a small bird out of a bag, he added, 'It takes six weeks and a lot of work to train them to fight good. These ones are ten weeks old. They're not fighting yet.' Khan then led me downstairs to a dark, rat-infested cellar crammed with broken television sets and building material, where he kept another eight birds. They were caged individually in empty plastic paint pots with an opening in the side covered with chicken wire. Seizing a couple of the birds, he put them on the floor and encouraged them to fight. 'That one won a £2,300 fight the other week. Once they've had a good fight, I leave them to rest for a while and re-feather again. You have to starve them so that when they see another bird, they just want to kill it.' Grabbing a third quail from a cardboard box, Khan demonstrated the 'streamlining' process. As he tugged out the feathers, the squirming bird began to bleed. 'This one had a fight last week – it's a champion bird. Anybody will pay me £200 for that bird, but you can have it for £60. It's a good fighter bird, that. You can have these other two as well – they've had fights, but not for money, practice fights. In eight weeks, they'll be ready for a money fight. I've got to knock a few ounces off that one and it will be a killer bird. It will rip birds to pieces.'

Another plastic tub contained three quail that Khan said he used as sparring partners for his prize birds. He said: 'They're rubbish, they're just for killing.'

Khan then produced a razor blade and chiselled away at the delicate beak until it was a needle-like point, and revealed how he and others like him fought a constant battle with the law. 'You have to be careful,' he warned. 'There have been a lot of raids in Bradford. We had one £40,000 fight and only three people from each party were allowed to watch. But somebody reported it and the police raided. It was a party from Scotland that came down. We've gone underground now.'

I bought three of his fighting quail to rescue them from the cruel death that awaited them. I had planned to drop them off at a small farm in north Yorkshire, where they would stay until the RSPCA inspected them. However, when I arrived at the farm, there was no one there. It was a Friday afternoon and the farmer had gone out and wasn't due back until late. I couldn't wait around, so with three quail shuffling around in a cardboard box on the back seat of my car, and a dinner party to attend in London, I had to find somewhere quick to leave the quail. I rang my father in Birmingham, who helpfully suggested I leave the quail with my Auntie Zubaida in Bradford who would look after them. It was a good tip, and my Aunt happily took custody of the birds.

I returned to Bradford after the weekend to Auntie Zubaida's to collect the birds, which I would have to hand over to the RSPCA. But when I turned up and asked how the quail were, my Aunt replied: 'They were very tasty, son. I cooked them and we all ate them yesterday.'

I desperately raced round to buy another three fighting quail from Khan. This time I personally chauffeured them to London, where I handed them to my colleague Harry Scott, the chief sub-editor at the paper who owned a farm. I tipped off the RSPCA who raided Khan's home along with local police, rescuing scores of birds.

In court, Khan was ordered to do 200 hours of community service and pay £500 costs and was warned that he had escaped jail by a whisker.

I felt pleased but a little bit guilty as a spokesman for the RSPCA praised my work: 'The *News of the World* has done a great job in infiltrating this cruelty. This prosecution would not have taken place without the *News of the World*. It was investigative journalism of the highest order.' The fact my family ate the bloody evidence didn't make it into the paper – I thought it best to leave that bit out.

CHAPTER 5

TARGET PRACTICE WITH BIN LADEN'S MEN

It was just a few days after 9/11 and Conrad, Jaws, and I were about to cross the Afghan border from Pakistan, to infiltrate the enemy who had sworn their allegiance to Osama bin Laden.

In the back of a battered old pick-up truck I squatted next to Conrad and Jaws, all of us dressed in traditional Pakistani *shalwaar kameez*, a long shirt and baggy trousers. Sandwiched in between us were four Taliban fighters clutching AK-47 sub-machine guns. Our bones shook every time the vehicle went over a pothole in the winding dirt track, high in the Afghan mountains. Suddenly Conrad whispered behind me, 'Fucking hell!' I quickly turned to look at him as he sat nervously on a sack of flour. One of the elderly Afghan warriors, who had a huge grin on his face, was gently stroking Conrad's knee. It was the first time these Taliban had seen a white boy, and in an area where homosexuality is not uncommon, the fighter had clearly taken a shine to Conrad.

Conrad's suitor had a loaded AK-47 propped up beside him, so I diplomatically explained that Conrad had recently converted to Islam after marrying a Muslim girl. Despite my best attempts to quash the Afghan's amorous advances by implying that Conrad was straight, he continued to stare at him throughout the uncomfortable and perilous journey. The Taliban believed we were Muslim sympathizers from London, who were willing to help them financially and would recruit foreign Muslims to join them in their *jihad*, or holy war, against the West.

A High Court judge in Lahore who was a family friend had put me in touch with a veteran *mujahideen* leader in Peshawar called Ghulam Khan. Khan, a man in his sixties with a long white beard who had fought bravely against the Russians for several years, was a feared and respected figure among the young Taliban. We had been warmly welcomed by Khan, who didn't know our true identities, when we went to meet him at the back of a nondescript mosque near the Main Chowk, or Square, in the bustling city.

A meeting of Muslim brothers was already in full flow and we were invited to join them. Around twenty men sat drinking *kava*, a herbal tea, discussing the inevitable Western backlash against their hero, bin Laden. Unnervingly, I noticed a pile of guns stacked up on the floor just outside the room. It was the first time I'd seen weapons in a mosque. Khan introduced us as Muslim brothers from England who had come to help in the battle against the West, and we were greeted by a round of handshakes and chants of: 'Praise Be To Allah!' We were each handed a small cup of the tea that tasted foul. While Conrad and I politely sipped the unpleasant brew, Jaws interrupted the meeting by requesting milk and sugar.

This was an insult to our Taliban hosts and I gave Jaws a dirty look, telling him firmly: 'This ain't bloody Starbucks, just drink it as it fucking comes!' Luckily, no one in the room spoke English; otherwise they would have heard us arguing over their tea while they discussed ways to fight the infidel invaders who were en-route.

Khan announced: 'If America strikes our Muslim brothers next door, we will have to take to arms again and go into the hills and fight them. There are many Taliban among us here and supporters who have vowed to rise up and fight against the Americans, or even Pakistan forces here if they side with the West.'

One man stroked his long henna-dyed beard and piped up: 'We have been betrayed by our own Pakistani government. To support the West is to be in league with the devil. The Afghanis are our own people. We speak the same language [Pushto], have the same religious beliefs and customs, it is our duty to do whatever we can to help them. They are our brothers in Islam.'

Another man, in his thirties, added: 'A lot of our brothers here have fought before and will not hesitate to go back.' Khan told the group that he was going over the border to meet a Taliban Commander to find out how they could assist them in the impending war.

After the meeting, which was followed by prayers in the mosque, Khan agreed to take my pals and me over the border to introduce us to a Taliban leader. He bundled us into the back of his unroadworthy truck, alongside seven of his sidekicks, all bearded men, a couple of them wearing distinctive black Taliban turbans. With black toxic fumes bellowing out of the exhaust, Khan drove his truck from Peshawar towards the Khyber Pass, which leads to the Afghan border. But at a Pakistan army checkpoint on the edge of the city, the vehicle was flagged down. A sign declared: 'No foreigners beyond this point.'

Two military guards came over and said special passes were required to go any further. Even if we had passes, we would be escorted by Pakistani troops who would take us no closer than five miles from the Afghan border; but Khan dismissed the restrictions with a knowing smile. 'Don't worry about papers; you are friends of ours and guests of the Taliban. We know ways to get you wherever we want. These are our mountains,' reassured Khan. 'Allah is Great!' His henchmen joined in the response: 'Allah Is Great!'

As Khan drove north towards Torkham border crossing, in the Nangarhar province of Afghanistan, he asked us to hide under hessian sacks containing flour. By now we were all getting frightened, we didn't know what would happen to us if we were caught trying to cross the border illegally, but, more importantly, how the hell would we get back?

Conrad had been particularly concerned about going to Afghanistan. We knew that President George Bush had declared his 'war on terror' and staying in a Taliban camp we could easily become casualties of US bombardment. In addition to that threat, Conrad feared that as a Westerner in Afghanistan, the Taliban might see through his feeble cover story and turn on him. Assuming the worst, Conrad had penned a letter to his girlfriend Carly Jay back in Enfield, north London. He'd left the romantic epic with one of my relatives, asking him, in the event that he was killed in Afghanistan, to post it to England.

After around ten minutes almost suffocating under the weight of the sacks of flour, one of the men in the back of the truck shouted that it was now ok for us to emerge. As we looked up we could see the barren landscape of the Afghan mountains. We were on the road to Kabul. A rugged mountainous terrain littered with caves and natural hiding places, it was clear that any foreign infantry would struggle to locate the enemy, never mind engage them in battle. With the onset of winter looming, conditions in the snow-capped Hindu Kush, where temperatures can drop to minus 50°F, would be intolerable for the allied forces. The so-called 'war on terror' was going to be long and tough.

'One youngster, aged about 12, casually appeared clutching a rocket launcher and ammunition. "This can finish off a tank from 700 yards ..."'

The *mujahideens* had successfully taken on the might of the Soviet Union in a ten-year war and defeated them. It was a testament to their incredible resilience and sheer courage. The Russians had committed 642,000 men to the war. A total of 15,000 died. And nearly 470,000 soldiers – 70 per cent of their force – were wounded or struck down by hepatitis and typhoid fever. In return, Soviet troops reportedly killed 1.3 million Afghans. They also forced five and a half million people, one-third of the pre-war population, to leave the country as refugees. Ironically, the *mujahideen* fighters had been financed and armed by the West. US President Ronald Reagan had praised them as 'freedom fighters'. These were the men who had now become our enemy.

As we drove along the mountain road, another truck on a dirt track higher up was travelling towards us. As it approached, it slowed down and our hosts instinctively eyed up their Kalashnikov rifles and spoke furiously among themselves in Pushto. I asked them if there was a problem. 'It's a rival warlord and they may have seen your white friend.

Khan is a bit worried that they might try and kill him, but tell your friend it's a matter of honour. He is our guest. If they kill him, we will kill two of their people,' he reassured us. Conrad asked what the commotion was. I couldn't bring myself to translate what the *mujahideen* had just told me. Instead I told him they thought it might be Pakistani intelligence officers, but they were now satisfied that they were just locals.

Again, our hosts ordered us all to keep our heads down. I was beginning to get just as nervous as Conrad, although I tried my best not to show it. I felt that at least one of the men in the truck with us was not totally convinced that we were genuine. He hadn't uttered a single word to me in the two-hour journey so far, and looked at me with his bloodshot eyes filled with suspicion.

I realized that one of the reasons they wanted us to hide under the sacks again was so that we would not remember the route. The last thing we saw before ducking under the flour was a painted sign on a mountainside. It read: 'Go Back America. Death!' After what seemed like an eternity racing along the winding mountain road through the pass, the journey became increasingly rough and painful. It was a huge relief when the truck eventually screeched to a halt. We were told to get up. 'We have to stop here and continue on foot,' explained Khan. 'But this is war time, so everyone must be careful.' We trekked in our Pakistani sandals, through the breathtaking mountainous region, for about an hour until we finally arrived at the Taliban hideout. We were the first Western journalists to cross the mountains into Afghanistan, since President Bush had issued his threat of military retribution.

A high mud wall enclosed a courtyard and two large rooms. Several armed men sat in the yard with their weapons beside them. Another group were praying.

'This is Afghanistan and those mountains behind us are Pakistan. There are lots of Pakistani troops hiding there,' gestured Khan. 'We have our brothers scattered all over this area. The West can't dream of tackling us here. They will surely be defeated.'

A man named Raim Ullah warmly greeted Khan and his pals. His beard was thick and black, but his head was shaved. He had a permanent bruise on his forehead, a mark of beauty among Muslims, as it had been earned by bowing his head on the floor in prayer five times a day over many years. After several minutes of discussion between them, we were introduced to a succession of men, some carrying AK-47s over their shoulders. Each man came into the courtyard in turn to shake hands with us before leaving.

Janzer, the Taliban Commander, was one of the men at prayer. The bearded man in his forties wore a black turban and a flowing white robe. After finishing his devotions he picked up his rifle. Janzer sat on a string-woven bed and spoke with pride and enthusiasm about his preparations for war. 'We are not afraid of anything except Allah,' he said. 'We have young boys who are with us, and older brothers who are with us. We have youth and we have experience.' He invited us to share a silver bowl of water with him.

Janzer wanted to explain the reasons for his anger at the West and Pakistan President Pervaiz Musharraf, who has declared his support for George Bush in the war on terrorism. 'Osama bin Laden is like us, someone who is fighting for Islam,' said Janzer. 'We cannot and will not betray him like Musharraf has done.'

Islam is unequivocal. The very word Islam, means peace. Nowhere in the Holy Koran is there any justification for acts of terrorism against innocent people. But arguing with Janzer about his twisted interpretation of Islam would have been suicidal. 'We are not terrorists, we are religious people fighting for our rights. The West has no evidence to say that Osama bin Laden has done anything wrong,' he claimed. 'They just want someone to blame and the Islamic world to be finished. But Islam is too powerful. This is a holy war and the whole Muslim world should be with us.' It was a ludicrous belief that was not only held by the uneducated and misguided Taliban, but also shared by a large proportion of Muslims living in Britain.

Throughout our short stay in Afghanistan we did not see a single female. The Taliban's distorted view of the

Koran had resulted in women being treated worse than pets in British households. It was a hellish existence for women; they had to be covered from head to toe in a *burka*, were not allowed to work, and couldn't leave home without a close male relative escorting them. Neither could they wear cosmetics, laugh loudly (in case strangers heard their voices), or wear high-heeled shoes, which might make a noise and attract the attention of men as they walked. Women caught violating the tough Sharia laws could be brutally beaten by religious police wielding sticks, publicly flogged, and stoned to death.

Janzer and his thirty-odd men wanted to give us a display of their firepower. They took us to the edge of the mountain and produced an arsenal of weapons. We counted over a dozen Russian AK-47s and other small arms. They proudly took it in turns to fire bullets into the skies, chanting words from the Koran. One youngster aged about 12 casually appeared clutching a rocket launcher and ammunition. 'This can finish off a tank from 700 yards. We used it against the Russians. It works well,' explained a proud Taliban fighter.

The weapon certainly looked as if it had been well used. The rocket-propelled grenade (RPG) was held together by brown packaging tape. The fighter politely asked us if we wanted a demonstration. Without thinking, Jaws foolishly asked to see the RPG in action. I quickly butted in to halt the demonstration. We were behind enemy lines. In an attempt to show off their unlimited military might, the Taliban could be inviting an assault by allied forces, which were massing in the mountains. The Taliban fighter was just as pleased as me when I declined his offer. 'I'd rather save every rocket for American tanks. Each rocket costs us $5,' he said. 'We have been told to sit tight until the Americans attack.'

The gang then asked us to join them for target practice as they fired bullets down the mountainside, shattering large rocks. They laughed as Conrad hit the target with the Kalashnikov. 'You can join the Jihad!' they said.

Janzer, who was crouched down on the floor with three other men, then stood up, picked up his AK-47 and stared at the bleak mountains in front of him. 'God willing, we will wipe out the Americans', he said. 'Don't forget to tell your people that we Muslim brothers are prepared to die for our beliefs. Tell the British and the Americans!'

I asked Janzer how the group received battle orders. He explained: 'We don't need any orders. We are all equals and have the same goal. If anyone moves in these mountains, we know about it.' In a dramatic demonstration of his power he raised his Kalashnikov automatic rifle above his head and emptied a magazine of bullets into the sky.

As the deafening sound echoed back from the rock-strewn landscape he yelled: 'Death to Bush and the great Satan America! Jihad!'

Night was near and we suggested it was time to go, but Khan refused. 'You cannot go back at night,' he said. 'It's not safe, there are too many patrols.' Janzer added: 'Because you are a Muslim brother and have been introduced by an old friend, you are welcome here. While you are here as my guest, it is my duty to take care of you.'

The Taliban invited us to join them for chicken curry, rice, and naan bread. An elderly man called Baba, who doubled up as lookout, cooked it over an open fire. We sat on the ground and ate off a tablecloth spread on the floor. The meal was eaten in deadly silence. The food was well cooked. There was no doubting that the Taliban were very hospitable and likeable people. While they all drank water from a well, we as special guests were entertained with lukewarm bottles of Coca-Cola. After dinner, the men all sat burping loudly as a sign of appreciation of the food. It was expected of us too; I looked over at Jaws and we both smiled. No matter how hard we tried to expel a burp, we couldn't. So I faked one, and it seemed to be well received.

As night fell, lanterns were set around the rugged camp. It was like going back in time with all the usual luxuries that we take for granted banned by the Taliban's draconian decrees. There were no televisions or newspapers, and even listening to music had been banned. At precisely 9pm nearly half of the men laid down on rugs and string-beds, still with their weapons next to them, and went to sleep. Janzer explained: 'We work in shifts. We will wake for morning prayers at 5am and then take over the watch.'

All three of us were given one of the two rooms to sleep in. But we didn't get much sleep. We were woken at 5am to join the morning shift in prayer. Conrad looked close to tears and was shaking with fear. 'I'm fucked. How am I going to pray?' he whimpered. I told him to follow me, and tried to convince him that nobody would notice. After performing *wuzu*, the ritual ablutions, Conrad stood in the line-up next to me and five Taliban soldiers. He mimicked my actions as I knelt down in prayer. Conrad managed to get through prayers without arousing any suspicion.

After prayers, we were treated to breakfast of tea and bread with jam and honey, again eaten while sitting in a line-up on the floor. I joined Janzer who was squatting on a mountain with his piercing eyes scanning the breathtaking terrain for signs of a US invasion.

'We are ready and waiting to sacrifice our lives for Allah. That is our strength as an army,' he said. 'We saw off the Russians and now, god willing, we will see off the Americans, the British and anyone else who dares to come on our soil!'

History proved that no invading army could take Janzer's threat lightly. The Soviet invasion had devastated the country, and in a bitter civil war that followed, the Islamic-inspired movement called the Taliban took command. Two million refugees joined those already abroad, and what was left of the country was torn to pieces. While I didn't agree with Janzer's support for terrorism I knew that Western leaders would be wrong to underestimate the total commitment of Janzer and the rest of the Taliban fighters. The unrelenting will of the men left in Afghanistan today has been forged in fire. The men are unmoved by starvation, cruelty, threats, or even death – which makes them a formidable enemy.

As Khan bundled us back into the truck for the long road back to Pakistan, Janzer embraced me and said: 'God willing, we will meet again!' And, as Conrad clambered into the back of the truck, his Taliban admirer rushed over and handed him a gift as a souvenir – his Islamic prayer cap!

CHAPTER 6
THE MEN
IN BLACK

An Albanian gangster pulled out a 9mm semi-automatic pistol and fired four bullets into an old metal tin 30 yards away. The deafening sound of gunshots echoed around the deserted mountains of Ardenice as three of the bullets pierced the tin. Freddi, the burly minder to a mafia boss, handed the weapon to me and said: 'Now let's see how good you are.'

I tried hard to control my trembling hands as the small criminal gang gathered round to watch the spectacle. I turned to my informant-cum-interpreter and told him that I didn't know how to shoot. A worried look crossed his face. 'Just do it, pull the trigger. If they want to play, you have to play. If these people don't like you they kill you and me too,' he said.

These were less than comforting words. I grasped the handgun, stretched out my arm and took aim. As I fired the gun I felt a painful shudder run right through to my shoulder. I missed the target by a mile. A fat unshaven man standing a few feet behind me laughed as he quickly pulled out his weapon and fired a shot. The bullet whistled past my ear, narrowly missing my head before clipping the side of the metal tin. With a bulky recorder weighing heavy in my denim jacket, and a pinhole camera in the button, the sweat started to roll down my face. But I couldn't appear scared or intimidated, so I asked: 'Do you have an AK-47 here? That's the weapon I'm used to.' Luckily they didn't.

Freddi reloaded the handgun with a single bullet and handed it to Conrad – they wouldn't hand over a gun with a full magazine in case we turned it on them. Conrad seemed more comfortable holding the weapon; I knew he was a good shot as he had displayed his shooting skills to me in amusement arcades around the world. Luckily his practice paid off. Conrad hit the centre of the metal tin and our hosts were suitably impressed. After handing the gun back to Freddi, Conrad whispered to me: 'I've got to get a proper job, you're going to get me killed one day. These people are crazy!'

We were in Albania attempting to nail a mafia kingpin who headed an international people smuggling racket. Asylum seekers were flooding into Britain claiming to be victims of the war in neighbouring Kosovo; more than 80,000 applications were submitted to the Home Office, but most were economic migrants fleeing Albania. Home Office officials seemed unable to differentiate between bogus and genuine Kosovar refugees, and the route from Albania to London was regarded as a fast track to a life of scrounging in Britain.

We'd flown to Tirana, the Albanian capital, accompanied by our informant Bekim, a young Albanian who worked as a translator for a London law firm. He wanted to blow the whistle on the racket because the gangsters had killed several members of his family. They'd been promised a life of luxury in Britain, but once at sea the gangsters simply took their money and forced them at gunpoint to jump to their deaths. Bekim had read several of my immigration investigations and for a fee was willing to lead us through his distant cousin Freddi to the Mr Big, Artian Yzer – the feared mafia boss who was making a fortune from the human trafficking racket. Freddi believed I was a Pakistani criminal who wanted to send people to Britain via Albania.

Freddi had kindly sent his driver to pick us up. He was a middle-aged man called Afrim who drove a battered old saloon car, with a handgun wedged between the driver's seat and the handbrake. 'Too much bandits, too much bandits,' explained Afrim as I pointed to the gun. We drove for three hours across countryside that made it hard to believe we were in 21st-century Europe. It was like driving through poor Indian villages, with the occasional donkey or cow wandering on the roads and people selling vegetables from wooden carts at the roadside.

We checked into a £9-a-night hotel, a one-star establishment advertising hot water as one of its luxuries, in the small town of Fier. I asked for the best suite in the eight-bedroom hotel and was led by the receptionist to a dingy room on the third floor, which had a small single bed in one corner and an old black and white TV set on a small table. As it was in the middle of winter the room was of course freezing cold. Freddi, who invited us for dinner that evening at his local taverna, had arranged the hotel.

Freddi, a thirty-something with a cigarette hanging from his lip, arrived wearing a black T-shirt under his leather jacket; a Beretta pistol was stuffed in his waistband, and for good measure he had a Colt 45 in a shoulder holster. 'Before business comes friendship,' he said as he introduced us to four of his fellow henchmen. Shot glasses were passed round the table and filled with a clear liquid. 'It's Raki, best drink,' announced Freddi, lighting up again.

I quietly told Bekim that I was a Muslim and didn't drink alcohol. Freddi overheard me and shouted: 'We are all Muslim, this is good drink for friendship!' A nervous Bekim warned me: 'It will be a big insult if you don't drink Raki with them.' As the first course of bread and feta cheese arrived, Freddi asked me where I was born. I told him London. Everyone at the table joined Freddi as he raised his glass and toasted: 'To London!' I downed the Raki in one. It was like drinking white spirit, and fire ran down my throat to my stomach. The things I do for my job.

Next Freddi asked me my father's name; again he led the toast. It was the same for my mother a few minutes later, then my son, my school, and my car. I asked Bekim if Freddi was taking the piss. He reassured me: 'He is just showing you respect. It is their custom.'

While the Albanians downed Raki as if it were water, Conrad and I were getting more and more intoxicated – for me, this was the first and only time in my life. My head was spinning. Then the main course of steak was served and just when I thought Freddi's toasting had come to an end he turned his attention to my sidekick, Conrad. Freddi asked Conrad where he had been born. Fearing that it would result in another ten shots of Raki, Conrad drunkenly quipped: 'I'm an orphan, I have no parents and was found in a bush!' I kicked Conrad under the table, as these were not people to joke with. There was a long pause. Freddi lifted his glass, laughed loudly, and toasted: 'To the Bush!' By the end of dinner, Freddi had leant over the table and thrown an arm around my shoulder. 'Tomorrow I will take you to see my boss, Artian. He is the biggest boss in the whole of Albania,' he said in a heavy Eastern bloc accent.

We staggered back to the hotel, past scary groups of men in their black leather jackets and unsmiling faces, and went up to our rooms, which, after a dozen shots of Raki, seemed like the Ritz. The room was in darkness; there was a power cut. Conrad came and handed me a torch. I climbed into bed, pulled up a blanket riddled with cigarette burns, shivering with the cold and the Raki roaring around my bloodstream, and tried to sleep.

The following day Freddi arrived in an old white Mercedes 190E to pick us up for our big meeting. He drove us 20 miles across country roads and a winding track to the top of a mountain in Ardenice. Afrim and another giant in black T-shirt and leather jacket called Edwart followed us in another vehicle. At the top of the deserted mountain there was a small restaurant, normally closed in the winter but opened specially just for us. As we waited for the mafia boss to arrive, we took part in Freddi's impromptu shooting challenge with the tin box.

Two flash cars drew up outside the remote bar, and a short while later Freddi summoned me inside to introduce me to his boss. Artian was a fat man in his forties who also wore a black leather jacket but was dripping in gold chains. He sat drinking whisky and smoking a cigar as two of his men stood guard behind him. Bekim translated as he told me how he sent illegal immigrants to Britain every week. 'We send people from Vlore (a south Albanian port) to Brindisi in Italy using small boats. I cannot guarantee your people will always make it across the sea, 59 of them died last week when one of our boats sank. But you will only pay for the ones that make it across. I send around 30 to 40 people in one boat. They are small speedboats with fast engines.' The ruthless racket had made Artian one of Albania's richest crooks.

'Everyone wants to go to England because the government give them good money there,' he explained. 'They claim asylum and say they are from Kosovo. Easy!'

He was right. A notorious Albanian pimp, Luan Plakici, and a murderer called Mane Driza had been welcomed into Britain as Kosovans, even though the pair lived 300 miles away from the nearest fighting in the Balkans. Plakici smuggled sixty women into Britain, having promised them jobs as cleaners and waitresses, but instead forced them into prostitution. He made £1 million before he was imprisoned for ten years for pimping, kidnapping, and incitement to rape.

> **"Just do it, pull the trigger. If they want to play, you have to play. If these people don't like you, they kill you and me too."**

Scotland Yard's vice squad officers estimate that Albanians today control more than 75 per cent of brothels in the United Kingdom and their operations in London's Soho alone are worth more than £15 million a year. They are present in every big city, with Albanian-run brothels recently uncovered in Glasgow, Liverpool, and Cardiff as well as in provincial strongholds including Telford and Lancaster. Armed Albanian pimps have scared off underworld rivals including the Jamaican Yardies and the Chinese Triads.

Artian explained how his travel scheme worked: 'I have houses all over Vlore where we keep people until it's time to go. It's your job to get your people to me and it's mine to send them onto England. I want $500 per person, that is a price for large groups, and only if it is regular business.' In a highly organized international network, Artian controlled several boats and drivers who would pick up the illegals in Brindisi and drive them via Calais to Dover concealed in the back of lorries. He claimed he had sent nearly 1,000 immigrants to Britain including Turks, Jordanians, Algerians, and Pakistanis. Artian was so confident that he offered a money-back guarantee. 'You only pay if they arrive in Italy and phone you to confirm they are safe.'

Not all of the travellers were favoured with the same guarantee. Later Freddi revealed that the mafia speedboat drivers themselves were responsible for the brutal deaths of scores of people. 'There is always a man with a machine-gun on board. If they see Italian police boats they simply point the weapon at the passengers and order them to jump to their deaths into the sea. If they refuse, they shoot them. This means when the police approach the boat, all they find is a couple of Albanians who say they are sailing.'

With all the evidence on tape, I returned to the hotel, which had started to feel like home. I was writing the story when my mobile rang; it was Bekim, who frantically told me to get out of the hotel. 'Freddi has found out who you are,' he said. 'His friend owns the hotel and has checked the name on your passport and knows who you really are. If he finds you, you're dead.'

I immediately woke Conrad, we quickly packed our bags and headed for the town square to try and find a cab. The streets were crammed full of men, all wearing leather or suede coats, seemingly staring at us. The fact that I was the only Asian in town made it easy to spot me. We jumped into a taxi and asked the driver to take us to Tirana airport. But as we headed out of town, I realized that the airport would be the first place Artian's men would look for us.

I phoned a friend of mine, Robert Cole, a senior producer at the BBC, who had been in Albania during the civil war. He suggested we head to Vlore, the port Artian used, where we could try and get on a ship. After a two-hour taxi ride to the port, we were desperate to jump aboard any ship leaving Albania, but were told that the first ferry out would be in the morning. We checked into a small family hotel in the once thriving sea-side resort, which had been ravaged by civil war; fortunately the owner of the hotel didn't ask for our passports. At the crack of dawn we walked towards the ferry port and joined scores of men, women, and children milling around the locked gates. Ferry tickets were being sold by a number of ticket touts loitering outside the bustling port. We bought our £30 tickets, which resembled a handwritten cab receipt, unsure whether they were genuine. As the gates opened we joined the scrum outside the port office – queuing clearly wasn't an Albanian custom. After an hour of being pushed and shoved by our fellow passengers, we finally had our tickets validated by a port official.

We were directed to the quay where we joined another crowd jostling to get on board the old rusting ferry in front of us. Two armed police officers wearing dark blue uniforms were checking travel documents at the boarding ramp. The cops started shouting at the Albanian family in front of us as they inspected their passports. Then to my astonishment, the police officer tossed their passports into the sea before sending them away. I was worried what the officer would make of an Asian man trying to leave Albania by sea with a British passport. I quickly slipped a $100 bill in the pages of my passport and handed it to him. The officer flicked through the book and with a magician's sleight of hand, gave me back my passport minus the crisp green bill. No receipt for my expenses claim there, then.

Conrad and I both breathed a huge sigh of relief as we were allowed up the gangway and boarded the vessel. Passengers on board were already rolling out blankets and lying on the floor. We endured a six-hour crossing before arriving at Brindisi, on the eastern coast of Italy. Our hotel, the five-star Masseria San Domenico, with swimming pool, tennis courts, golf course, and a colour TV in my bedroom, seemed like heaven. Despite the luxury of the hotel room, it was hard to sleep as I thought how easily I could have lost my life just a few hours earlier.

But the time I came closest to losing my life, though, wasn't with the Albanian mafia, or even with the Taliban in the Afghan mountains – it was in a north London park. Two teenage girls had been shot dead outside a New Year's Eve party in a hairdresser's salon in Birmingham. The tragic deaths of Charlene Ellis, 18, and Latisha Shakespeare, 17, who had died in a hail of bullets from an automatic weapon in Aston dominated the news.

Inevitably I was asked by the news desk to try and buy a gun to demonstrate how easy it was to obtain firearms in Britain. But in the wake of a high-profile gun incident, when villains are extra cautious who they deal with, it is never easy.

One of my informants put me in touch with a Yardie gang in north London who were told I was an Asian drug dealer and were willing to sell me weapons. I turned up to collect two overpriced handguns for £1,500 from a pub in Edmonton, north London. I was accompanied by my informant, an African called Paul who had negotiated the deal. When we arrived at the pub at around 10pm, one of the dread-locked villains, Tito, a crack-addict who had had dealings with Paul before, told us the handover would take place in Pymmes Park around the corner.

As arranged, Paul and I waited in the park by the toilets in pitch darkness. Soon we were approached by Tito and four other black men wearing balaclavas. One of them shouted, 'You want to see a gun? Well here it is bro!'. He held the gun to my head as one of his pals pulled out a huge machete. 'Now give me your money,' he demanded.

Paul started screaming hysterically as the two men began to punch and kick him to the ground. I tried to calm down the man with the gun, telling him they could have the £1,500 if he left us alone. As I pulled out the bundle of cash from my pocket he lowered the gun from my head. Paul continued to scream as a tall black man held the machete to his throat. Tito, said, 'Hurry up,' but they decided to give us a good kicking before they left. We were both punched in the ribs and head by three of the men and left lying battered and bruised on the muddy grass. Paul was kicked unconscious. Given the circumstances we'd got off lightly. These men could easily have shot us or slashed our throats without a second thought.

I rang Conrad who had been sitting in his van trying to film the scenes using a special night vision camera. He said he'd managed to get photos of two of our assailants as they left the park and removed their balaclavas. I told Paul, who was shaking like a leaf, that we should call the police and get him to a hospital.

'Please don't. If you grass on these people, they know where I live and they will kill me and my family,' he pleaded. I rang news editor

Greg Miskiw and told him that I had been robbed at gunpoint. Greg asked me if I was alright and, as soon as I'd shakily said, 'yeah, I think I'm okay,' continued, 'Ok don't worry about the money, but you have got to get me a gun for this week. The editor really wants the story.'

It was a reminder to me that in the ruthless world of newspapers, few things are more important than the story.

I headed to my old patch, Birmingham, where I linked up with one of my contacts and asked him for a favour. With police scouring the city to track down the cold-blooded killers of the two teenagers, getting hold of a weapon in Birmingham of all places was a difficult task.

But my contact came good. I was put in touch with a Jamaican villain called Dee, who was told I desperately needed a gun to settle a score. He told me: 'It's real hot here, if you want the piece bad, you do it my way. I've got a 9mm (handgun) for £600. It'll do the business. But if you want something really right, you got to pay two grand. I'll give you something special, an AK. This would do serious damage, worse than what you've seen in the news.'

I agreed to the £2,000 fee for the deadly weapon that could fire 600 rounds a minute, and arranged to pick up the weapon in a deserted country road off the M4 near Bristol. Dee warned: 'Any Five-O [street slang for police] and bullets will fly!' I drove down there and, following the directions I'd been given, trudged into a field where I left the money under a bucket of foul-smelling chicken manure. A half-hour later I returned, as instructed, and picked up the gun. I wrote the story and came into the office on Saturday night just as the first edition of the paper was rolling off the presses.

I was livid when I saw that my efforts had made just six paragraphs at the bottom of page nine in the paper. Without saying a word to Greg, who was sitting on the newsdesk, I pulled the lethal AK-47 out of the black bin liner I'd kept it in, dumped it in front of him and stormed out of the office.

I'd almost lost my life for just six bloody paragraphs. But it wasn't the first – and certainly not the last – time that I put my neck on the line for the *News of the World*.

CHAPTER 7
EXCEEDINGLY
GOOD BORDER
CONTROLS

Inside the 38-tonne lorry trailer it was practically pitch black. The only chink of light came through a small gap in the tarpaulin covering which flapped against the lorry making an eerie noise. There were around a dozen of us inside, many huddling together to survive the freezing night. We were perched on top of large metal drums, cardboard boxes containing Zanussi vending machines, and huge metal pipes destined for oil rigs. With the sharp rims of a container digging into my back, it was just as uncomfortable sitting as lying down. My fellow passengers, who believed me to be a Pakistani refugee, included people from Turkey, Iraq, and Kosovo. I could just about make out a woman opposite me crouched on a cold steel pipe; balanced delicately beside her, wrapped in an old worn blanket, was her two-and-a-half-year-old son. Nearest to me was a man called Huysen, unshaven and looking fearful in his shell suit. He was travelling with his wife Liri and their three-year-old son, who was using a carrier bag of luggage as a pillow, next to him.

Posing as an illegal immigrant, I had been shoved into the container at a lorry park in Calais by an Albanian people smuggler called Olsi. Together with his sidekicks, Olsi had calmly strolled between the lorries in the ferry terminal's car park, looking for ones heading to Britain. Olsi, who claimed to have sent more than 300 people to Britain, would prise open the trailers and bundle in the supposed refugees. Pointing to a lorry he said, like a bus conductor: 'That one there is leaving shortly. How much money do you have? It's $600 dollars for one person. You will have no problem with the police.'

I paid him the money and he helped me clamber on board by undoing the straps at the side of the trailer and pushing me unceremoniously under the tarpaulin.

Each illegal immigrant crammed inside the lorry had paid between £100 and £400 a head for the final leg of their journey to Britain – the promised land of free housing, cash handouts, jobs, free medical care, and education. Conditions inside the 40-foot-long trailer deteriorated as it began to rain; the canvas ceiling rattled above us as rain spat down like shrapnel and the icy wind blew through the flapping sides. A couple of the kids began to cry, as their parents desperately tried to muffle the noise. Liri, shivering with cold and shaking with fright, started to cry too. Loud whispers from the other end of the lorry urged her in her own language, Albanian probably, to shut up – any sound and we would all be caught and arrested.

In the darkness we couldn't see our watches and minutes seemed like hours.

As we waited for the lorry to leave, all of a sudden I spotted a small flame lighting up a corner of the lorry. I could see the rugged face of an unshaven Turk with a cigarette in his cupped hands. I quickly dived across the gaps between the cargo, bruising my ribs in the process, to grab the fag from his mouth, before stubbing it out on his cigarette box. The contents of the lorry could have been flammable and we would all have gone up in a ball of fire. Struggling to catch my breath and with sweat dripping from my brow despite the freezing conditions, I tried to explain to the man that we had to observe a no smoking policy.

Sadly I couldn't enforce a no pissing or vomiting policy. In the early hours, as the lorry finally moved and boarded the P&O ferry to take us across the Channel, several of the passengers started throwing up. The stench among the human cargo was unbearable.

The crossing was nerve-racking with the effect of the waves exaggerated in the dark; as we continued to perch uncomfortably in silence, I had plenty of time to think about some of the less glamorous assignments I had undertaken for the *News of the World*, I suppose because I was trying to block out this one.

Once Conrad and I got jobs through a local agency in Mr Kipling's huge bakery in Eastleigh, Southampton. We were there because a drug ring was operating inside the factory where workers churned out millions of cakes and pies for Britain's supermarkets. The pushers were using Mr Kipling's exceedingly accurate weighing scales to measure out their wraps of cannabis. Some of the workers worryingly claimed they had slipped cannabis into cakes on the production line to make hash cakes to share among them later. They laughed at the thought that some of the pies and chocolate mini-rolls that they'd laced with cannabis might have ended up in boxes destined for teatime treats.

At the start, my job in the factory really was a piece of cake. I donned my white overalls and an unglamorous hat, and was appointed as a 'quality controller' on Plant 5. My cushy job involved weighing and measuring Cadbury's flake cakes as they flooded off the production line by putting every twentieth one on the scales. During my tea break I wandered over to see Conrad, who was labouring away on Plant 2, stacking finished Sainsbury's mini-rolls into cardboard boxes. I had a laugh at his expense; he was having a tough time doing what was a monotonous and unpleasant job.

In between shifts we managed to buy drugs from some of the dealers and secretly videoed them in action on the factory floor. But then my fortune changed. The foreman called me over and asked me to work nights. I agreed as we still needed more evidence, and after all, I thought, weighing a few cakes throughout the night wouldn't be too difficult.

However, when I reported for my nightshift, I was sent to the end of the production line. My new job entailed lifting heavy cake-filled cardboard boxes off the conveyor belt and loading them by hand onto large wooden pallets. I then had to wrap the pallets in cellophane tape before a colleague drove them away in a fork-lift truck. It was back-breaking work, and to make matters worse I couldn't pause for breath as the boxes flooding through on the conveyor belt would stack up and hold up the entire production line. It was Conrad's turn to laugh as he was still employed putting cakes into the cardboard boxes.

I'd picked fruit on a farm alongside illegal immigrants and joined others to work as a labourer on building sites, but this was in a different league – it was work for a robot. After a couple of hours of really hard work, I pulled a muscle in my back and was left in agony. I complained to the unsympathetic charge hand, who simply laughed and told me that there was no one to replace me. He demonstrated, in his experienced robotic manner, how to stack the crates properly. I continued throughout the night in extreme pain. Since then, the very sight of Mr Kipling's cakes sends a shooting pain up my spine.

Suddenly the journey across the Channel lurched back into the forefront of my mind, as I sat shivering in the back of the lorry. Huysen had dozed off resting his head on my leg, when suddenly his little son, who was also asleep, slid along the packing case he was lying on. I watched in horror as he came closer to the edge – there was a 10ft drop below between the boxes – when the toddler slipped and plunged headfirst down the gap. I leapt forward and just managed to grab the poor child's leg. I desperately clung to his foot as he dangled down, screaming with fear, and slowly pulled him back up. Another second and the toddler could easily have been dead.

His father and mother cried out loud as they realized how close they had come to tragedy, and continued crying as they reached out to clasp my freezing cold hand in thanks.

A few moments later we heard the muffled sounds of the announcement by the ship's captain that we had arrived in Dover. As the lorry drove out of the port and headed towards London, Conrad and reporter Neville Thurlbeck flagged it down to alert the driver to the fact that he had illegals in the back. The nervous driver quickly phoned the police. They turned up and hauled us all off to jail, from where I was eventually released with the help of the *News of the World*'s legal team, and the illegal immigrants taken off to a detention centre.

This was an unpleasant but run-of-the-mill job for me. My very first investigation for the *News of the World* back in December 1991 had involved a similar journey in the back of a lorry from Rotterdam, with another batch of illegal immigrants. I have also been recruited as a van driver to bring illegals over the Channel on three separate occasions. The last time, I was taken on by David 'Scarface' Weir, from Luton, who asked me to drive a gang of economic migrants who had been loaded in a van concealed behind stacks of toilet rolls.

Alan Smith and I drove the van around the French countryside for a couple of hours with our unusual cargo, followed by a car containing two photographers and minders. Eventually, I pulled up in a field, opened the rear doors of the van and the men emerged. As we off-loaded the illegals, shepherded by my minders, loo rolls went flying across the picturesque Upper Normandy countryside.

'Is this London?' asked one of the Indian immigrants, who bizarrely was smartly dressed in a suit and tie and carrying a leather briefcase. I told him it was and watched as he grinned broadly and punched the air. I asked him to sit down in the field and wait for a smaller van to come and pick him and his pals up. A van did come, only it was the local gendarmerie who rounded them up and drove them away.

Despite all the supposedly stringent measures including new X-ray equipment and CO_2 sensing devices, illegal immigrants still flood into Britain every week hidden in vans and lorries. I confronted then Home Secretary Charles Clarke about the government's inability to cope with the burgeoning problem, which has the potential to make Britain an open house for terrorists. 'Your investigations have shown that at times we are not policing it properly. There is a feeling that the system isn't under control. That's why I put a pledge in Labour's general election campaign to address the problem,' reassured Clarke. His replacement, Dr John Reid went further and confessed that the Home Office was 'unfit for purpose'.

Successive governments have failed to tackle the issue, either to remain within the vote-gathering arena of political correctness, or through sheer incompetence coupled with a lack of adequate funding.

There is no topic that elicits a larger response from our readers than exposés of bogus asylum seekers and illegal immigrants, and so it should; the rogues exploiting 'soft touch' Britain cost us taxpayers a staggering £2 billion a year.

I myself have controversially rounded up two coach loads of illegal immigrants and delivered them to the Home Office detention centre in Harmondsworth, near Heathrow. Once, I took a lorry down to Southall – on another occasion East Ham – and said I was a hotel owner looking for people to help with building work. I'd make it clear that papers weren't really required, and usher those who came up looking for work without papers into the back of my lorry, before driving them promptly round to the detention centre. Ironically, I exposed two uniformed guards working at that very same detention centre who were illegal immigrants themselves. The government were paying these men to guard fellow illegals. I have also caught illegals working at our airports, posing as bogus students, posing as fake priests, and even one working in the kitchens at Buckingham Palace who joked how he could poison the Queen.

> '**The Russian brides racket was run by a mafia gang who were organizing three weddings a week and charging brides £7k a time.**'

I have a cupboard full of fake passports and identity documents with my photograph affixed, which purport to show that I am American, Portuguese, Czech, French, Pakistani, Polish, Kosovan, Dutch, or Afghani. Beside them is a pile of fake British passports. I have slipped past immigration officials at our ports using these documents on numerous occasions to highlight the problem.

The government still faces a horrendous task in dealing with illegal immigration. We could fill the paper every week with immigration stories, and over the years I have come across almost every variation.

Endless solicitors, barristers – and even crooked Home Office officials – have been nailed for brazenly exploiting our lax immigration rules.

I have also exposed numerous marriage scams, whereby illegals pay to undergo a 'paper-marriage' to gain citizenship. In one story, headlined 'Wedded Blitz', I posed as a British groom and jilted three brides in one morning. It was like a scene from a comedy, as together with my wedding party, I raced from registry office to registry office to marry my unfortunate fiancées. My mum was horrified when she rang to ask me round for dinner and I casually told her that I was busy because I was getting married in the morning. She thought I had lined up a secret wedding for myself with an unworthy bride.

But my blushing brides – all willing to pay me sums of up to £3,000 – were even more horrified. Shortly after posing for their wedding-day photographs with their groom, wearing their specially chosen wedding dresses, the women were arrested and led away by Home Office officials.

In another wedding story a blonde Russian twenty-one-year-old model, Alona Samoluka, was willing to pay me £5,000 to marry her. The marriage was to take place in Latvia where formalities are more lax and officials are easily bribed. All I had to do was to marry her and then accompany her to an interview at the British High Commission, as she would then be able to apply for a spouse visa to come and live in Britain. She listed some inviting statistics and promised not only an all-expenses paid holiday in Latvia but also a week of happily married sex. Sadly I jilted my beautiful bride in Latvia.

Our switchboards were jammed after the story was published featuring a glamorous photo of the Russian beauty. Readers from up and down the country phoned in, but not to congratulate me on exposing the gang, but to ask for contact details for Alona – they all wanted to marry her.

The Russian brides racket was run by a mafia gang who were organizing three weddings a week and charging brides £7k a time. The boss, Antonio Russo, always accompanied by his bodyguard Alexanders Kudryashouos, was arrested following my story. When the police raided his premises in north London they uncovered one of the biggest fake document factories ever found in Britain. The place was littered with blank passports, birth certificates, and driving licences from around the world, as well as professional printing equipment.

Russo was jailed for four years at Isleworth Crown Court, and Kudryashouos pleaded guilty to charges of conspiracy to defraud the Secretary of State; he was sentenced to fourteen months. But after the sentencing, worried officers frantically summoned me to Scotland Yard. There, the police warned me that Russo had put out a £30,000 contract on me from his prison cell. Russo owned four houses including a mansion in Essex, and the police had applied to the courts to seize his £3.5 million assets. He had good reason to be angry.

When he was fingerprinted, though, the authorities discovered he was a double-murderer called Antonov Russo who had escaped from an Italian prison where he was serving a 23-year sentence. Judge Sam Katkhuda recommended Russo be deported back to prison in Italy after finishing his stretch in Britain.

However, the most prolific bride I uncovered was Farjana Patel from Blackburn. She married eight husbands, all illegal immigrants, at register offices in Lancashire – only she didn't even know it. Illegal wedding planner, Ismail Pirbhai, who charged £8,000 a time for sham marriages, had used Farjana's birth certificate. Having stolen her identity, Pirbhai used different local girls to pretend to be Farjana, in the bogus ceremonies. It was devastatingly simple because there is no national computer database, which would allow register offices to check if the person applying to marry is already wed. Pirbhai was sentenced at Preston Crown Court to six years' imprisonment.

But while Pirbhai's racket required duping register offices, a London priest was running his own marriage scam performing fake weddings. Minister Adeola Magbagebeola, who headed the Celestial Church of Christ in north London, worked in conjunction with a fraudster called Paul Singh, who provided fake documents.

The Nigerian priest charged £1,000 a time to perform wedding services for illegal immigrants and was responsible for more than *eighty* fake marriages. He had even married the same woman *twice* on the same day wearing the same wedding dress, but to different grooms.

Magbagebeola was finally caught when he demanded a backhander from me – posing as an illegal immigrant – to perform a fake marriage ceremony at his imposing church in Islington, north London. Thanks to that evidence, police raided the church as he was about to carry out yet another fake ceremony. The priest and the groom were both arrested in the dramatic swoop. When cops searched the vestry they found a register of marriages revealing the true extent of the long-running scam. They also found a large number of fake passports hidden in the church. The resulting police inquiry led to several men and women being arrested and jailed. The minister pleaded guilty at Snaresbrook Crown Court to a 'sophisticated criminal conspiracy'. The pastor escaped jail because of his failing health but was given a two years' suspended sentence and ordered to pay £20,000 in costs. His partner Singh was jailed for five years.

But the most bizarre immigration scam – which remains a testament to the stupidity of the Home Office – involved a 'Messiah' who was turning his false prophecies to profit by pretending he was Jesus reborn. Pakistani Sadat Miran Sufi proclaimed himself the reincarnation of 'God's prophet Jesus'; Muslims do not regard Jesus as the Son of God. Sufi claimed the call came in a message from the Angel Gabriel in the form of 'strange noises'. Soon after his transformation the clowns at the Home Office granted him political asylum, with housing benefit and income support thrown in, as Sufi told them he faced persecution in his native land on the basis that he had been born a Muslim.

He told me, posing as a potential disciple: 'I regularly get messages from God. I stand in front of a mirror and see a crown of light above my head. I am Jesus, and that's why I got asylum. My case was straightforward; people want to murder me back home. Nobody can categorically say I am not Jesus. Even the cynics must think maybe I could be.'

Alas, the officials who dealt with his case failed to recall the biblical warning of the real Jesus – contained in Matthew's Gospel – that 'many shall come in my name, saying, I am Christ; and shall deceive many.' As a result, Sufi repaid the Home Office's gullibility by rounding up a mob of fellow spongers to rip off his adopted land of milk and honey.

From his Holy HQ in Leytonstone, east London – ironically located in Church Lane – he charged bogus asylum seekers £200 a time to help them stay in Britain by claiming they were his disciples. He spread the word about his unique immigration scam through adverts in local Urdu-language newspapers.

He promised me a miracle: 'I can apply for asylum for you, or tell you how to apply. You'll get money from the social services and you'll be able to work after six months. You'll get money for accommodation too. It's £200 to open a file, then you pay again when I send a solicitor with you to the Home Office,' he preached. 'You can claim to be one of my followers and therefore you will also be persecuted if you go back home.'

I was only too happy to play Judas to Jesus of Leytonstone and crucify him in the hallowed pages of the *News of the World*. Although he couldn't be deported, having been granted asylum, he thought it better to simply disappear. An unsatisfactory end to that story, perhaps, but nowhere near as unsatisfactory as the story that has become one of the most well known I have ever been involved in. And it all started so simply, too.

CHAPTER 8
SHEIK
IT LIKE
BECKHAM

NEWS OF THE WORLD

WORLD EXCLUSIVE
We stop £5m ransom gang

POSH KIDNAP

Moment saves Victoria and her sons from thugs

On a Saturday afternoon in October 2002, squashed inside a toilet cubicle at the Tower hotel in St Katherine's dock, an Albanian criminal with a cigarette dangling from his mouth brushed against the video camera concealed in the button of my denim jacket. He reached into a rustling carrier bag and pulled out an antique diamond-, ruby- and pearl-encrusted crown for me to examine, and told me it was worth a quarter of a million pounds.

I held it up before the lens. Made of faded green cloth, and resembling an old turban more than a crown, it wasn't much to look at. After a few seconds I flushed the loo, left the cubicle and headed back to the bar to join the two men who had brought the stolen item for me to inspect. With the viewing over, we all headed downstairs and out of the hotel.

It was a run-of-the-mill job that would probably not even make the paper and I wanted to get away quickly. I'd popped in on the way to go shopping in Green Street in east London, I can't even remember what for now. My six-month-old son, Danyal, was playing with a balloon, waiting in my car. I glanced to check he was ok – he was smiling and banging on the car window – as I briskly walked past with the thieves and stood by a fountain overlooking Tower Bridge.

The meeting had been arranged by one of my informants, a Kosovan asylum seeker called Florin Gashi who had provided me with information in the past that had resulted in criminal convictions. Gashi told me that these men were heavy-duty Eastern bloc criminals who had stolen a valuable crown from a museum and were also deeply involved in other crimes. I agreed to meet them posing as Mohammed, a middle-man who might be able to source a buyer.

The men, Luli Azem Krifsha, a slim man wearing a black suit and black T-shirt, and his stocky pal, Jay Sorin, told me that the item I had just seen had been stolen from the vault at Sotheby's; they were offering it to me for a bargain £40,000, less than a fifth its actual value.

'It dates back to the 18th century. It comes from a safe in Sotheby's,' Luli said in his heavy Eastern European accent. 'We've taken £4 million worth of stuff. It won't show up as stolen.' He also said he had a painting by a 17th-century Dutch master plus some rare books. The entire package was on offer for £45,000. They also wanted to sell me cars they'd driven over from France, one an S-class Mercedes worth £60,000 but which could be mine for just £20,000; and, Sorin added in his gravel voice, 'we have many businesses,' as he casually offered to sell me bundles of fake American dollars.

I told them that I would speak to my contacts and get back to them. I couldn't have imagined that this meeting would lead to one of the biggest and most controversial stories of my career – the Beckham kidnap plot.

Back at the office a few days later, news editor Greg Miskiw felt that there would be no real interest in the story, so I decided to tip off Sotheby's who could confirm whether the crown had in fact been stolen. If so, I would fulfil my public duty and help the police nab the villains. I emailed photos taken from our secret video to Helen Griffiths, the press officer at Sotheby's. It was then that I received a call from Gashi in which he told me that the men I'd met were not just petty burglars but were part of a dangerous gang who were planning to kidnap a Saudi prince who lived in London. I met Gashi and asked him if he would help gather evidence so we could prevent them from carrying out the kidnap.

Police officers from the Met investigating the stolen crown came to see me at the office: Detective Inspector Ian Horrocks, Detective Sergeant Greetham and Detective Constable Hulme. The officers were from Scotland Yard's Kidnap and Specialist Investigations team, and it was they who would end up investigating the crown thieves for conspiracy to kidnap. It was the first time in all my years of dealing with police that three senior officers had turned up for what seemed like a straightforward case of theft. It clearly meant that the gang were considered to be serious criminals of interest to the police.

Gashi had secretly taped members of the gang talking about the Arab target. I heard Luli say, 'The Arab sheik lives in a hotel in Knightsbridge and he's got two expert bodyguards who follow him everywhere. You have to tackle the bodyguards from behind, hit them on the heads and use knockout gas as well. We have to be very quick. We can't hesitate. It's not easy. It will take months of planning.' The Arab named Abdullah had first caught the attention of one of the gang members, Romanian Sorin, who had spotted him in a London casino spending thousands and decided to follow him. But the gang decided to drop the Arab target because it would be too difficult to abduct him as his bodyguards might be armed.

It was then that Luli had decided upon an easier target – Victoria Beckham, because one of her former hairdressers had indiscreetly spoken of weaknesses in her security arrangements. Luli, who lived in Battersea, explained: 'I asked a girl today who is a friend of mine, she works in a hairdressers where Victoria had her hair done and that time she had only one minder outside the shop. Victoria will be easy. But we have to watch her for a month. She'll definitely pay. I can't believe that she doesn't have a bodyguard with her all the time.'

Gashi slowly earned the gang's trust over a period of several weeks and made covert video recordings of them discussing their various criminal activities. When they asked him to find a getaway driver for the kidnap, it created the ideal opportunity for me to get my own man to infiltrate the gang. Jaws fitted the bill perfectly; they were told that he had just come out of Strangeways prison in Manchester. At the Prince of Wales pub in Brixton, south London, Adrian Pasareanu told Jaws was that he would get £10,000 to act as the getaway driver. When Jaws asked for more, Adrian told him he would discuss it with the boss, Luli.

In a meeting at the Atoca restaurant in Wandsworth, south London, Gashi joined Luli and his cronies including Adrian, Sorin, and Joe Rivas, who claimed to be the one who had stolen the crown from Sotheby's. Gashi filmed the gang with a camera concealed in a jacket discussing the amount of money they should demand as a ransom.

'I will ask Beckham for £5 million, for him that's like spending a few pence on a cup of coffee,' said Luli. '£5 million for Beckham is nothing, he's got flash cars worth that amount!' Adrian argued that it would be better to ask for just £1 million and guarantee a quick pay out: 'They will pay immediately, less than 24 hours,' he said. Luli ridiculed the suggestion. 'For £1 million you can take me, and my brother will pay that to get me back! You think I am going to risk prison for just £1 million. People like that could transfer millions to a bank account instantly. People like that just have to call the bank.' Rivas agreed with Luli: 'We'll ask for £5 million.' There was then a discussion about how they would ask Beckham to transfer the money to an account in Romania. 'There's no way we take the money here, it's got to be in another country. I think £5 million is fine. We go to Romania and they bring us two bags of money and we get together and take our shares. Everybody is happy,' said Sorin. 'We ask David Beckham for £5 million. It's 100 per cent he pays. But if something happens and he doesn't, Victoria is going to die of course.'

Luli had a sideline – selling fake identity documents. Gashi handed him my photographs together with £250, and, within a day, he handed back a near-perfect copy of a computerized UK driving licence complete with my photograph. In another meeting, at Gashi's flat, Luli told how he had smuggled a knockout gas spray from Italy, which would be used to sedate Victoria before bundling her into a van. 'Even if you don't point it at the face it still works. The person will be asleep for half an hour. In three seconds they will be asleep. I got it from Italy for jobs like this,' said Luli. 'If police catch me with it, I'll end up doing five years for it.'

In a separate meeting in a pub, this time with Jaws present, Sorin confirmed Luli had the deadly spray. 'When you shoot it, it's like gas.

Terrorists use it. You also get it in bottles, if you break it, everyone goes to sleep,' he explained. Jaws captured Adrian on video, waving a semi-automatic handgun about: 'This is my best friend. I keep it with me all the time. I'll supply you with one. It's a Mauser. It's very good, very safe, very powerful and quiet.'

Over just a few weeks we gathered evidence that showed that the gang were serious criminals involved in cashpoint fraud, burglary, guns, importing stolen cars, drug dealing, handling stolen goods, false documentation, and planning robberies.

But even that list seemed trivial when Jaws played back the tape of a meeting at Sorin's home in Croydon. Sorin had been drinking whisky and was asked how they would react if Victoria had Brooklyn and baby Romeo with her: 'Fuck off the baby. That is not a problem. If she is with her kids that will be even better. If the money is not in there we are going to cut her in pieces, that's all. We ask David for the money, if she's still alive he can talk with her.' The plan was for Victoria to be rolled up in a carpet and rushed to their safe house. 'She has to disappear; nobody can see her face, nothing. They are very fucking proper persons. Victoria and Beckham are the most loved couple in Britain. They are representatives for Britain. We can be certain that the police will be on our asses. It's not something you talk about today and do tomorrow. Once everything is set up we start to follow Victoria. They have a lot of cameras there. Victoria has got a fucking palace. And at every hour of the day there are a lot of reporters and paparazzi there.'

Sorin took Gashi to visit the Beckhams' £5.5 million home, dubbed Beckingham Palace in Sawbridgeworth, Hertfordshire. I sat in the back of Conrad's van and watched as Sorin and some other men – two of whom were never identified – walked past the Beckhams' home to case the joint.

Once we had enough detailed evidence about the gang's kidnap plan, I rang DI Horrocks and met him at the Thistle hotel at Victoria train station. *News of the World*'s editor Rebekah Wade had asked me not to reveal the name of the target but to give them details of the plot to kidnap a well-known celebrity. After discussions with SO19, the elite firearms unit, it was agreed that I would lure the gang to the Ibis hotel car park in east London. It was easily done, as Luli was expecting me to hand over £45,000 in cash for the stolen art treasures.

On the morning of the arrests I attended a meeting at Leman Street police station for a briefing. An officer told me: 'We don't know how many of the gang will be armed. They think you'll be paying them £45,000 for the goods, so they may just try to pull a gun on you, take the money and keep the merchandise. If that happens, put your hands in the air and we'll come immediately. Do not put your hands up for any other reason.' If everything went smoothly the plan was that I would take a look at the goods and then take out my mobile phone supposedly to call a henchman to bring the money to the site. In fact I would be calling a police officer and it would act as the signal for them to pounce.

Everything was in place, with undercover officers hiding around the hotel complex. We picked a deserted part of the car park so there would be no danger to members of the public. As part of the same operation an armed police team headed for an address in Surrey where they expected to pick up other gang members. At 12.35pm on a Saturday, three members of the gang, Luli, Rivas, and Sorin arrived at the Ibis in two separate cars. Both pulled up next to my Mercedes sports car that I had hired for the day. 'We want to do this quickly,' said Luli. 'You inspect the goods, we count the money and we're out of here.' Rivas added: 'We don't want to hang around.'

The men gathered around the boot of Luli's green Renault Laguna as he proudly showed off his haul. Hidden in a black bin liner was a valuable landscape painting. Next to it in carrier bags, were the jewelled crown and rare antiquarian books. I nodded my approval and reached for my mobile phone to call for the cash. Almost immediately a nondescript white van screeched to a halt beside the Laguna, the back doors flew open and twelve officers, wearing Day-Glo blue jackets with POLICE SO19 in yellow on their backs, and pointing automatic weapons at us, jumped out.

The officers shouted at us, 'Armed police, get on the floor.' It had been agreed that I would also be handcuffed and bundled into a police vehicle so that the gang did not realize that I was actually an under-cover reporter. 'These guys could be armed and it would be putting your life at risk if they thought you were behind their arrest,' explained DI Horrocks. But he failed to mention that I would be hurled onto the tarmac in the pouring rain, have a Heckler and Koch automatic pressed hard against the back of my head and forced to lie spread-eagled on the ground.

It was a successful operation for the paper and the police. DI Horrocks said: 'You've done a fantastic job and taken on dangerous crim-inals. We're extremely grateful for your information. This demonstrates the importance of close cooperation between the police and investigative reporters.'

Victoria Beckham was shocked by the news and thanked me for bringing the horrifying drama to an end. 'I'm stunned by what has happened today. It's clear these people were serious. It's terrifying that someone would want to do that to you and your children. I'm in absolute and total shock.' She insisted that her gratitude be reported in the paper and said, 'I'm incredibly grateful to the *News of the World* and to Mazher Mahmood for everything you've done here. You've clearly had the best interests of my family at heart and we appreciate it very much. We have good security. We are very aware of the risks. But if people want to do this to my family how can you be 100 per cent sure you'll prevent it? If someone is mad, that sick, what can you do?'

Police officers were waiting for David in the changing room as he came off the pitch at Old Trafford after Man Utd's 2–1 win over Southampton. Victoria was there too. In his autobiography, David wrote:

'As soon as I got to the dressing room, the gaffer said we needed to talk in his office. Not after I'd changed, not as soon as I could – *now*. I don't know what I was expecting but it wasn't that Victoria would be there waiting for us. She looked pale and nervous ... I half recognized a Manchester-based police officer and he introduced me to the other

three. They were from SO7, the Serious and Organised Crime
Command Unit and had driven up from Scotland Yard.'

He recalled reading the article in the *News of the World*:

'We might have been used to seeing and hearing stories about
ourselves, often to do with things we've had no idea about beforehand,
but this was different. There were pictures of the gang at the gates of
the house down south and details of the threats they'd made about
what would happen to Victoria if I didn't pay up. That kind of
wickedness and on my own doorstep made my blood run cold. I think
it was overnight that the shock really sank in for us both. We were
upset and scared.'

The Beckhams made drastic improvements to their security. Even Her
Majesty The Queen had heard about the kidnap plot and asked David
about it when he met her along with the England team. The story
shocked the nation and made international headlines.

The five men who were arrested were charged with theft and conspiracy to rob. Scotland Yard launched its own investigation code-
named Operation Rumpus. Together with my team, we spent days on
end making detailed statements to the police. Months later, after the
police had assessed every inch of our evidence and satisfied the
Crown Prosecution Service (CPS), the men were charged with conspiracy to kidnap. The case was sent to trial.

A trial, though, wasn't always the end of the story. Giving evidence
in court is unappealing but remains an integral part of investigative
journalism. It often involves days on end providing police with statements and evidence, followed by weeks hanging around courts, and
then a gladiatorial battle inside the courtroom with defence barristers
determined to slay the tabloid reporter in front of a jury. There is the
inevitable post-mortem from media commentators, who are equally
keen to put the boot in even when villains are jailed. Just as in the
Beckham case – one of the scores of cases I have been involved in

which did not result in prosecutions – there have been endless stories reporting the premature demise of the Sheik and his covert support team. The slightest criticism of our methods is blown out of all proportion.

> ❝ "We just don't know how many of the gang will be armed...they might just pull a gun on you, take the money and keep the merchandise." ❞

The same media commentators seldom report the successes; no mention of the man jailed for conspiracy to murder, the men selling arms, those jailed for immigration rackets and no mention of the paedophiles sent down. Neither have I read reports of judges who have praised and thanked me for helping to bring those villains to book.

Another high-profile sting that has been unfairly criticized involved three men who were allegedly trying to buy 'Red Mercury'. The informant, a respectable man with a scientific background and no criminal record, told me he had been asked to supply this substance used to make dirty bombs and one allegedly made by the Russians. He had already gone to the police but felt that they had failed to investigate the threat properly, so he turned to me.

The events of 9/11 and 7/7 and the other foiled terrorism attempts are evidence if it were needed that terrorism poses a huge threat to our country. Senior officers privately concede that they are fighting an uphill battle against a new lethal breed of homegrown Muslim terrorists, and it is only a question of time before these terrorists manage to strike in Britain again. With the Muslim community too scared, too protective of their radical elements, or instinctively – and wrongly – closing ranks to protect itself, to help expose potential terrorists, I feel an even greater duty to investigate every terror tip I get and to pass it onto the police.

That's exactly what I did when the dirty bomb story came my way. After establishing that the informant had indeed been asked to supply a substance to make bombs for a Muslim buyer, I immediately contacted Scotland Yard's SO13 anti-terrorist squad. They signed me up as an official participating police informant.

In a potentially dangerous investigation, I took orders directly from Detective Inspector Adrian Swarm, though sometimes I disagreed with police tactics. The police even read my story, and made minor amendments, before it was published on the front page in September 2004. As a result of our joint collaboration, three men were arrested – Abdurahman Kanyare, Roque Fernandes, and Dominic Martins – and charged with two counts of entering into a funding arrangement for the purposes of terrorism.

My evidence had clearly been of a sufficient standard to satisfy highly experienced anti-terror officers, the Crown Prosecution Service who decided on the charges, and the Attorney General who had to personally sign off the prosecution. The evidence was also good enough to satisfy one of the most respected judges in the land, the Recorder of London, Peter Beaumont. I spent almost a whole week in a witness box at the Old Bailey being attacked from every angle by three different defence barristers determined to discredit the newspaper and myself so that the case would be thrown out of court. During the legal argument, every single story I had ever worked on was dissected and closely examined in a desperate attempt to stop the case from going before a jury. But the judge ruled that the case should go ahead.

A three-month trial ensued, and once again I was subjected to several days of relentless assaults by barristers. I was described as 'corrupt', 'dangerously deceitful' and a man with an 'egotistical obsession' for terrorism stories. The barristers spent more time discussing other stories I had worked on than arguing over the taped evidence I had gathered on the dirty bomb story. During the trial DI Swarm said that I was as experienced as any of his undercover policemen and had performed just as well; a nice tribute from a senior officer amid all the mud that was being slung at me.

The mud slinging was worse than anything I had every experienced before. Even the judge felt it necessary to redress the balance in his summing up, telling the jury: 'It is not about showing distaste for the

News of the World's style of journalism, it is not about cutting Mazher Mahmood down to size – we have a free press, we have a choice about which newspaper we buy. The Press Complaints Commission polices the press and they are bound by the law of defamation. Rather more significantly you are not some sort of posse, empowered by the processes of the trial to punish the newspaper.'

The judge went on to say that the criticisms that defence lawyers had heaped on me and the police were irrelevant to the case, as we were not the ones on trial. He told them how I had refuted the defence claims made against me, that over my fifteen-year career I had produced more than 500 stories and had about 100 successful prosecutions. I had also never had any Press Complaints Commission matters upheld against me; this, the judge told the jury, indicated that I had a 'very experienced legal mind'. Most importantly the judge said that when I became involved in the police operation, I had 'followed police instructions to the dot although [I] disagreed with the police strategy'.

The judge summed up the defence arguments of the three men. (1) Martins had admitted he was in the deal for money but he had no idea that the chemical was to be used for terrorism purposes. (2) Fernandes had a 'completely different' motive – and that was to find out as much information as he could to tip off the police and stop the chemical from falling into the wrong hands, claiming, in effect, that he was an undercover agent. (3) Kanyare was an anti-terrorist, due to be located at the US embassy in Nairobi before terrorists bombed it in 1998. The judge also added that one of his other main defences was that he wanted Red Mercury liquid – not powder – to wash banknotes with. During the trial the court was told that the practice is used frequently in Middle East and African countries, where the United States government attempted to bring in American currency covertly by painting it black. To remove the paint or dye a series of chemicals are used and according to Kanyare one of the chemicals included Red Mercury.

After deliberating, a jury of four men and eight women cleared the trio of all charges.

While we all accept the decisions of juries, this one left me disappointed. The Metropolitan Police issued a statement saying: 'The fact that defendants have been acquitted does not mean the case was not properly brought to court. The Crown Prosecution Service assessed the evidence and decided there was a case to answer, a decision later confirmed by the trial judge. The Attorney General was required to give formal consent to the prosecution under the Terrorism Act 2000. The verdict is then a matter for the jury.' The CPS also made a statement. Sue Hemming, the CPS's head of counter-terrorism, said: 'It was right to bring this case. We regarded the evidence as credible and the trial ran its full course.'

Despite this, the media commentators-cum-vultures still chose to attack the Fake Sheik over the case. A story published in the *Guardian* on 31 July 2006 was headlined: *'Clouds Gather Around The Fake Sheik'*. The article claimed that following the Red Mercury trial, my reputation was now in question. The reporter also interviewed Mr Kanyare, who claimed that he wanted the Red Mercury not only to wash notes but because it is also the 'Middle-Eastern equivalent of Viagra'.

In the eyes of my critics the dirty bomb trial is a black mark on my career and is used to question my methods. How the *Guardian* think I should have acted when tipped off about potential terrorists is not clear, as they never address that in their article. Should I have ignored the call about a possible terror threat? Should I have not gone to police and followed their instructions? They must know that, despite the flak, my 'egotistical obsession' with terror stories remains intact and I will continue to root out any potential terror threats.

I was on holiday in Los Angeles in June 2003 when the *News of the World*'s editor Andy Coulson rang me with the shock news that the prosecution had abandoned the charges in the Beckham kidnap case and offered no evidence against the accused. I didn't even know that a court hearing was scheduled to take place. The CPS made the decision on the basis that Gashi could not be regarded as a reliable witness, because he had deceived the police about payments he had received for the story.

I was angry with the CPS and totally bewildered. Like me, the CPS knew full well that Gashi was a villain. Informants from the underworld will always be dubious characters, otherwise they would never have access to the information nor be able to get close to villains; a fact that the police live with every day. The CPS knew all about the £10,000 payment we had made to Gashi months ago; I'd told the police, the payment was made by cheque and there was no question of us seeking to hide it. It covered his work on the Beckham story and two other stories he'd worked on in the past. From my dealings with Gashi I knew that his main motivation was never money, he could easily have demanded five times that amount for the Beckham story. He seemed to be more concerned with gaining permission to stay in the United Kingdom; he felt that by helping me, I would be in a position to use my Home Office contacts to help to assist his asylum claim. When he was subsequently deported Gashi turned against me saying that I had failed to help him so he would do his utmost to discredit me.

One of the defence team, Martin Hicks QC, accused me of setting up the kidnap plot: 'On the face of it, it was designed to further Mr Mahmood's notorious career.' It was the same Mr Hicks who had successfully used my evidence to prosecute actor John Alford for dealing drugs back in 1999. The Press Complaints Commission, which launched its own inquiry into our conduct, ruled that our payment to Gashi had been perfectly proper under their guidelines.

Rivas pleaded guilty to the theft of the Sotheby's turban, a painting, and four books. Luli pleaded guilty to handling the stolen goods. Sorin was deported before his trial. But the collapse of the trial was a godsend for our critics. In one particularly spiteful attack, the *Guardian* chose to publish my photograph on the front page, knowing full well that I had been subjected to endless death threats. The *Press Gazette* – the newspaper industry's magazine – published a sympathetic leader headlined, *'Don't kill investigations in rush to bury Mahmood'*. It summarized my plight:

The national press had one victim in its sights on Tuesday morning. It was one of their own, Mazher Mahmood, award-winning *News of the World* reporter, [who] was suddenly on the wrong side of an investigation. Popular investigative journalism has a crucial role to play in a robust and free press. It's vital that this fact – of the 100 plus successful convictions he's helped to secure – isn't forgotten in the rush to bury Mahmood.

Nevertheless, the same old armchair media commentators who have never undertaken an investigation in their lives came out of the wood-work to attack the *News of the World* and me. The so-called posh papers that routinely attack our methods but steal our exclusives had an absolute field day. Ludicrous allegations were made, suggesting that the plot was a 'set up job' by myself and the paper, or that the plot had been nothing more than 'idle pub banter'. In effect it meant that the police who studied our evidence for months were incompetent, as were the CPS who decide on charges. But all the allegations were put to rest when I got my day in court by virtue of a libel action brought by one of the alleged kidnappers. The man who admitted using a false name sued on a no-win, no-fee basis and I gave detailed evidence before the Hon. Mr Justice Eady at the High Court.

At the end of the two-week trial, Mr Justice Eady concluded that although there were some inaccuracies in the story, such as us sug-gesting that the gang were 'on the brink' of the kidnap, the story was true.

The judge said: 'There was an attack on Mr Mahmood's character, suggesting that he knew that the story was false and that he had picked on vulnerable asylum seekers, who would not be able to sue the news-paper, just to sell more newspapers. The object of this exercise was largely to aggravate the award of damages and to set up a case for exemplary damages. This got nowhere at all. Mr Mahmood may be hard-bitten and cynical, but I found no support for the proposition that he had made the whole thing up. Indeed, I have seen recorded exchanges between him and Gashi that make it clear that he believed the plot to be genuine. Nor do I accept, having heard his explanation, that he misled the police about Gashi's role in the undercover investigation. He did not pretend dishonestly that Gashi had received no money. He told them, as he told me, that Gashi was not motivated by purely financial considerations. I accept that money was not discussed before he agreed to take part and, what is more, that he could have asked for much more than he ultimately received. There was a certain amount of embellishment of the story or "hype", but I have no reason to think Mr Mahmood did not believe it to be true in its essentials. It is important not to confuse "hype" with substance.'

The *News of the World* later acknowledged that Bogdan Maris, the man who brought the libel action, was not part of the gang.

An eminent barrister, John Kelsey-Fry QC, a familiar face at the Old Bailey, approached me after the trial and told me that my performance in the witness box was the best that he'd seen in his entire career. I immediately rang my father to tell him; he was thrilled, as he had been equally angered by the negative publicity the Beckham kidnap case had received in rival newspapers. My father died of cancer less than a week after the case ended.

A few months later the then commissioner of the Metropolitan police, Sir John Stevens, invited me for a private drink together with Andy Coulson. We sat in his plush offices at the Yard and Sir John praised my work, singling out the Newcastle United bosses story as one of his all-time favourites. He also told me that he felt that my work on the Beckham kidnap case had been excellent and that in his view the evidence was overwhelming. He shared my disappointment at the CPS decision.

Coming from the most decorated police officer in the land, I considered it a huge honour.

Honour was in very short supply in my next story.

CHAPTER 9

PARENTING, AND 'BRITAIN'S MOST DESPICABLE MUM'

There are rare occasions when good investigations have to be dropped because of unexpected circumstances; one such was when editor Colin Myler sent me to Bulgaria to expose the secret trade in babies and toddlers. Their parents were selling the children for a few thousand pounds, and with the country having recently joined the European Union, it meant they could easily travel to Britain. It was a great human-interest story and was about to go into the paper when news of English toddler Madeleine McCann's disappearance from a hotel complex in Praia da Luz, Portugal, broke on 3 May 2007.

Colin Myler had to ditch our investigation because it would have been insensitive to run a piece about babies being sold in Europe at a time when everybody was joining in the desperate hunt for Maddie. Kate and Gerry McCann's case touched the world, even thick-skinned tabloid editors; Colin agreed to make a massive contribution towards a £1.5 million reward for information leading to her safe return, and printed hundreds of thousands of 'Find Maddie' posters which were plastered across Europe.

In Bulgaria, it had taken me just a couple of hours to be put in touch with women offering to sell me three different children. Child trafficking is a major business in Bulgaria, with poor families seeing it as a quick way to get out of poverty; some women get pregnant just so that they can sell their babies to childless couples around the world. Others even hand over babies to pay off debts to local loan sharks, who in turn sell them to the highest bidder. Only a couple of months earlier ten Bulgarians were sentenced to up to six years' imprisonment for selling twenty-three babies to French families for around £4,500 each. Police investigated hundreds of similar cases of Bulgarian and Romanian babies sold in neighbouring Greece and Italy. Police arrested one 16-year-old Romanian girl after she complained she had been short changed by a British woman who offered to pay her £9,000 for her baby but only paid her £7,000 and took the child.

'Despite police activity it is easy to buy a baby or young child in Bulgaria as long as you have the money,' my Bulgarian informant told me. 'Nobody is going to ask you whether you are a child sex abuser or what you want to do with the child. As long as you have the money you can take the child straight away. It's just like buying something from the market.' He was right; a couple of hours' drive from Sofia, I was taken to the poor district of Pleven where I was introduced to a woman who was desperate to strike a deal for her unborn child. She had previously sold another of her offspring.

Fidanka, 28, lived in the village of Trevene, with her husband Alex. They had five young children and the sixth was on the way. The family survive on a pittance provided by the government in a one-bedroom near-derelict shack, with the stench of sewage hanging in the air. Father Alex – who used to work as a labourer until he became ill – sleeps on a rusty iron bed in the outdoor kitchen.

'The children have no shoes, no clothes. I am sick and my husband has asthma,' explained Fidanka. She led me to the bedroom, where plaster was hanging off the walls because of the damp caused by a leaking roof. There, she sleeps with her five children on makeshift mattresses strewn across the floor of the dingy room. The family don't have basic amenities like a toilet or clean running water in the house. 'I have five kids, I tell you it is misery. Our money goes to pay debts at shops because we buy food on credit, we're not left with a penny,' explained Fidanka. 'We don't have beds, we don't have proper mattresses. We have no windows so in wintertime we are dying from cold, there isn't even wood to burn. There is no life for us, we live in poverty, like dogs.'

Fidanka and other Roma gypsy families see children as an extra burden and many used to be simply abandoned at birth. It was traditional for gypsies to have large families, and she herself had fourteen brothers and sisters; contraception is rarely used in their culture. But now ruthless mafia gangsters have moved in and the families quickly learned that, by selling children through them, they have a chance to escape a life of poverty.

As Fidanka showed off her children she pointed to a cute baby girl nearly two years old playing by the well in the yard with her older sisters. Her ten-year-old son Todor was busy throwing stones and mud down the well that provides water for the household. 'This one, two years ago I wanted to give to the government. We didn't have the money,' she explained pointing to the two-year-old. She told me how she had sold the baby to a family in Spain but the deal fell through. 'At the last moment the buyers changed their mind,' she said, slapping her forehead. 'They gave me some money and clothes afterwards.'

Then stroking her bump, the bare-footed mother-to-be asked: 'And this one. How am I going to look after it after the birth when we don't have enough money? I don't have money to feed the baby. I have nothing. I don't even have shoes.' We were told the family receive 200 lev ($80) a month in benefits from the government. 'It's not enough,' said Fidanka. 'I was wondering what to cook. The pot is empty. Look at the time, the children haven't even eaten yet.' It was way past 4pm; luckily, Conrad and I had bought a bag of sweets and biscuits for the kids, which they grabbed and devoured in seconds.

Fidanka claimed that the previous winter the whole family suffered from pneumonia because of the cold but the family did not even have enough money to buy medicines. In a bid to secure the deal, Fidanka reached under a dirty blanket and pulled out a hospital document, which she proudly handed to me. The letter confirmed that she had been for a check-up and that her baby was healthy. 'They did a scan and said it is a boy,' she said. 'I may give him to the government if we don't have money. If we don't have money why I should look after him, I'll give him.'

But she said that she would rather sell the unborn child to me and would be willing to travel to London for the delivery. 'If there is such a possibility it can be done.' Then she quoted her fee: 'Fifteen thousand Euros,' which is £10,000. My interpreter confirmed that £4,000 of that fee would go to the mafia Mr-Fix-It who had arranged our meeting. Asked if she might change her mind once the child was born in London, she reassured me that she definitely would not.

It would be easy for Fidanka to travel to Britain, as her Bulgarian passport would allow her instant access. And if her child were born in Britain with a British father named on the birth certificate, the child could stay here, bypassing protracted adoption procedures.

As his wife discussed the deal, Alex dressed in a vest and shorts, casually smoked a roll-up outside. I asked him if he was happy with the deal. He said: 'You would be happy if your children have another choice of life. If they live in some rich country, if they are born in another place.' Fidanka added: 'We decided to give them because there is nothing here and they will live nice lives abroad.' Neither Fidanka, nor her husband asked a single question about me or how I would look after their child.

An hour's drive away in another village called Brashlyanitsa another desperately poor family were also trying to sell two children. More than a dozen members of the family live in a disused barn along with their prized possession – a pig. Old mattresses and dirty worn blankets were heaped on the floor of the two dark rooms in the barn; a pile of pig manure was in one corner of the bedroom, where a baby lay in a hammock made from an old towel.

Family elder, grandma Anka, who stood bare-footed, spoke on behalf of the family: 'Poor, we are poor. We have nothing. The children are naked and hungry. We have no bread, we have nothing,' said the frail seventy-year-old woman. She said recently the family had sold twins, a boy and a girl. 'We gave them because we didn't have money to look after them,' she said. 'We survive on 55 lev a month.' That's £22.

Pavlinka, her daughter, was holding her pretty baby daughter Desislava in her arms; she quickly offered to hand her over for cash.

Pavlinka, who had given birth to another child only three weeks earlier, said: 'I want to give this child. It's because it's hunger all day, miserable. What can I do?' Asked how much she wanted for the baby girl, Pavlinka replied: '20,000 levs [£8,000]. This is Desislava. She is one year and ten months old.' Desislava, who was clutching her milk bottle, listened to her mother, unaware that she was making an illegal deal to sell her to a stranger.

This may not seem a lot of money to a childless couple in Britain, but Pavlinka said her husband slaved all day in the fields for just one Euro a day – 60-odd pence. The family spoke about selling their children with the coolness and detachment a farmer might display in selling his livestock. Anka greedily offered me a 'cut-price deal' for another of the children, pointing to a scruffy bare-footed toddler who was busy chasing the family pig. 'This is Dimitar. He is an orphan. His parents died,' she explained. Anka demanded 10,000 lev [£4,000] for the child who was wearing a dirty old sweatshirt and was naked from the waist down.

As somebody who loves children, it was upsetting for me to hear the women selling their own flesh and blood like produce in the market. I told them that I would think about it, and get back to them. But as I headed towards the car, walking away as if from her market stall, Anka shouted after me: 'Ok you can have Dimitar for 6,000 lev [£2,400]. You can take him with you now.'

This sad tale never reached our readers; Colin planned to run the story at a later date but a rival newspaper beat us to it by printing a similar story about the baby trade in neighbouring Romania. The racket still continues to this day, not just in Bulgaria but also in other countries such as India; in April 2008, when it emerged that pop queen Madonna was considering adopting another child from India, I visited the country and wrote a virtually identical story. There, I was offered young children for sale, including an unborn baby by a social worker for £1,200.

These are tragic tales involving poverty and the tantalizing prospect, for the parents, of an escape from its grinding realities offered by greedy middlemen. No one asked me, as a potential buyer, what I intended to do with their child, and sadly I am only too well aware of the awful fate that might have awaited some of them. As an investigative reporter for the *News of the World*, I am routinely required to delve into the depths of human depravity. Just like war correspondents, I inevitably become immune to horrific sights that would take the average person years of psychiatric counselling to come to terms with. Nevertheless, even after years of infiltrating pae-dophile groups around the world, befriending some of them and pre-tending to share their interests, it still remains a stomach-churning experience. Among the most sickening pair I have had the good for-tune to nail was Terry Valvona and his common-law wife Rosemary Iredale in 1993; they ran a council-approved hostel for the homeless in Huddersfield, west Yorkshire, and had scores of vulnerable chil-dren in their care.

Local officials were convinced that middle-aged businessman Valvona could be trusted with the care of the kids, particularly since he lived at the hostel himself with Rosemary and her two children from a previous marriage. The impressive hostel boasted a crèche complete with slides, a trampoline, and a large array of toys to keep children amused. But the children's paradise in a council 'safe-house' con-cealed a secret; the pair were systematically abusing children and even videotaped their abuse.

Geoff and Joan Bailey, a homeless couple who had been sent to live at the 27-bedroom hostel by Kirklees Council, tipped me off about the home. A few days after arriving at the hostel, Rosemary propositioned Joan, asking if she and her husband would like to swap partners for a night. Joan, an attractive and innocent young mum of three small chil-dren, was shocked at Rosemary's blunt approach and immediately refused. Over the next few weeks, though, Rosemary and Valvona both harassed the couple, making crude comments as they tried to lure them into bed.

The couple, who had nowhere else to go, managed to fob off the unwanted sexual advances, but things got out of hand when Joan went with Rosemary to pick up a 13-year-old schoolgirl who she thought was coming round to earn some pocket money by cleaning. 'I was horrified when Rose told me that she was going out for the evening with some girlfriends and that the child was there as a "sex treat" for her partner Terry,' a tearful Joan explained to me. 'I thought it was a sick joke, but Rose went into detail about the things they "enjoyed" with children in their care – blow jobs, buggery, that kind of thing. Rose said she was planning to have sex with a 14-year-old boy in the hostel. I didn't believe her but to show me that she was telling the truth she said they videoed themselves when they had sex with kids and I could watch.'

Later, Geoff sneaked into Valvona's room and put on one of the small pile of VHS tapes stored in a bedroom cupboard; he was horrified at what he saw. The videos showed both Valvona and Rose having sex with a child inside the hostel.

The Baileys were scared to go to the police as millionaire Valvona was known to have links with local criminal gangs. 'When you are homeless and have a young family, you have to think twice about grassing up the owner of the hostel you are staying at to the police. When he's known to have a few heavy connections you have to be all the more careful,' explained Geoff. While they did not want to make statements to the police or give evidence in court, the couple desperately wanted the monsters brought to justice. As regular *News of the World* readers, the Baileys felt that I would be able to help. I spoke to both of them and was convinced they were living with a predatory paedophile, so I dropped everything and drove straight up to Huddersfield. Eric Walters, a handyman who worked at the hostel, accompanied the Baileys; all three claimed Valvona and his girlfriend were guilty of child abuse.

The following day, I arranged to visit the hostel, as a straight reporter but not in my name, allegedly writing a piece for the local paper about the good work Valvona was doing for the community. He lapped it up, posing for pics with his wife in the crèche and bragging about their charitable work. It was easy to see how the couple had managed to dupe the local authorities; the Cambridge Road hostel was well equipped, nicely decorated and the proprietors seemed like a mature caring couple. I even began to question the validity of the Baileys' allegations; was this just a nasty smear campaign? If he were a paedophile, why the hell would somebody like Valvona risk everything by videoing himself having sex with kids, and then leave the taped evidence lying around?

Valvona gave me a guided tour of the hostel: 'This is the only place of its kind to have a crèche; so much is laid on for the children. What's more the crèche is free. From six in the evening I've set up a children's video club where we show them films. At one time last year we had twenty-six kids in here. We do a lot for kids; we've recently added a library for them. We also had a massive Christmas party for them, and on bonfire night I paid £1,000 to get a good firework display together for the children.' Valvona was in his fifties and claimed to have made his money as a 'property tycoon'; he now said he worked as an 'unpaid social worker'.

Rosemary, a seemingly respectable mother who served me tea, told how she empathized with the plight of the homeless. 'I know what it's like to be homeless, hard up, and desperate, because many moons ago I was in that situation,' she said. 'It's hard work here, seven days a week, but satisfying.' Valvona also mentioned that the hostel catered for battered women fleeing abusive partners and had a high level of security as a result: 'We've been designated by the council as a safe-house. We have lots of women here who are fleeing violence. That's why we have external and internal video cameras, microphones, two dogs, and two shotguns.'

Maintenance man Eric was lurking around as I chatted to Valvona, and as I went to the toilet he signalled for me to follow him. He showed me Valvona's bedroom and pointed to the stash of videotapes in the cupboard. I contemplated swiping them there and then, but realized I had nowhere to hide the bulky VHS tapes; I couldn't have taken my briefcase to the toilet, and neither could I return to Valvona with more than one tape shoved down the back of my trousers.

After the interview, I pleaded with the very nervous Eric to help me get my hands on the supposedly incriminating videos as, without the tapes, there was absolutely no evidence to suggest that Valvona and his lover were involved in anything illegal or immoral. Eric reluctantly agreed, and I met him later that night outside the hostel where he handed me a black bin liner containing four VHS tapes.

Back at the George hotel in Huddersfield, I put the tapes into the video player and watched in disbelief. The first showed Valvona having full and oral sex with a 13-year-old girl half his size in the very crèche where I had interviewed the evil duo. Bald-headed Valvona smirked at the camera while he pleasured himself with the child, who had a look of fear on her face.

Another video filmed at their holiday home in Lanzarote, Canary Islands, showed Rosemary having sex with a young girl maybe twelve years old, who appeared to be drugged. The child was then forced to film as Valvona had sex with Rosemary – he could be heard giving the child instructions on how to use the camera to make sure that the action remained sharply in focus. But the most nauseating image from the tapes was of a child, still partly dressed in her school uniform, clutching her knickers in her hands, as she was made to perform oral sex on Valvona while he lay on the bed smoking a fat cigar, a huge grin on his face and making a V-sign to the camera. Rosemary, who filmed the session, could be heard encouraging the child to satisfy her husband's perverted desires. I have seen a lot of vile videos in my time depicting all manner of appalling sexual practices, but these horrific tapes made me feel both sick and angry in equal measure.

By now Valvona was pretty angry too, as he'd seen that the tapes were missing; someone had tipped him off that I was from the *News of the World*. He knew that if the incriminating tapes were handed to the police it would mean the collapse of his business and a lengthy prison stretch for both him and his wife.

Geoff Bailey rang to tell me that Valvona was desperately trying to track me down. I hardly had time to find out who had betrayed me, as there was a knock on the door of my bedroom. It was the hotel manager, looking as if he'd seen a ghost and shaking with fear. He told me to leave the hotel immediately through the fire exit as two villains had turned up at reception clutching large bags, demanding to know my room number. 'We've got two shotguns. Tell him he's a dead man. We know what he's up to,' they told the shocked hotel manager. The hotel staff rang the police after the men left, but the threats continued as Valvona made increasingly desperate attempts to get the damning videos back. He even offered money for the tapes, saying that he would call off the hitmen and pay me a hefty fee, if I returned the tapes. There was no way I was going to let sex beast Valvona get his hands on the evidence. I delivered them straight to the local police station. Social services were immediately called to take any children at the hostel into care. Valvona and Rosemary went on the run, but were soon arrested as they attempted to leave the country. Both Valvona and Iredale were later jailed for five years each.

> ❝"This is Dimitar. He is an orphan. His parents died." … Anka demanded 10,000 lev [£4,000] for the child … who was naked from the waist down.❞

A few days after the story was published, I received a letter from the 13-year-old girl who had been abused by the couple on the video I handed to police. The scrawled note, riddled with spelling mistakes, said: 'Thank you for rescuing me and saving my life. You are like Superman! You are my hero. You saved me from this evil man.' I framed the letter and put it up on the wall of my office in Wapping. It was acknowledgement that my work had saved at least one child from the clutches of a sex monster. It was one of the proudest moments of my career and certainly the most touching accolade I have ever received.

One of their victims, Hazel Walsh, now grown up, gave up her anonymity to publicly thank me. She spoke about her horrific ordeal in a TV documentary, explaining that Valvona would drug her to make her compliant, and had even pointed a gun at her head to force her to have sex not only with him but at least fifteen other men. She fell pregnant twice, Valvona kicked her in the stomach to try and abort the baby, but his plan failed, so he dragged her to a backstreet abortion clinic for secret terminations. Hazel attempted suicide on several occasions, and said her adult life has been scarred by her childhood trauma. Valvona robbed her of her childhood.

I wish I could say that Valvona was the sickest paedophile I have exposed. Sadly he is not. Grotesque monster Clifford Davies groomed his *own* 15-year-old daughter and her school friends, plying them with drink and drugs to ready them for sex with his friends. The repulsive, weasel-like figure whose lanky, grey shoulder-length hair and straggly moustache made him the image of a Fagin, offered his services as a babysitter – he was a retired painter and decorator. His lair, a backstreet hovel in Little Horton in west Yorkshire, was a magnet for local school kids, who started out simply bored or lonely, hanging out at his dingy home. They ended up locked into drugs, drink, crime, and abuse.

'There's kids around my house all the time,' Davies told me in July 1997, as he explained how he corrupted young children. 'I give 'em a bit of leb [cannabis] and they'll do anything for me. If I tell 'em to go and nick something for me they'll do it no problem. They all love me.' Within two minutes of meeting the man who believed I was part of a paedophile ring, conversation turned to sex. 'I'm a wheeler-dealer. I deal in girls and boys, sex, videos, everything. It's not soft stuff, it's proper stuff, kids of 14. These are definitely kids,' he said as he peddled child porn videos for £120 each. Davies also sold me a roll of film for £50 containing, so he said, obscene photos of his daughter and another 13-year-old girl photographed stripping out of her school uniform. 'They both go in for it,' leered Davies. 'I've had sex with one of them … yeah.'

He offered his daughter and her friend for an afternoon of sex: 'It's £100 a piece and you can have them for the afternoon, but they have to be back by 10pm,' he said. 'The girls will do everything. They won't say ow't to nobody. I take them, go somewhere, and bring them back home. I tell them exactly what to do. I've got another girl who's 15 and one who's 12,' he said matter-of-factly. 'They hang round here all day. The twelve-year-old won't have full sex, but she'll do other things. I can get you anything as long as the money is there. It's all about money.'

The kids were lured to his home, strewn with rubbish, cigarette ends, and worn rugs thrown over the rotting floorboards, because it doubled up as a puppy farm. 'Lots of the kids don't go to school,' he explained. 'They've run away from homes and stuff. They come here to play with the pups, smoke, drink, and watch telly. At the moment there's loads of kids around because it's school holidays. They've got nothing to do – and I get them drunk.'

We parked our surveillance van outside Davies's run-down home on a council estate and watched as a steady stream of young children turned up. Eventually I went in too. An intolerable stench of urine and cannabis filled the air. From beneath a blanket, Davies yanked out three tiny pups. 'I've just sold two,' he told me. 'This one's £25. They're half Alsatian and part wolf. You can take them but make sure you give 'em a good home.' He seemed more concerned about the welfare of his animals than the children.

We rescued the children and the puppies from his clutches, but in a controversial decision Judge John Cockroft jailed Davies for just twelve months after he admitted taking indecent photographs of children.

For another equally challenging 'undercover' job, Conrad and I had to shed cover and strip naked to track down a paedophile at a nudist camp in France. Nudity provides insurmountable problems for under-cover reporters – there's nowhere to hide your tape recorders and camera equipment for a start – but the ever-resourceful Conrad came up with an answer, installing a covert video camera in a thick English-French dictionary.

We were in Barjac, south France, in the summer of 2001, in pursuit of convicted paedophile Thomas O'Carroll, one of the founders of the notorious Paedophile Information Exchange, which had campaigned for legalization of sex between adults and children (it was closed down in 1984, ten years after it was founded). O'Carroll, who had not been photographed for twenty years, was prowling the naturist holiday camp in search of young boys, as he had confessed in the past – but also to me that week – to liking young boys aged nine to eleven.

Also at the camp was former teacher Simon St Clair Terry, a paedophile from Canterbury, who had been jailed for indecently assaulting a 12-year-old girl pupil.

We emerged from our log-cabin chalet nervous and stark naked and walked through the forest towards the swimming pool at the La Sablière complex. It's a weird experience, being naked in front of colleagues; I felt uncomfortable and extremely self-conscious, and of course I tried very hard not to notice anything below Conrad's chin.

Walking around the site naked was no better; there was something creepy about mingling with naked young children, and I wondered why any parent would want to bring their young kids to play naked in what appeared to me as no more or less than a sun-kissed nonce's paradise. It was a surreal experience having dinner served in the café by naked waitresses, with all the guests also nude. After a couple of days we'd just about overcome our coyness, and got used to the sights of naked men and women of all shapes and sizes, while we hunted for our targets. However, when I visited the camp's own supermarket and stood queuing behind a fat grey haired woman in her seventies carrying a basket full of groceries, I was taken aback as I reached the counter. The teenage girl serving me was fully clothed; all of a sudden my embarrassment returned.

Fortunately though it didn't take long to home in on the two paedophiles; they were lounging by the pool, ogling children. We sat at the bar leafing through Conrad's cunning book-cam as we videoed O'Carroll and befriended him. 'I'm really enjoying myself here, it's a fantastic place. It's full of children because of the school holidays,' he told us. 'This place was highly recommended and is living up to all expectations. I'm going to Blackpool next week but I don't think that will be this good.' Luckily, O'Carroll had to cancel his tour of the amusement arcades of Blackpool, as we tipped off the authorities and he was later arrested in Britain.

Most mums would go to any lengths to protect their child from the likes of O'Carroll, but in an article the paper billed as '*the most sickening story you will ever read,*' I uncovered one mother, who looked every bit the loving, affectionate mum, who was trying to sell her daughter's virginity to the highest bidder, to any pervert who would pay £30,000. It wasn't some desperate starving Bulgarian gypsy mother; it was Claire Kent, a glamour model from Essex, who wanted the cash so she could buy herself a new car and some drugs. The woman the *News of the World* called 'Britain's most despicable mum' told me: 'It's a one-off thing, isn't it? It is a thing that she can never offer to anybody again which is why it is such a high price. The money is hers but because she loves me she'll make sure her mum is alright.'

The story came to me in late 2004 from one of my contacts in Las Vegas, a pornographer called Paulie. Claire Kent, who had worked in porn films, approached him to try to sell her daughter's innocence, believing the deflowering could make a great porn flick. 'I'm in the porn industry, but even we have some morals,' said Paulie, who was so revolted that he rang me. 'This woman is basically asking me to film the rape of a child. She should be behind bars.' He provided me with Kent's contact details and was happy for me to use him as a reference.

I asked Alex to approach Kent posing as the personal assistant to the Sheik, willing to negotiate a deal for the child's virginity. Kent turned up with her daughter, Sharon (whose name I have changed to protect her identity) and her toddler son, at the Kensington Rooms hotel in south Kensington to discuss the deal. Sharon looked much younger than 13 in her T-shirt with pink bunnies on it and a Parka jacket.

As the little boy lay on the bed in the hotel room, Kent got straight down to business with Sharon listening nervously alongside her. 'The sooner we do it the better 'cos Madam's getting a bit nervous,' she said.

'It's £30,000. The price is not so much the time, it's not even on her age. The price is that she is losing her virginity to this guy. That is it, that is what he is paying for, he is paying for her virginity – it's a big thing for a girl isn't it? It's a big deal for a girl, it's a big time in their life, isn't it?'

Kent had readied Sharon for that 'big time' in her life by letting her watch some of the hardcore videos she herself has starred in. Now it was her turn. 'Obviously I will be there – I'm not going to be there in the room unless he actually wants me to. If he wants me to be there in the room that's not a problem, I won't physically join in with them, but if he wants me to watch I will. I don't know what he wants really. I mean for £30,000 I'll be there.'

She then told Alex that Sharon might not be able to fly to the Middle East to satisfy the pervert Sheik because her daughter's passport had expired. But she quickly added: 'I could get a passport, I mean 'cos she's got to get it anyway 'cos she's coming out to Vegas with me in January.' Kent told Alex the trip was to attend the Adult Video Awards.

The business meeting was suddenly interrupted by the toddler demanding a doughnut. 'I like jam doughnuts,' said the infant, who started to bounce about. As Alex was ringing room service, greedy Kent said impatiently: 'I think we need to discuss business really.' She continued: 'Once we arrive at the hotel and she's in the room I would like him then to sort out the funds 'cos then that way he's happy 'cos he knows that we've shown up, but then we got the assurance that she is going to get paid before she does anything. I really am in some financial trouble at this moment in time, I crashed my car, I desperately need some cash because we need to get a car fast.'

She reassured Alex, 'We will 100 per cent be there, Sharon and I have spoken about it at great length.' She asked a few questions about the 40-year-old who would be abusing her child. 'You wouldn't know the size of his dick would you?' she asked. 'He's not hung like a donkey is he? It's not going to hurt or anything.' Sharon sat beside her mum biting her nails as she listened anxiously to the conversation. Kent asked her daughter if there was anything she wanted to know about the man who would be abusing her. Sharon softly replied: 'No.'

From Afghanistan...

...To Albania

◆ Conrad and I firing AK 47s with the Mujahideen in Afghanistan. Later on, I went to Albania where I had to shoot a pistol. I've always felt uneasy around guns, particularly when they're pointing at me. My new Albanian friend seemed a bit concerned at my poor marksmanship, and was furious when he found out I wasn't a people smuggler.

Kidnap rescue

◆ Rescuing 8-year-old Zira (inset) from kidnappers in Pakistan. Working underco as a reporter isn't easy; the intelligence services have surveillance equipment, satellites and spies. I had Conrad, in a dress, with make up. But it worked...

Galloway on the Warpath

George Galloway.
large gentleman
Galloway's left is
bodyguard, Jaws;
r our dinner,
loway went home
read about Jaws
book that carried
ece about me.
penny dropped
he was on the
path.

nother man in
ial was footballer
n Fashanu (right)
I exposed for
g football
ches for cash.
was so greedy
ven took the
overs from our
h in a brown bag.

Paul Burrell & Sven:

◆ The world's most luxurious hotel, the Burj Al-Arab in Dubai (below right); the £2 million yacht (bottom) we hired in Dubai marina for the sting on Paul Burrell, just like the one Sven-Goran Eriksson is on, with me and the team (below); and the ex-Royal butler (right), a man with an over-inflated opinion of himself, on board. I so wanted Sven to wear the headdress I'd bought him, but he was too canny for that.

overinflated?

Toon on Fire

◆ Exposing Freddie Shepherd and Doug Hall, the two big cheeses at Newcastle football club, was so simple and they couldn't wait to say and do the stupidest things while I secretly filmed them. This award-winning story was raised in Parliament by Prime Minister Tony Blair, and it remains one of the most famous stings I've ever done.

◆ Toe-sucking Johnny Bryant (right) couldn't wait to brag to the Sheik how Sarah Ferguson, Duchess of York, was 'on fire' in bed.

'Go Jerry! Spring Loaded!'

◆ A warning to all those who are thinking of appearing on a *Jerry Springer Show*; if you're a porn star, and your stepmother's a porn star too, then he might ask you for a little pre-show action, as long as step-mom joins in. And I might be there to tape it.

Sophie and Jodie: Wild Things

◆ I really liked Sophie Anderton (below) and I'd tried to help her stay off cocaine. But the grip of addiction was too strong, so much so that this lovely young woman ended up selling her body to pay for more drugs. I'd wanted to like Jodie Kidd (above) as much, but she disappointed me.

Faria – Caught Offside

◆ Faria Alam, the sultry Eastern beauty, used her charms to seduce her rich and famous bosses at the Football Association and became a kiss-and-tell queen. But she had a secret sideline that she was determined to deny despite our video recordings.

Kent, sounding like a saleswoman with a Christmas offer, continued: 'This is like a once-in-a-lifetime thing and it is quite a big deal. Do you like me to bring along her passport, which is out of date, but at least proves [her age]?' Alex asked what Sharon would do for the money, and the little girl replied 'whatever'. Kent chipped in and said to her daughter, 'Not whatever, you can't just say whatever.' She then asked her daughter, to Alex's horror and astonishment, if she would let the man have anal sex with her. Sharon looked at her mum and nodded that yes, she would do it. Her mother just laughed and said: 'Oh you are, oh, I wasn't expecting that!' She then asked her daughter: 'How can you say that you are happy with that when you've never even done it?' Sharon replied: 'You've got to do it once to try it, ain't you?'

The toddler demanding his doughnuts interrupted the conversation once more. Alex reassured him they were on their way, and the child continued jumping on the bed. Sharon asked her first question, wanting to know where her four-year-old kid brother would go while she and her mum entertained the Sheik. Kent turned to Alex and asked him if he could baby-sit the toddler. 'Get a video, some cartoons. He'll be no trouble,' she said. Just when it appeared Kent had sunk as low as any mother could, she shocked Alex again by saying: 'I am OK for her not to use condoms ... if he's been tested. He's not going to catch anything from her. You've just heard for yourself she's quite happy to try anything and she's never done it before.'

Kent asked her daughter to pose for few photographs so that Alex could tempt the Sheik. As Alex walked away the greedy mum was concerned about protecting her investment, and he heard her say to her daughter, 'Don't you go having sex.'

Back at the office, I had a meeting with Neil Wallis who was editing the paper that week. He watched the covert video we had shot and shouted: 'This woman is fucking evil. I can't believe it. Drop everything and concentrate on nailing this evil woman. Rescue the kid, talk to the cops and get this woman banged up. She's got to be the lowest scum you've exposed. And I want you to write a few hundred words on how you've travelled the world and met all sorts of lowlifes, but she had got to be the most evil.' Neil was disgusted. For a man hardened by years on the tabloid treadmill to be moved to such anger showed it really was a sickening story.

I went round with Jaws to see Kent at her home in the picturesque village of Maldon, Essex, to finalize the deal; she believed me to be the Sheik's right-hand man. The three-bedroom semi was decorated with fairy lights outside and inside her little boy sat on the sofa with his sister watching cartoons. 'We're cool to talk in front of her, we can discuss whatever you want in front of her,' said Kent. I didn't want Sharon to know any more than she had to so I insisted on talking to the mother alone; she led us upstairs to a bedroom. We walked past the well-decorated children's room full of toys and DVDs of children's movies and cartoons. In the bedroom, Kent bizarrely had her prized collection of ornate thimbles on a shelf, but I didn't have time to comment on that oddity as she proudly revealed that she had introduced her daughter to drugs. 'She smokes crack. If she had her way she'd smoke it all the time, but I tend to give her the occasional pipe here and there,' said Kent. 'She's always with me and we smoke it nearly all the time. I mean we smoke it every day.'

She attempted to justify getting her child involved in a deadly drug addiction. 'She's breathing in the fumes anyway and I thought what hope has the girl got? I smoke crack, everyone around her is taking drugs, what hope has she got of not taking them? Let's be honest about it, she's going to, isn't she? Well I'd rather, if she's going to do it, she did it with me, with my knowledge, with my consent, so that we can build up the honesty. And I thought it's a nice experience, the first pipe she has, she has with her mum.' Jaws and I were stunned by this revelation, but there was worse. 'The first time she ever sniffed a line of cocaine was with me,' said Kent. She offered to supply us with drugs too. 'I can actually get crack better than I can Charlie [cocaine]. That's my drug. I can get tons of it. An eighth is £130,' she said.

After hearing her speak both Jaws and I were as angry as Neil – she really was the most evil mother I'd ever met. She handed me her daughter's passport to confirm her identity and age, reassuring me that Sharon wouldn't say a word to anybody if the Sheik had sex with her. 'Me and her are very, very close. We have a lot of secrets together. A lot of important secrets that if people knew about I'd be in a lot of trouble. If word got out about some of them I'd be in a lot of trouble and so would she.'

It took all my strength to sit there and listen to her when she came up with her final perverted idea: she would join in. 'Obviously I don't want to do anything with my daughter because it borders on incest,' Kent said. 'I'm not going to kiss her or touch her or anything like that. I'm happy to watch and to perhaps give him a blowjob or whatever while she's there as well. I know she'd have a great time with me there.'

She then said she'd 'rather' the man wore a condom. 'I don't want to be a grandma just yet!' she said, as she had already mapped out the poor girl's future, which was to follow her mum's footsteps into prostitution and porn. As I left, Kent predicted her own future: 'I'm looking at either a really good opportunity to get myself out of debt or I'm looking at 15 years in jail.'

It was the latter. As she arrived at the Kensington Palace hotel with her daughter and sat waiting for the Sheik, it was the police who turned up to greet her. Officers from Scotland Yard's Child Abuse Investigations Command arrested her and her children were immediately taken into Social Services care.

Our switchboards and email boxes were jammed after the story appeared, with readers shocked and appalled – many simply wanted to know if the story was true. There is nothing more infuriating for an investigative journalist than to be told: 'You can't believe all you read in the papers!' You definitely *can* believe what you read in the *News of the World*, as we risk our lives on a daily basis to gather the evidence required to get articles past our lawyers. If anything inaccurate is published we get sued. Nowadays, with solicitors keen to cash in on 'no-win, no-fee' libel cases, there is absolutely no room for error. But in this instance I wasn't annoyed by the callers and bloggers who questioned the truthfulness of the story, because it was hard to believe –

even the cops who nabbed the evil mum were shocked. Detective Inspector Colin Burgess who led the inquiry praised our work and commented: 'That a woman can be so callous and greedy as to prostitute a 13-year-old, and worse, sell her virginity, is an appalling example of child abuse.'

At Snaresbrook Court Claire Kent pleaded guilty to 'arranging or facilitating a child sex offence' and possessing crack cocaine with intent to supply.

CHAPTER 10

'THEY CALL ME THE BALL-BREAKER'

Society is made up of people who achieve great success through sheer hard work, education or through natural talents, excelling in sports or the arts. And then there are the bullshitters, and, worse, those who have refined bullshitting – also referred to as blagging – into an art form. The world is riddled with lightweights masquerading as heavyweights and it never ceases to amaze me how easy it is for them to reach the dizzy heights of fame and fortune.

One great exponent of this skill is 'lifestyle guru' Carole Caplin who started life as a soft porn model and, after befriending Cherie Blair in the late 1980s, ended up as style advisor to her – and confidante to Prime Minister Tony Blair. It's hard to fathom that this woman had a security pass to enter No.10 and Chequers and offered advice to a man entrusted to make decisions that would change the world.

In an interview in *Vanity Fair*, Caplin's former lover Peter Foster, a convicted conman, claimed Blair had sought her advice over his repeated clashes with Gordon Brown; Caplin would ask her mother Sylvia to do a New Age 'reading' involving a hidden force called The Light. Foster said: 'Tony would call and Carole would say, "I'll ask mum to channel on this and ring you back." Then she'd call back and say, "You must not confront him on this. Now isn't the right time."'

My colleague Alex D'Souza signed up for her 'Lifesmart' programme, which promised to restructure your entire 'spectrum of health, fitness and well-being'. After being ordered to buy her £16 lifestyle book, he had to fork out £100 plus VAT an hour for Caplin's twice-weekly sessions. The first session took place at her home, a comfortable flat in Holloway, north London littered with photos of Caplin and her famous clients. There, she plunged him into a Jacuzzi complete with a concoction of salts and minerals. After twenty minutes Caplin gave him a painful massage.

Next she wanted to visit Alex's home to inspect the toiletries in his bathroom, food in his cupboards and fridge, and even the clothes hanging in his wardrobe. 'I have to examine every aspect of your life. I even have to see what detergents your cleaner uses,' explained Caplin. 'If you use moisturizer than you have to stop because all cosmetics contain petroleum. You might as well go to a petrol station and rub petrol over you.' Then she took Alex on a shopping spree, running up a £343 bill in an hour at Planet Organic in west London, buying approved shaving creams, deodorants, vitamin supplements, a Chinese wok, and even healthy dental floss. I kept getting phone calls from a distraught Alex pleading with me to bring the investigation to a speedy close.

After one gym session with Caplin, Alex was left in agony after she made him perform a bench press using his legs rather than his arms to lift heavy weights. 'A lot of exercises I do I have devised myself,' she had reassured him as he considered heading to the local casualty.

While I have every faith in the merits of alternative medicine, I have no time for cranks, fortune-tellers, and mystics who simply prey on the vulnerable and the insecure in pursuit of money or power. I have fought many battles over the years against the mad, sad, and weird world of spiritualists and fortune-tellers.

One Muslim mystic, Peer Abul Fateh Chishti – who was later jailed for sexually abusing women who came to visit him – claimed to have conversations with the souls of the dead. He was so confident that he invited me to have an exclusive interview with Princess Diana from beyond the grave. He chanted verses from the Koran before a large group of his devoted followers as he spiritually dialled up her soul. Relaying messages via his heavy Pakistani accent, Diana told me the Establishment had murdered her. I thanked Diana for giving me a world exclusive, but when I asked her if she would kindly confirm her date of birth and if she would let me have her direct line phone number at Kensington Palace, just to convince the lawyers back in the office, she refused. When I dared to suggest that he might be making it all up, I was quickly escorted out of his home by a burly henchman.

My own partner once visited an Indian *jyotshi*, or mystic, in Los Angeles, out of curiosity. She was told not to marry me unless she married a clay pot first and was warned that she would die within days if she ever visited Dubai. We have been to Dubai together on numerous occasions and she is still alive, although I still worry at nights about that clay pot …

After subjecting Alex to two months of Caplin's equally nutty programme he could bear no more. 'The woman is absolutely mad,' he bleated. 'Put me on any other job you want, I'll go and live in Baghdad or Afghanistan if you want, but I can't take any more of Caplin.' My mum always said that you are judged by the company you keep. I wondered how this special friendship reflected on our Prime Minister; if Tony and Cherie followed Caplin's 'lifestyle advice' to the letter, what did it say about their judgement?

Alex arranged for her to meet his wealthy employer, the Fake Sheik, at a rented apartment in the heart of Mayfair. Caplin was keen to meet me because she wanted funding for her all-in-one health and fitness centre with complementary medicine. She waltzed into the apartment clutching a wad of promotional material. 'I look after people's health and well-being. I'm known in this country as a bit of a ball-breaker. I walk into homes, you know, whether it be Downing Street, wherever, where there is money, and people don't know how to live,' she claimed. She then started trying to impress me by cashing in on her trusted relationship with the Prime Minister and his wife. 'We had dinner last Saturday and he's in dire straits, he's put on weight,' she said before going on to brand the PM an overweight boozer. 'I can't believe the change in him since I've not been there. You know I'm a nag. I'm horrible. You know I got him off coffee, alcohol and he's gone into all those things again.'

She claimed the PM was drinking too much. 'It's the constant drip. It makes you get into the habit of maybe two or three glasses a night and it builds up and the body is not designed to take all that all the time, and the more you are under stress the more you reach for [a drink].' I didn't like Caplin at all. Here she was talking her head off to a complete stranger, laying bare confidences of people who rather foolishly trusted her. And she had the cheek to tell me: 'I never talk about my clients in any way. I've never spoken about the Blairs to anyone.'

Caplin left the meeting happy that I had been suitably impressed by her performance and would reach into my deep pockets to fund her project. But just in case I had not realized her importance, Caplin biked round a copy of *Hello!* magazine featuring an article about her close relationship with the Blairs, and even rang my assistant to make sure that the Sheik had read the article. I had. Now it was her turn to read my piece. It appeared across five pages in the paper under the headline: '*The Blairs Betrayed – The Fake Sheik Strikes Again*'.

She complained about the article to the PCC on the grounds of harassment, use of clandestine recording devices, and subterfuge. Her media advisor, Phil Hall – one of my former editors – told our ombudsman, Bob Warren: 'You're going to lose this one, I'm afraid.' Phil was wrong. Our defence was simple yet solid; this was a publicity-hungry woman who was an associate of a known criminal and had caused the Blairs great embarrassment. There was a huge public interest argument to justify our probe. Her complaint was duly slung out.

While Caplin was just greedy and mad, another lifestyle guru Dr Mosaraf Ali proved to be greedy and a complete fraudster – and he had the ear of our future King, Prince Charles. Somehow the quack from Calcutta had managed to become a royal healer by persuading Prince Charles of his amazing powers; Charles even wrote the foreword for his book, *The Integrated Health Bible*, claiming, 'I am wholly convinced that the integrated health approach has the power to really make immense difference to many people's lives and to our society as a whole.' The Royal endorsement had opened the doors to a long list of celebrity patients including Kate Moss, Geri Halliwell, Michael

Douglas, Catherine Zeta-Jones, and Tara Palmer-Tomkinson. It was time to add the Fake Sheik to his list.

Despite claiming to have qualified as a medic in Russia, Mosaraf was not registered to practice as a medical doctor in the United Kingdom. Instead he had set himself up as an alternative medicine practitioner running the Integrated Medical Centre, in central London. I was worried that he might rumble me and recognize me as a fellow Asian, and I also suspected that he might be able to speak Arabic, while I couldn't. I had to take precautions as I'd almost come unstuck once before.

> **❛It's hard to fathom that this woman had a security pass to enter No.10 and Chequers and offered advice to a man entrusted to make decisions that would change the world.❜**

It was when I exposed a group of elite troops responsible for guarding the Queen who were moonlighting as private bodyguards. I'd taken on Staff Sergeant John Twells, a platoon commander of the Royal Military Police to guard me, posing as the Fake Sheik. He came into my suite at the Royal Gardens hotel, next to Kensington Palace, saluted and then started speaking to me in Arabic. The officer had served in the Middle East and spoke fluently, while I could barely understand a word. Seeing the expensive operation collapsing before my eyes, I quickly stormed out of the room and in my best Arabic rage shouted: 'I never speak Arabic with white men. This man has insulted me!' Sergeant Twells sheepishly apologized and went on to provide me with prostitutes, and a two-page spread in the paper.

So for Mosaraf I recruited a *fake* Fake Sheik – my reliable Palestinian plumber, Marwan. He'd worked wonders with my leaking Jacuzzi, and had told me that he had always wanted to be an actor. After sending him for a manicure to remove the filth from his workman's hands, he donned the robes and looked the part. I was playing the role of his assistant and I ran through a rough script with Marwan.

Baby-faced Mosaraf oozed all the charm of an Indian mystic. Within minutes of entering our suite he proudly announced: 'I am the personal physician to Charles and Camilla. I sometimes travel with the Prince. I keep him healthy.' Marwan, the plumber-turned-Sheik, was enjoying his role, but went off script when he told Mosaraf that I suffered from a bad back. Mosaraf immediately leapt into action and in a move which would have done a Chinese martial arts practitioner proud, he twisted my neck in a lightning-fast manoeuvre until a dull cracking noise was heard. 'You are properly aligned now,' he proclaimed as Jaws stood in the background, grinding his gold teeth, waiting for me to scream. Surprisingly it didn't hurt that much at the time, but over the next ten days I cursed Mosaraf as I couldn't sleep because of the pain in my neck.

Mosaraf claimed to have cures for every ailment and said he could make paralysed people walk again. 'I can treat anything. Conventional medicine is rubbish.' The man dubbed a 'miracle worker' even claimed to have 'cured' brain-damaged boxer Michael Watson. 'He is one of my patients. I helped him with his walking,' bragged Mosaraf. This was news to Watson's agent, Geraldine Davis, who later told me: 'I should know if he has treated Michael because I pay the bills. He has played no part in his rehabilitation.'

Over dinner, Mosaraf spoke fondly about his pal Charles, but was less forgiving about Diana: 'Diana was beautiful, but all beautiful women have some bad quality you don't see, either a disease or something. God took her mind. Camilla is not beautiful but she makes you laugh,' he said.

My entire team including the minders, technician, photographer, driver, and not forgetting the plumber, simply couldn't understand how this man could get anywhere near a member of our Royal family. Besides his ludicrous miracle-cure claims, Mosaraf was a crook – we trapped him helping illegal immigrants stay in the country by providing fake medical reports to dupe the Home Office.

At his office in New Cavendish Street, where a photo of Mosaraf with Prince Charles taken at Highgrove held pride of place on his desk and doubled up as a sort of Royal seal of approval, Mosaraf handed over a false report to our reporter who claimed to know a refugee. As he handed over the note, Mosaraf promised: 'It means he is not well and can't be sent back. We can keep him continually sick.' Mosaraf lied in the letter, claiming he had examined the patient who suffered from 'chronic backache, vertigo, depression, occasional panic attacks, continuous headache, and severe fatigue.' For good measure he suggested: 'We could say he had an accident and whiplash and suffers from all these neurological symptoms.' Mosaraf demanded £70 as his 'standard fee' for the fake report.

Bizarrely, Dr Mosaraf still to this day retains the friendship of Prince Charles. He is not registered here so cannot be struck off; and he writes, occasionally, for one of the Sunday newspapers.

It wasn't the first time I'd uncovered the malpractices of some doctors. I'd exposed a whole list of them including eminent Harley Street consultant Dr Naveed Hasan who sold fake medical reports to help people put in bogus insurance claims. There was even the Birmingham doctor, Dr Anwar Ali, who prescribed himself sex on the floor of his surgery three times a week with local prostitutes from an escort agency. But the most corrupt doctor I ever came across was Dr James Allan Muir who was the doctor for the House of Commons. Dr Muir was a greedy practitioner who would do almost anything for money. In between treating MPs and Lords, Dr Muir was taking backhanders from drug users, illegal immigrants, crooks, and fraudsters. He sold methadone – the controlled drug substitute for heroin – to anyone who could pay. He referred foreign nationals who were not entitled to NHS treatment to our hospitals to undergo expensive operations, helped rip off the DSS and insurance companies with bogus medical reports and arranged abortions to enable women to get rid of a child of the 'wrong sex'. During my investigation he even admitted how he had covered up the cause of death of one of his VIP patients who had died of a drug overdose, by diagnosing another ailment on the death certificate. It was a joy to give evidence before the General Medical Council (GMC) and to witness him getting struck off.

It was second only to the pleasure I got when I came up before Cherie Blair QC at another GMC tribunal. She was representing Dr Mohinder Singh who had made £1 million in three years by making up a list of 5,000 fake patients with fictitious addresses including a fly-over on the A13. The Sikh doctor from East Ham was also selling false medical reports, raking in another £300k a year. He offered to help me con the DSS into paying out increased housing and incapacity benefits, even though he knew I was perfectly healthy. He said that I'd get a disabled badge thrown in as an added perk.

I was up most of the night preparing a speech for the GMC tribunal, which would have caused great embarrassment to Cherie. The case came in the very week that her husband had been extolling the virtues of the National Health Service and fighting criticism over the lack of funding. Here was his wife trying to defend a man who had robbed the NHS blind of over a million quid. But as Cherie sat hearing my evidence – which included covert video recordings of the turbaned doc in action – she played nervously with her pencil. She could see the mauling I was about to give her, and was no doubt imagining the headlines in the following Sunday's paper. Cherie whispered to her client for several minutes and then told the hearing that he had changed his mind and was now pleading guilty. She stood up and made a feeble speech in mitigation for his indefensible behaviour, claiming that it was important that it be noted that this hearing was the result of an elaborate tabloid sting. My sentiments exactly.

CHAPTER 11

'BEWARE
OF THIS
MAN'

Sometimes the story I'd set out to do wasn't the one that made it into the paper. Circumstances would change our plans literally overnight, and, just as the Sheik had to think on his feet at times, so too did I as a journalist, and write something entirely different for the paper.

Like the time I met actress Michelle Collins, Cindy Beale of *East-Enders* fame. I sacrificed a story to save her getting battered by her violent boyfriend but you wouldn't have known I'd done the right thing as she instead chose to fire off a complaint to the PCC about me.

One of her closest friends had contacted me and made serious allegations about Michelle's private life. Michelle was a soap queen in the middle of a major storyline in the show and, if the information proved true, it would make a front-page splash, as most of our readers were big *EastEnders* fans (as it turned out, it wasn't true). I did have slight reservations about meeting her though; a few years earlier I'd spent the evening partying with Michelle and her fellow *EastEnders* actress, Danniella Westbrook.

I've made it a rule never to go to any parties where there is the slightest chance of my bumping into potential future targets – at least, not as myself anyway. But this was a lavish *News of the World* bash to celebrate the paper's 150th birthday and I had been ordered to attend by editor Patsy Chapman. In the end I'd made a fool of myself by attempting to do the twist on the dance floor with Michelle, goaded on by a former colleague of mine, Lorraine Kelly from GMTV. The embarrassing moment had been captured by one of our photographers and the photo of Michelle and me dancing ended up pinned on a notice board in our newsroom. Someone had scrawled the vulgar – but soon to prove prophetic – caption, 'Sheik Shafts Cindy' underneath it.

Away from the dance floor Michelle and I had talked a bit, and she told me that she thoroughly enjoyed reading my exposés but couldn't believe how celebrities were stupid enough to fall prey to my tactics, the implication being that she was far too wise to fall for the ploy. I laughed this off, never dreaming for a moment that I'd be testing her theory out on her in the not-too-distant future. So with a fear of being rumbled lurking in the back of my mind I pulled out my newly dry-cleaned Arab robes and summoned her to come and see Sheik Mohammed Al-Jamal at his holiday retreat in Marbella. Editor Rebekah Wade gave me the usual speech about budgetary constraints before I flew out there: 'Keep me posted. Let me know everything she says, and try your best to keep the costs down.'

The man who arranged the meeting was one of my team of minders, John Miller, an ex-soldier Michelle knew and respected. Miller, who'd served in the Scots Guards regiment, rose to fame when he kidnapped Great Train Robber Ronnie Biggs from his bolthole in Brazil in 1981. Biggs, who was on the run from British police, was found on Miller's rented yacht, which had broken down seven miles from the coast of Barbados. He was later returned to Rio de Janeiro. Soldier of fortune Miller had more recently turned to running a themed restaurant called School Dinners in central London, which was where he'd befriended Michelle.

Michelle was told that Saudi Sheik Al-Jamal was the biggest fan of *EastEnders* in the Arabian desert. He wanted to open a nightclub in Marbella and wanted her to be the chief guest. Besides, the maverick Sheik was financing a Hollywood film and would obviously want Michelle to play a prominent role in his forthcoming production.

Michelle, who was about to leave *EastEnders*, was keen to consider new projects and so was eager to meet me. I laid on first class airline tickets and a luxurious room for Michelle to stay at the exclusive Marbella Club hotel. She'd told Miller that her Italian boyfriend Fabrizio Tassalini insisted on coming too, as he couldn't look after their

15-month-old daughter Maia alone, but Miller reassured her that the Sheik loved children and would be happy for her boyfriend and daughter to come along too. Michelle had met Fabrizio at a bar in Miami over Christmas a couple of years or so before, in 1995. She had almost immediately got pregnant, and Fabrizio had given up his job selling motorbikes in Milan to move to Britain to live off Michelle.

The newspaper had put me in the Marbella hotel and golf club complex too, but in a £1,500-a-night Andalucian-style three bedroom apartment, with my own private swimming pool, private beach, and stables nearby. The Sheik had arranged to meet Michelle in the evening for dinner, which meant that during the day I had to keep out of her way – I was still unsure whether or not she'd recognize me even though it had been two years, maybe more, since I'd danced with her. Also, I had to make sure Michelle didn't see me in my jeans and M&S T-shirt nipping to the local Spanish off-licence to pick up cheap bottles of champagne. It was important to make her first meeting with the Sheik a grand event, but as always part of my job was to make sure I kept the hotel bill and other expenses down. Photographer Bradley Page was tasked with keeping a close eye on her every movement, which he relayed to me via a two-way radio.

Miller is a very resourceful minder to have around as his military training often comes in handy. The Sheik's robes had been crushed in my suitcase on the non-VIP EasyJet flight over, and I was struggling to get the creases out when Miller stepped in. He pulled out a steam iron and moments later he handed me my rags, perfectly ironed, fit for a Prince. He then got to work on my footwear, making the pointed fake crocodile skin shoes, complete with large fake gold buckle, shine like they had never shone before.

I'm not sure who was more nervous when Michelle strolled from her plush hotel room across the sun-kissed Mediterranean gardens to my imposing Royal villa – her or me. She asked Miller on the way in: 'How do I address him, what do I call him?' She needn't have worried about protocol; my only concern at that moment was would she recognize me.

I knew that even if she did recognize my face it would certainly take a few minutes, because I'd made sure that the room was full of thick plumes of smoke rising from my Arabian sheesha pipe stuffed full with strawberry-flavoured tobacco. Through the cloud of smoke Michelle caught sight of me in my long white Arab robe and red chequered headdress. Added to this, I'd tuned the TV in the room to an Arab news channel that I had on loudly – the intention being to totally disorient her and hit all her senses at once.

So with Arabic commentary blaring full volume, her eyes blinded by smoke and her nostrils attacked by strawberry tobacco and my sickly Arabian aftershave, I stood up to greet Michelle. She appeared to curtsy.

It's amazing the effect that the Arab outfit has on people. Almost like a reflex action they instantly feel inferior and are compelled to bow. HRH Sophie Wessex had bowed before me, and Princess Michael of Kent had lowered her head out of respect and handed me a rose.

The secret of the Sheik is to present people with what they are willing to believe: so if they want to see an Arab prince, with the robes and headdress and expensive things about his person, in a hotel suite or on a boat they could never afford, you make it look like it is so. So what if the robes cost me £9.99 on the Coventry Road in Birmingham, and I can't speak a word of Arabic – it's the acting, and the behaviour of those around me, that convinces the target they're meeting a Sheik.

My diamond-studded Rolex and diamond rings were catching the light perfectly as they twinkled before Michelle's eyes. As I rested my red and gold snaking mouthpiece for the Arab pipe on my armchair, I welcomed her in my best broken English.

She looked older. Despite her best attempts to look glamorous in a black figure-hugging blouse, tight satin trousers and a leather jacket, her face looked tired and prematurely wrinkled. Michelle spoke nervously as she positioned and repositioned her Prada handbag and struggled to make small talk. Her demeanour was a world apart from her TV character of super-bitch Cindy Beale.

She was clearly overawed by the formality of the situation; after all, it's not everyday a mere soap star gets to rub shoulders with a billionaire Saudi Sheik. Which she wasn't, of course. I continued to talk in my bad English, asking her about the show, while John Miller, smartly dressed in a suit and tie, stood to attention with his arms behind his back by the door. He would occasionally step forward to pour drinks for us, always referring to me as 'Sir'.

Michelle proudly handed me a copy of *Hello!* magazine, which contained a feature about her spread across several pages. I continued to relax her with some general chit-chat, aided by my grey-haired assistant Gerry Brown. Gerry was a veteran *News of the World* reporter, who we referred to as Morse, as with his broken nose and silver hair he bore a striking resemblance to the actor John Thaw. I even signalled to Miller to break with protocol and sit down and join us.

As Michelle struggled to understand my broken English, Gerry would regularly chip in to keep the conversation flowing. Power and wealth overcomes most hurdles, though, and by the time we got to the main course over dinner at the romantic hotel restaurant, Michelle and I were the best of friends.

I sat twirling my mother-of-pearl worry beads as Michelle revealed secret *EastEnders* storylines and criticized her fellow stars. She claimed Ross Kemp who played Grant Mitchell was someone who 'has a bit of an ego'. When I reminded her that Ross, who was going out with my editor Rebekah Wade at the time, was very popular she replied simply, 'I don't know why.'

I knew I'd truly gained her trust as Michelle admitted having experimented with Ecstasy. 'Ten years ago when E's first came out they were so pure and that's when they were good. But now there's so much rubbish and that's why it's so dangerous,' she said. 'I took them a long time ago but I wouldn't touch it now.'

By the time dessert arrived we were howling with laughter and she repeatedly grabbed my arm as she cracked jokes and reeled off anecdotes. We recorded everything, on the machine stitched into my robe as well as on other recording devices hidden about the room. Later, I listened to the tapes and realized that my Arab accent was turning more and more into the Queen's English as the night went on, but luckily Michelle didn't notice.

That was largely because she kept getting distracted by phone calls on her mobile from her boyfriend. She became visibly annoyed as Fabrizio kept phoning her from the hotel bedroom a minute's walk away. After about the fourth call, an embarrassed Michelle, who kept twirling her fingers in her blonde bob, made an excuse and left saying she had to check up on Maia. She returned later and rejoined me at the dinner table looking very uneasy. I twigged she was having problems with Fabrizio.

We quickly finished off our coffees and arranged to meet by the pool the following day. Before she left, Michelle told me how she had spent a lot of time in Marbella because her ex-boyfriend called Nick ran a nightclub there. 'But don't mention it in front of Fabrizio, he gets a bit funny about it,' she warned before lighting up a cigarette.

As she left the restaurant and quickly returned to her room, I shoved the earpiece back into my ear – we had a private communications system that Conrad had rigged up for us. Bradley, who we'd stationed in the room next door to Michelle's, told me that while we were dining Fabrizio had been screaming abuse down the phone at Michelle, ordering her to get back to the room immediately. Fabrizio had told her that he would kidnap their daughter unless she came back to the room within two minutes. In light of the circumstances, she'd done well to keep her composure during dinner.

As soon as Michelle returned to the room, the pair started rowing. In a jealous rage, Fabrizio repeatedly called her a prostitute, branding her an 'Arab's whore!' When the furious Italian ran out of English expletives, he resorted to hurling Italian swear words at her.

Conrad, who was in the hotel room on the other side of our celebrity guests, reported that Fabrizio was shouting so loud that he could hear it clearly through the wall; so loud in fact that he switched on a tape recorder and recorded the disturbing exchanges for me to hear.

The following day, I thought it would not be a good ideal to lounge by the pool with Michelle. Instead, I sent one of my entourage over to invite the family to dinner with me that evening. I insisted that she bring along Maia too. And just to make it absolutely clear to Fabrizio that I was not interested in Michelle, I arranged for an attractive female assistant to be by my side during dinner posing as the Sheik's secretary-cum-fourth wife!

In another flamboyant show of wealth, I arranged a fleet of stretch limos complete with a small army of drivers and minders to ferry us to nearby Puerto Banus. En route, I tried to engage Fabrizio in conversation but he seemed very cold towards me. The only thing I could remember him telling me was that he was from Sicily, home of the Mafiosi. I felt like telling him you don't frighten me mate, I'm from the backstreets of Birmingham!

Michelle, who was wearing a green dress and £200 designer high-heeled shoes she'd bought in Puerto Banus earlier, tried to compensate for his rudeness by being even more friendly towards me. Or maybe she was just trying to annoy her boyfriend.

We dined at the Antonio restaurant in the heart of the marina surrounded by row upon row of luxurious yachts in an area dubbed the 'millionaires' playground'. Miller acted as minder to Michelle's beautiful young daughter Maia, who was clearly having a nice time running around the restaurant.

Fabrizio ordered the most expensive item on the menu, fresh lobster thermidor, which he washed down with vintage champagne. I thought that I had finally dispelled any seeds of jealousy from Fabrizio's twisted mind and even began to think that his limited conversation was due to the fact that his English was even worse than the Sheik's. I saw Michelle on several occasions encourage him to behave by giving her lover her hallmark Cindy Beale cold stare.

I had arranged for a friendly Spanish photographer to come to our table and ask if we wanted a group photo as a souvenir of the memorable dinner. It meant that we would have a photo for the paper without having aroused any suspicions that we were journalists. Like the famous Princess Diana photo at the Taj Mahal, the picture I was handed spoke a thousand words. I had my arm around my attractive assistant and we were both grinning broadly. Fabrizio stared menacingly at the lens, while Michelle next to him rested her head in her hands, unable to raise a smile for the camera.

I remembered dancing with her at the Christmas party, and how nice and friendly she'd been, and I thought to myself, you are a top soap star who could have your pick of men in Britain; why the hell would you want to go out with this unemployed scumbag? But then it seemed to be the trend among *EastEnders* actresses at the time; almost the entire female cast on the hit show had been going out with villains or lowlifes who either cheated on them, beat them up, or cashed in on their celebrity partner's fame.

Unbeknown to Michelle, I already knew that the slippery rat she was sitting next to had not that long ago approached the *News of the World* to sell a story about her. Fabrizio had demanded £20,000 for his sordid tale and promised to reveal Michelle's secrets. We had shown him the door.

> ❝"I need £300 up front to sort out your union card. I'll have you on *EastEnders* in no time."❞

Nevertheless, to try and keep the Latin lover sweet, I ordered one of my burly Spanish minders to bring him a £20 cigar as a peace offering. It didn't work. By the end of dinner it was plainly obvious that he still didn't like me. I didn't like him much either. In fact, by the end of the night I hated the bastard.

Back at the hotel, Fabrizio flew into a jealous rage again and events in Room 488 were about to get completely out of hand. Bradley buzzed me in my earpiece and whispered in his Cockney tones: 'The Italian has gone mad, he's screaming at her, he's going mental!'

Fabrizio was screaming so loudly that I could hear him down my earpiece. I heard the sound of glass smashing as the hot-headed Latin hurled objects around the room and repeatedly shouted at Michelle at the top of his voice: 'You are a fucking disgrace.' Then he lashed out at Michelle, who was holding baby Maia in her arms. Michelle's screams of pain were drowned out by baby Maia's hysterical crying as her parents battled in front of her.

Michelle shrieked: 'Look at me! Look what you've done to me! You've hit me right across the room. Do you think you are clever? You are the disgrace – you're the one who takes my money. You're just a sponger! Who's paid for your air fare? Who's paid for your hotel? It's fine for you to take my money isn't it? You already owe me £6,000. When will I get that back?' she screamed. 'You've spoiled everything again, you always do.'

It wasn't the first time that mad Fabrizio had assaulted Michelle. 'I can't believe you've just hit me in front of our child and made her scream,' Michelle told him. 'This is the fourth time you've done this, you Italian pig. You've marked my face. That's it, we're finished – get out!'

Just hearing what was going on made it clear that this was a shocking scene, rivalling anything Michelle had done on screen. And as Fabrizio tried to attack her yet again, Maia screamed hysterically. Michelle threatened to call Miller to sort him out. 'I'm going to call John Miller, he'll be round here and deal with you!' she warned.

She didn't have to wait long.

A large part of being an investigative reporter involves thinking on your feet and making instant decisions. I decided to drop the investigation into Michelle and simply rescue her from this monster. I ordered Miller to steam in. I stood next to Gerry at the end of the corridor, while Miller banged hard on Michelle's bedroom door.

She regained her composure, opened the door and told Miller that she was having a row with Fabrizio but everything was alright. He told her he would be outside if he was needed.

Michelle told Fabrizio: 'I don't want to sleep in this room with you. You're a sick man, you need help.'

When he refused to leave the room, scared that Miller was lurking outside, Michelle rang her mum in London for support. 'He's just hit me right across the room,' she sobbed down the line. 'He just went completely off his head. He's crazy. He's disgusting. My face is all red and I'm just sitting here in shock.'

Fabrizio eventually stormed out of the room and went for a walk by the beach to cool off.

With Bradley and Conrad taking it in turns to keep their ears to the bedroom wall throughout the night, we headed to the Marbella Club bar to discuss what to do next. It was clear that the only person that warranted being exposed in the *News of the World* was evil Fabrizio.

With each pint he downed, Miller became more and more concerned at the situation. He felt more responsible than he should have for the unbelievable events, because he had encouraged Michelle to fly out to meet the Sheik. At about 4am, Miller couldn't cope with his guilt or the alcohol he'd guzzled anymore. He stood up with a scary glazed look and announced: 'That's it, I'm going over there to give that fucker a kicking, I'll kill the bastard!'

He meant business, and my pleas to calm him down went unheard, as Miller walked past the hotel swimming pool towards Fabrizio's room. I tried to grab him by his arm and pull him back, but my short 5ft 8in flabby frame was no match for the 6ft 3in, 17-stone mass of muscle in front of me. Miller simply pushed me away. Next I tried shouting at him, hoping that his military discipline would kick in and Miller would respond to orders. After all he had been one of the elite fighting men operating secretly in the brutal undercover war against the Provisional IRA in Ulster.

But he failed to take any notice of my orders. Gerry joined in as we struggled to restrain him. By now staff from the bar – who still believed me to be an Arab Sheik as I still hadn't removed my robes after dinner – were pacing towards the pool. I took a few steps back and ran straight at Miller, jumping on him to stop him in his tracks. He stumbled and fell onto the finely manicured grass lawn beside a sun lounger.

I radioed to the photographers for urgent back-up and, half-dressed and dishevelled Conrad and Bradley raced downstairs. It took all of us to control Miller's rage and to pin him to the ground as he tried to throw us off with every limb, while continuously shouting threats to kill. By now lights in several hotel rooms above us were being switched on and curtains were twitching as guests were woken by the noisy fiasco.

The hotel manager and a Spanish security man arrived at the extraordinary scene and saw the Sheik sitting on Miller's chest under a palm tree. 'What is the problem, Sir?' the manager asked me. In my finest broken Spanish, I told him: '*Ingles! Quando bibere loco!*' (When Englishmen have a few too many they go mad!). It seemed to strike a chord with him and he thought he understood the problem.

With his puffed-out bright red cheeks and fury still in his eyes, it took our entire *News of the World* crew, all four of us grappling with him, plus three Spanish hotel staff; together we dragged Miller into the back of one of the waiting limousines. I told Gerry, who was an old pal of Miller's, to take him round to Nigel Bowden's place and lock him in a room. Bowden, a close friend of mine, was a British freelance journalist who lived on the Costa Del Sol and was well versed in handling our tabloid adventures and Sangria-soaked journos.

As the car left the hotel grounds, I wiped the sweat from my brow and breathed a sigh of relief. Then Miller opened the door of the moving limo and shouted at me: 'Maz I'm going to kill that bastard! I'll fucking have him!' Gerry leaned over and pulled the door shut as I shouted back: 'Ok John but do it in the morning when you're not pissed!'

The following morning it was apologies all round. Miller turned up at dawn and apologized for his behaviour. I rang the office and apologized for dropping the story. Fabrizio woke up and ordered Michelle to apologize to him!

I wrote a piece about the battered *EastEnders* beauty which appeared on the cover of the paper; but when writing the piece I was careful not to make it look as if Michelle had fallen for the Fake Sheik routine, as that could have triggered a whole new round of violence from Fabrizio. The story read as if it had come from British guests staying next door to the celeb at the hotel; of course it had but the 'guests' were our boys.

As Michelle came down for breakfast wearing large sunglasses to hide her bruised face, I asked Nigel Bowden to approach her and ask her about the alleged violence she had suffered the previous night. She turned to woman-beater Fabrizio, who was walking a few steps behind her and said angrily: 'Fabrizio, you better handle this!'

The maniac claimed the information Bowden had received was not true. 'The baby was awake at night and was making a lot of noise. You know what they're like at this age. There are no problems between me and Michelle. We are on holiday,' he said lying through his teeth.

Before I checked out of the hotel, Michelle walked over to my villa and popped a handwritten note under my door. It read: 'Dear Mohammed, Thank you so much for your hospitality and kindness, (especially to Maia!) I must admit I wasn't sure what to expect having never met an Arab Sheik before. But I was amazed how normal and human you are. Thank you. Kind Regards, Michelle, Fabrizio and Maia. PS. I hope to see you in London in February.' She wrote her home address and phone number at the bottom of the note scribbled on the hotel notepad.

Back in Britain, Michelle went to the trouble of writing to me again, but this time it was through her solicitors Shillings. Michelle threatened legal action. I was accused of 'a very serious breach of the new Code of Conduct of the Press Complaints Commission.' The letter claimed that the story I had written had been 'seriously inaccurate'.

I was asked by News International's Legal Manager, Tom Crone, to provide the usual memo, tapes, and transcripts. I simply wrote back a one-paragraph reply:

'In this case Tom, it is with regret that I have to concede my story was inaccurate. My story only claimed he said "You are a f***ing disgrace"; in fact Fabrizio called Michelle a "fucking disgrace and a fucking Arab's whore and a motherfucking bitch!" – Yours etc'

I never heard back from the lawyers or the PCC again. No one was more pleased than me when Michelle finally dumped Fabrizio, ending their three-year relationship.

I was just as relieved when she walked out of Albert Square, because I might have bumped into her on the *EastEnders* set, because the next time I was involved with anyone from the cast of the top soap it was when I'd paid the uncle of one of the stars a £3,000 bribe to get a part on the show.

The story began with a late-night phone call from another of my loyal minders and 'back watchers', Lenny McLean. Lenny, who was known as the Guv'nor, had made a name for himself in London's East End as a bare-knuckle fighter, bouncer, and criminal who had been linked to the Krays. We had a mutual respect for each other. He told me that I had more balls than most of the villains he'd met in his life, and I saw him as a real family man, a gentle giant who attempted to mete out justice in his own way.

His last brush with the law had been in 1992 when as a doorman at the Hippodrome nightclub in central London he'd ejected a man called Gary Humphries from the club who was allegedly harassing a young woman. Lenny admitted giving the drunken man a 'backhander', only Humphries died later that night and was found to have a broken jaw-bone and severe neck injuries. Lenny was arrested for murder but the charge was later reduced to manslaughter after it emerged that Humphries had been involved in a scuffle with police as he left the club and they had restrained him by putting him in a stranglehold.

But because Lenny was responsible for the broken jaw, he was sentenced at the Old Bailey to 18 months' imprisonment for grievous bodily harm. Lenny had no regrets. 'If any bloke treats women like that then he deserves a slap,' he explained to me. 'I don't like going to jail but if I saw a bloke treating a woman like that in front of me again, I'd still give him a backhander!'

On one occasion I was warned by police that a £10,000 contract had been taken out on my life after I exposed a south London gang of fraudsters. The cops offered me round-the-clock protection. But bizarrely a few days later, I received a call from the notorious villain who wanted me dead to let me know that we were 'all square' – meaning that there were no longer any hard feelings on his side.

I thought the cops had used their contacts and persuasion to reason with the bad guys, but years later I discovered that Lenny had heard about the contract and gone round to a south London pub and made it known that I was his personal friend and that anyone messing with me would be taking him on.

Lenny wanted to take up acting, and I encouraged him: 'I wanna have a go at the acting game but my memory ain't good and I don't think I can remember any lines,' Lenny told me. To help boost his confidence I gave Lenny a few lines to speak to a couple of my targets while he was working with me as the Sheik's minder. He was thrilled when we watched the covert video back and I told him he had performed really well. With a child-like innocence that belied his reputation, Lenny excitedly rang his wife Val to tell her that I rated him as an actor.

It seemed to do the trick. Lenny went on to receive real acclaim for his role in Guy Ritchie's gangster film *Lock, Stock and Two Smoking Barrels*, which also starred ex-footballer Vinnie Jones.

One night I received a phone call at around 1am from Lenny who told me in his distinctive gravel voice: 'This acting lark is full of criminals and scumbags. There's a slimy scroat who's taking money from people to get them parts in *EastEnders*. Come round and I'll tell you about it. I'd sort them all out myself but I'm busy fighting the biggest fight of my life, so it's down to you!' explained Lenny. Lenny's fight was with lung cancer and a brain tumour, which he sadly lost on 28 July 1998.

I went round to his house in Bexleyheath, Kent, where Lenny sat in the garden wearing shorts and a T-shirt, next to one of his trusted lackeys called Eric Brady. Brady, a short man with dark curly hair, was your archetypal East End wide boy who ran a pub called Taffy Brady's in Stratford, east London. Brady was at Lenny's 24-hour beck and call.

The pair of them briefed me about a man called John Quilty, whose claim to fame was that he was Gillian Taylforth's uncle. The family connection was a 'nice little earner' for Quilty, as he cashed in on Gillian's fame. She was at the peak of her soap career, starring as Kathy Mitchell in *EastEnders*.

Brady introduced me to John Quilty as Mo, an Asian businessman straight out of the *Sunday Times* Rich List, who fancied his chances as an actor.

Quilty, an old-aged pensioner with protruding false teeth, lapped it up. Within minutes of meeting him at Mezzo, in London's Wardour Street, he had convinced me that I could be the new Asian Tom Cruise.

'You've got the right look, and what you've got going for you is that you are Asian and we need more Asian actors,' Quilty told me. 'I can manage your career for you. Getting you onto *EastEnders* is easy, I've got all the contacts. My niece Gillian works there, she's a big star. But I believe you could do better than that and make it in films, you've got the personality for it.'

He certainly believed that I had the money for it as he guzzled yet more champagne, leaving me to pick up the tab. After promising to get me a much-sought-after Equity card through his dodgy contacts across the road in Soho, the 'cash for parts' offer was on the table – £3k would land me a role in *EastEnders* with an introduction to his niece Gillian.

'So you want to be on *EastEnders*, I could arrange that. To start with the actual performance is small, but I'll do my best to arrange a couple of lines so you get a share of the limelight,' promised Quilty in his warm soft-spoken voice. 'I'll have to see some of the storylines and then I'll get you on. I make it my business to represent you. I'll introduce you to agents too. This is a sideways way into the acting industry. I only do this for a select number, like friends, otherwise people start talking.'

'I need £300 up front to sort out your union card. I'll have you on *EastEnders* in no time,' he said.

As I picked up the hefty luncheon bill, worrying whether my expenses would get past our managing editor, Quilty cheekily asked whether my driver could drop him off home. My bald-headed burly driver, Alan Smith – another wide boy to rival Quilty – sped off to Surrey with Quilty relaxing in 'my' Rolls Royce. Waiting until the hired Roller had slipped off into the distance, I jumped onto the Tube and headed back to the office. Throughout the drive back to his home, Quilty quizzed my driver to establish the scale of my wealth. Reliable Smithy filled him in, saying he wasn't supposed to discuss my affairs, but casually let slip that I was a big name in the clothing industry up north and that I was certainly worth a few quid.

I later discovered that Quilty had mistaken me for Shami Ahmed, a Pakistani worth £75 million who set up the Joe Bloggs clothing label from his base in Manchester. It wasn't surprising then that Quilty fancied another expensive champagne-drenched lunch at my expense at celebrity haunt, the Ivy. At this meeting he handed me my union card – membership for BECTU – Broadcasting Entertainment Cinematography and Theatre Union.

With great fanfare my newfound mentor proudly announced: 'Right my love, I've started you off. I just had to go and vouch for you in front of a minor committee. This is the union that has actors, producers, and directors. It's powerful. This entitles you to work.'

He also provided me with an Equity card – which I took back to the office and had checked out: it was a clever forgery. To whet my appetite for stardom even further, or maybe just to try and get a bit more spending money off me, Quilty then took me to the *EastEnders* set in Elstree. At the studio gates he announced himself as 'Gillian Taylforth's Uncle John', and was waved in by security guards who obviously recognized him.

He gave me a quick tour of the set that had almost become a part of British culture. I strolled around the famous Albert Square which was a small area surrounded by façades of houses propped up by wooden beams. Most of the scenes including those inside the Queen Vic were actually filmed in an indoor studio nearby. 'Gillian's not here at the moment, she could have shown you round,' said Quilty. 'I wanted you to meet her here but when she rings me I'll arrange dinner with her.'

As I walked out of the Elstree studios with Quilty he claimed he had spoken to one of the show's production staff and promised me: 'You're on *EastEnders* my son! You'll be playing a solicitor. It's all sorted!' But with Quilty there was always a price tag attached. 'You're like my family now. You'll have to give my backroom boy something. You've got to look after him or you don't get the part. He's going to want a grand at least, sort him out for £2,000.' Quilty also demanded I hand him £200 immediately to 'cover taking the contact out for a good meal to discuss your career!'

Once it looked certain that Quilty had lined up a part for me on the soap, I went to see my editor Rebekah Wade, then engaged to Ross Kemp, who of course played the role of hardman Grant Mitchell on the soap. I sat in her office and discussed the story with her, seeking her reassurance that it wouldn't end up as another page 35 exclusive.

'What are you doing to me Maz?' she asked as she ran her fingers through her trademark ginger hair and subconsciously twisted the large diamond engagement ring on her finger. There clearly was a huge conflict of interest for Rebekah who was living with Ross in Battersea, south-west London. I was relieved when she turned to me and said: 'It'll make a great splash. Go do it, but I don't know anything about this story until it's finished and presented to me. If Ross finds out I knew what you were up to he will be furious!'

Quilty rang again with an invitation to lunch with Gillian Taylforth and her sister Kim; Gillian had asked to meet us at a modest American grill called Bennigan's in north London. However dreams of a cut-price luncheon faded fast as Quilty ordered me to bring a brown envelope stuffed with money. 'When you meet Gilly give her a present, a grand. Give her a little envelope with that in. Gillian will look after you,' said Quilty. In case I hadn't heard him clearly the first time, he reminded me before he hung up: 'Don't forget to bring money with you for Gillian.'

Gillian, who had no idea about Quilty's cash-for-parts scam, turned up for lunch wearing cream trousers and a light blue blouse. She was a bubbly, friendly character and we got on well. So well in fact that she said to me, 'If you'd got in earlier you could have appeared with me instead of this bloke I've got a kissing scene with. He rang me up the other day and said I've seen the script, how do you want to do this, we better practise. I said it's just a kiss. No tongues!'

Later, when Gillian and Kim weren't at the table, I asked Quilty if I should hand Gillian the envelope containing £1,000 as he had suggested. Sly Quilty replied: 'It's very delicate. She doesn't want to be seen ... give it to me and I'll give it to her. If you give it to her straight it looks like a bribe, which it is, but we don't want it to appear so.' Quilty literally snatched the envelope from my hands and slipped it into the pocket of his tweed jacket. Later as Gillian and Kim left the restaurant our photographer – who had spent a couple of hours crouched in the back of a small van in the restaurant car park – took a picture of Quilty as he opened the envelope and handed Gillian some money.

For a brief moment I thought that Quilty was right and Gillian might even be in on the scam. But I later discovered that her cunning uncle had used and conned her too.

A few days after meeting Gillian, the extras agency rang me and confirmed that I was to report for work on *EastEnders*. I joined a pool of some thirty men and women of all ages and ethnic backgrounds loitering on the sets waiting to be summoned by the floor manager. Small groups of us in turn would be called upon to sit in the background at the café, the Queen Vic or walk past a market stall as the main characters reeled off their lines. It was a strange and enlightening day as I stood lurking in the wings watching the characters who I'd seen on TV create the scenes which would entertain millions of regular viewers.

But the drama was only about to begin for me, as my moment of fame finally arrived. I was called into the Queen Vic to stand at the bar next to Nadia Sawalha as she chatted to the barman – Ross Kemp!

As Ross pulled a pint his eyes met mine and he almost dropped the beer glass. His facial expression read: 'What the fuck are you doing here?' He was Rebekah's partner and we'd met socially on several occasions. He was a fan of my work and was always flattering me by telling me that I was a better actor than him.

That day I certainly was. I kept my cool as Ross fluffed his lines several times, which surprised the crew as he was known as a thorough professional who seldom got things wrong. I could see the shock etched on his face as he struggled to deliver his lines. Ross was unexpectedly faced with a huge moral dilemma. Should he blow my cover and impress his BBC bosses or keep quiet? One thing was clear, Rebekah had definitely kept it quiet from him.

Ross was nothing like his screen character Grant Mitchell; I knew him to be not only a great actor but an intelligent man who could easily have carved himself a successful career in politics. I knew that he would rationally weigh up all the odds before deciding whether I should be escorted off the set by BBC security men. Fortunately for me he made the right choice.

As soon as he finished his scene Ross followed me to the toilets. Inside we both waited for Ian Beale – actor Adam Woodyatt – to finish having a piss. Then Ross asked me: 'Does Rebekah know you are here?' I lied. I gave him brief details of what I was doing there but left out the fact that I had discussed it with his fiancée. Ross invited me to join him for lunch, but even though it would have been at his expense, I thought it wise to turn him down.

Before heading back to the Queen Vic for my next scene, I quickly rang Rebekah to mark her card. 'Oh no. How did he react?' she asked.

My story went on to spark a major family crisis for Gillian Taylforth; I rang her to tell her that I was not a millionaire aspiring actor, but a reporter from the *News of the World*. She was just as shocked as Ross had been and almost broke down on the phone, saying that she felt that I had cheated and betrayed her. I did my utmost to make Gillian realize that it was not me but her greedy uncle John who had betrayed her and she shouldn't flog the messenger.

As Gillian struggled to control her emotions, it sounded like another dramatic scene straight from *EastEnders*: 'I can't believe it. The whole family will be very shocked. My mother will go mad. Kim and I knew nothing about this. I swear to you on my baby's life. I've never taken any money off this man except that day. He said to me, "I've never seen baby Jessica, buy her something from me". I said "Don't be silly," but he gave me the money and I took it. I went running back to him because when I saw how much it was, £60, I thought this is ridiculous. I said: "Uncle John I'm not taking this". He said no. I thought it was funny because I said to my sister Kim, "Why didn't he offer you anything for your two boys?"'

Gillian said that her streetwise partner Geoff Knights had commented that it was odd that every time Quilty turned up to see her, he always had people with him. 'He keeps bringing people up to Elstree and I thought that was strange. He has used my name and I hope people believe that I am innocent.'

By the end of our long conversation, Gillian was beginning to see things from my perspective and realized that I was not to blame for her being dragged into this scam. I knew I'd won her over when she said I should add the quote: 'He has brought shame on the whole family and I thank the *News of the World* for exposing him!'

When I rang Quilty and told him his game was up, he completely denied having given Gillian a penny. He admitted having taken backhanders from me but explained: 'Whatever I did was a service. You wanted me to do something for you and I told you the price for it. I wasn't bribing anybody, and I've never sold a dodgy union card in my life.'

Despite the story appearing on the cover of the paper, my soap career was still launched. Millions of viewers caught a fleeting glimpse of me sitting in the Queen Vic in an episode that went to air. Most wouldn't have noticed, let alone cared, but there was a group of people who took a keen interest – the *EastEnders* producers. They extracted my photograph from the footage and pinned it on the notice board in the *EastEnders* dressing room beneath a warning for all their actors: 'Beware of this man.'

As for Ross and Rebekah, they seemed to have put my *EastEnders* appearance behind them. I was invited to their star-studded wedding bash.

But the one person who was genuinely thrilled to read the article was Lenny McLean. On the day the story appeared he gave me a wake-up call. He simply said: 'Maz, I just want to say well sorted son!' and hung up the phone.

CHAPTER 12

SUPER-MODELS SELLING SEX OR DRUGS

I have scored drugs everywhere from crack dens in crumbling council tower blocks to the hallowed corridors of the House of Lords; I have bought drugs in Disneyland, Butlins, and over the bread counter at a branch of Sainsbury's. I have exposed school kids selling drugs; a woman who injected heroin into the arms of young children; actors, models, City traders, and even members of the legal profession hooked on drugs. Over the years, I have personally witnessed the tragic demise of scores of people who have fallen prey to drugs, and I have learned that no one is immune to the perils. It is an evil that surpasses all boundaries of class and creed to take over and ultimately destroy lives. And worryingly, it is an epidemic that is sweeping through Britain.

On the face of it, former Manchester United star Mark Bosnich and his girlfriend, supermodel Sophie Anderton, were an A-list couple blessed with fame and fortune, enjoying all the glitz and glamour of a celebrity lifestyle; but theirs was a blighted paradise. Bosnich confessed that at the height of his addiction, he spent a staggering £2,000 a week on cocaine. The keeper who'd also played for Chelsea, and who became the first Premiership player to be banned for drugs, revealed how he was once so high on coke that he held an air pistol to his dad's head believing him to be a burglar.

I admired his frank confessions and believed that Bosnich really was committed to beating his drug addiction; and I sympathized with Sophie as she spoke about the way drugs had taken over her life. 'When I was a 19-year-old model, someone put two grams of cocaine in front of me. He said, "If you want to get on you have to take coke." My life has been wrecked by drugs, but now I'm taking a firm grip of it. People have to understand that drugs are not cool. Drug addiction destroys your life. Cocaine doesn't make you thin. Cocaine doesn't make your career. Young models need to know that cocaine only destroys everything around you. It causes sorrow and disillusion.'

Having shared their lows when I spent some time with them in Nashville, Texas, I developed a friendship with both Bosnich and Sophie, who came to regard me as an advisor and round-the-clock confidante. I was invited to dinners at their favourite Italian restaurant, Scalini, and was a regular visitor to Bosnich's luxurious flat in Knightsbridge. Bosnich confessed that they liked having me around to share a pizza and Häagen-Dazs, as it meant that neither of them would be able to row or take cocaine, for fear of ending up in the paper. Inevitably the pair started living their turbulent relationship through the pages of the *News of the World*. They would each ring me every time they rowed – which was with great regularity and invariably after 2am – asking me to expose the other for acts of drug-induced violence. They were a high-profile couple regarded by many youngsters as role models, and writing about their antics was in the public interest and sold papers.

In one rant Bosnich, who I thought genuinely loved Sophie, told me that he was very concerned about some of her new friends. He said that two of the girls she was hanging around with were high-class prostitutes, and confided that Sophie had told him in a row that she would sleep with men for money rather than sponge off him. I didn't think much of it until a couple of months later, when I was contacted by Britain's biggest madam, Bella. She excitedly told me that she had Sophie on her books and asked if I wanted to expose her.

Millionairess Bella, who lives in St John's Wood, north London, has a list of clients including Arab Princes, celebrities, and well-known politicians to rival the notorious Hollywood madam Heidi Fleiss. In the hope that her vice empire would be safe from the prying eyes of the tabloid press, Bella befriended a couple of journalists, including myself. She became an informant who would occasionally ring to shop the odd model who was no longer of any use to her, or a VIP client who had cut off her commission by swapping numbers to deal directly with one of her prostitutes.

Sophie had upset one of Bella's regular clients; Sophie had flown abroad to see two wealthy clients, meeting the first at a five-star Eden hotel in Rome, where she was paid 10,000 Euros in cash for dinner with a wealthy businessman, and spent the night in his hotel suite. From there, she flew on to Nice and was chauffeured to Monaco where she stayed at the equally luxurious Hotel Hermitage. She had been booked by another super-wealthy client for a staggering 60,000 Euros fee for two nights. But the model infuriated her date and he sent her packing after one night.

'She basically got really drunk and was typical Sophie. He was expecting to sleep with one of the most famous models in the world but found himself with a silly girl who was off her head,' said a furious Bella. 'She was just going on about her relationship with Mark Bosnich and giving him her life story. She then started showing him scars on her wrists and saying how she had tried to hurt herself to get back at Mark. The guy got really pissed off when she asked him if he could supply any cocaine.'

The client rang Bella to complain about Sophie's behaviour; she was paid 30,000 Euros for one night and sent home early. But the drama continued when Sophie claimed to have lost all the money she'd been paid. 'She said she'd put it in her suitcase and that the money was stolen,' Bella told me angrily. 'There were scenes at the hotel as she cried and screamed at hotel staff before she left.' It meant that not only had Bella let down a wealthy client but had also lost out on her commission.

After returning to London, Sophie, who had split with Bosnich, checked into a hotel in Knightsbridge where she stayed for two weeks. I persuaded Bella to make a taped phone call to Sophie at the hotel to get her to admit that she had been working as a prostitute, but Sophie simply hung up. I turned up at the hotel soon afterwards and called

Sophie on the house phone and told her I needed to talk to her about a very serious matter. She instantly knew what it was about, and refused to see me.

Without an admission from Sophie, our lawyer Tom Crone was not prepared to run my story. Although very disappointed, I accepted Tom's judgement. Despite the circumstantial evidence including flight and hotel bookings, the word of a madam just wasn't enough to nail the supermodel as a hooker. But fearing that she was about to be exposed in the *News of the World*, Sophie turned to another journalist pal, *Sunday Mirror* showbiz reporter Suzanne Kerins, for advice.

In a damage limitation exercise, Sophie confessed to a night of 'vice-girl shame', revealing how she was paid £5,000 by a businessman to have sex with him in Italy after meeting a woman called Bella. 'I was so naive – and I am so angry with myself at getting sucked in by it all. But, yes, I was paid for my night with him. I felt dirty and abused afterwards,' she claimed in a tearful interview.

Sophie told how she had been on a date arranged by Bella and had sex with the Italian. She claimed she was 'horrified' the following morning when the man disappeared but left an envelope stuffed with Euros on the bed. 'I was horrified. I realized I'd literally been paid for sex. That made me a prostitute. There was also a letter from him saying "Thank you for a lovely time, stay in touch." He was a very respectable man, but I had never been treated like that before. I was shocked that he had disappeared without saying goodbye. I felt like I had been used. I was understandably disgusted. I cried myself to sleep that night,' she claimed.

Sophie survived the scandal and continued to grace billboards and covers of glossy magazines. Sophie's profile was boosted further when she appeared on the reality TV shows, *I'm A Celebrity … Get Me Out Of Here!* and *Love Island*. With her modelling career back on track and the press no longer sniffing around, Sophie continued to do the odd discreet escorting job to fund her exuberant lifestyle – which still included vast quantities of cocaine at £50 a gram, despite her public claims to have beaten her drug addiction.

In mid-2007, years after her 'night of vice' shame, I was tipped off that Sophie was openly demanding £10,000 a night for sex from wealthy punters and was now on the books of an American madam based in Los Angeles. I went to see editor Colin Myler to discuss the merits of the story. Colin is a highly experienced and respected journalist who edited the *Daily Mirror*, *Sunday Mirror* and was executive editor of the *New York Post* before taking the helm at the *News of the World* in January 2007.

Colin had given a widely reported speech to the Society of Editors in which he suggested that celebrity sex and drugs stings would be curtailed under his editorship; but he reassured me that his words had been misinterpreted. Colin merely felt that a lot of serious and important investigations undertaken by the *News of the World* were overshadowed by celebrity stings, and I agreed. Colin, a hard news man, told me that a story about a supermodel working as a prostitute and snorting cocaine would always have a place in his paper.

I knew I'd missed the story last time, but that only made me all the more determined to nail it this time. However, the Fake Sheik could not pose as the rich punter, as Sophie would recognize me, so I called in a freelance TV producer, Tommy Bryant. Tommy, a larger-than-life character with Northern charm, could easily pose as a spoilt wealthy businessman, and his number was passed to Sophie. In a phone call to Tommy, Sophie confirmed the deal and demanded: 'It's £10,000 for the night.'

Before she turned up for the secret rendezvous, Conrad – who dressed as a butler for the evening so that he could monitor the equipment without arousing any suspicion – installed covert cameras throughout the apartment. We had to take extra precautions as we'd had bad luck using the same apartment before. Our latest camera system failed when I invited a Muslim extremist round, in a bid to expose a terror ring. The Islamic fanatic was making door-to-door charity collections on the streets of High Wycombe and confessed to me that he was sending some of the money to terrorist groups in Pakistan. But his worrying support for Jihad was not captured on video as the high-tech device failed to record anything. Luckily, a back-up audio recorder concealed under the sofa did the trick and enabled me to expose him.

But with a supermodel turning up and a large sum of cash about to be handed over we had to get the evidence on video. A totally realistic disguise of a stick-on theatrical beard and turban, so that I could lurk around, enabled me to brief Tommy and the photographers and make sure everything went according to plan.

Sophie turned up at the swish flat wearing a skimpy black designer dress with a plunging neckline and £350 Louboutin shoes. She immediately relaxed in Tommy's company as she ordered champagne. 'I'm bored of everyone else making a fortune out of me,' she explained. 'I've been a top lingerie, bikini, and swimwear model since I was 18. I've done every single campaign I can possibly do. I'll be a lot of fun. I'll look great on your fucking arm. I'm a supermodel,' she boasted.

Sophie explained she had turned to vice to help pay for a new three-bedroom home in London's Notting Hill. 'I'm buying a place at the moment so things are tight,' she said. 'I just think short term, and at the end of the day nobody gets hurt.' Part of the problem for her was that there wasn't enough money in modelling any more. 'Russian girls are willing to do it for £500 a day,' moaned Sophie. 'I can command 25 grand a day, one shoot without all the advertising and stuff. But that's quite rare. For catalogues it used to be £10,000 a day and now it's about £4,000 or £3,000. Then there is 20 per cent for the agency and 40 per cent for tax. It goes down rapidly,' she explained.

Then she laid down the ground rules for sex. 'Definitely with condoms,' she said. 'Spanking is cool. But I'm not into any kinky shit, to be honest.' Sophie also said that she was 'cool' with giving her punter oral sex. 'I know that I'm great in bed,' she bragged. 'But if I don't feel comfortable with something I'm not going to go along with it and be fake. I don't do the whole fake thing.'

I was hiding in a small bedroom inside the apartment and was listening in on the conversation through headphones. Sophie told Tommy about a recent party she'd been to with her friend Prince Andrew; they spent the night rolling about with laughter as they joked about Harrods boss Mohamed Al-Fayed. Sophie had befriended Andrew when they played polo together when she was 18. 'He's never hit on me but I have seen him in a few situations,' she confided. 'I had Camilla Al-Fayed giving me so much attitude. She's Mohamed Al-Fayed's daughter. I said, "Listen, I don't know why you're so up your own arse, you are the daughter of a cunt!" Prince Andrew was on the floor laughing. He said, "You never change."'

> ❝ "I know that I'm great in bed," Sophie bragged. "But if I don't feel comfortable with something I'm not going to go along with it … I don't do the fake thing." ❞

Prince Andrew was spot on, I thought, as Sophie pulled out a wrap of cocaine from her designer handbag. 'Everyone takes drugs. You don't take coke?' she asked Tommy. 'I've got some on me. Do you want a line?'

When Tommy declined, saying he would have some later, she made lines of coke on the coffee table and snorted them through a rolled-up £20 note right in front of our hidden camera.

Then she called her dealer, a girl called Isabella and tried to get Tommy to buy two grams of the drug. 'It's £50 a gram. And it's in rocks as well, it's not cut,' said Sophie. 'She's very trustworthy. She's a friend of mine. This is the only person I go to and she stops working at 11.' Talking to her in code on the phone, Sophie asked her to bring 'two invites to the party', meaning two grams of cocaine. 'She's one of the few people I trust. She's 24 but she's been dealing since she was 16,' said Sophie, revealing her dealer's credentials. 'She would protect me if she ever got busted. She has my name in her phone under some Arabic name. She has everyone under different names.' Within half an hour Isabella was at the door – having asked a policeman for directions. 'Can you give him the rock stuff like you give me?' asked Sophie, handing the woman a tenner that she said she owed from the night before. 'It's £50 per gram,' said the dealer as she took money for the drugs. As Isabella left, Sophie handed over a small bag of cocaine to Tommy before pulling out some more of the drug herself and snorting it on the table. She then reminded Tommy that he would have to pay her £10,000 for a night of sex. 'I hate talking about money,' she said feigning coyness.

But Sophie seemed quite comfortable as she quoted her fees for a weekend romp in the Bahamas with Tommy. 'It'll be 15 grand a day,' she said.

Sophie even offered to arrange other girls for the foreign sex party and phoned three of them to check their availability. 'She's got long dark hair, she's a bit younger than me, she's one of my best friends,' said Sophie. 'If you are going to have fun, you are going to have a few drinks, a few lines, at the end of the day, it's quite laid back. I have another girlfriend who is Indian who is beautiful with blue eyes, she's really sexy, she's gorgeous. You'll like her. She's more outrageous than I am, she really is. The other thing is, she's like me, completely discreet.'

Asked if they would join him for a threesome, Sophie said: 'I can't honestly say, and I'll fucking hit you for extra for that! It's like me doing an advertising campaign, and they're, like, "Oh you do billboards for free?" No, I don't think so somehow. I'll be honest with you. Lesbian scene maybe, but yeah it'll be more.'

Sophie then went to the bedroom to prepare for her evening's sex session. She pulled a condom from her handbag and placed it on the bedside table. Then she peeled out of her skimpy dress and lay on the bed wearing nothing but her G-string and stilettos.

By this time I knew that we had more than enough evidence to prove that Sophie was on the game, complete with video footage of her virtually naked on the bed. From my hideaway next door, I phoned Tommy who was in the lounge and broke the terrible news to him. 'I'm sorry to say Tommy, your uncle who is in hospital has taken a turn for the worse. You better come to the hospital straight away,' I told him. This was his cue – it meant we had enough evidence and he could wrap things up now.

Over the years we have used this ruse a lot. Once the evidence was in the bag, the minder would either call or rush into the room and announce: 'Sir bad news, you're required at the hospital straight away. I'm afraid your uncle has just passed away!' The hooker, whoever she was, would feel sympathetic, so that the Sheik could make a quick getaway. Many a time the girls would feel so sorry for their distressed client, that they would waive their fees and leave with just their cab fares.

The only pitfall with this exit strategy was that because we repeatedly employed it, it became impossible for me and my crew to keep a straight face when the minder entered the room. We'd all start sniggering as soon as he walked in anticipating what was to follow. One occasion I started howling with uncontrollable laughter as soon as Jaws came in and uttered the words: 'Sir, bad news ...' As I rushed to the toilet with tears of laughter running down my face, the girl asked Jaws: 'Is he ok? I've never heard anyone cry like that before!' Jaws, struggling to control his own laughter, explained that the wailing noise from the toilet was just how Arabs mourn – which sent me into yet another fit of laughter!

Tommy acted shocked and relayed the tragic news to Sophie; he would have to miss out on sex with her to visit his dying relative. Sophie was sympathetic and quickly got dressed. But she didn't forget to grab the envelope bursting at the seams with crisp £20 notes before she left the apartment.

This time Sophie was bang to rights. There was no way she could claim that she had been duped, or had simply stumbled upon an envelope stuffed with notes after a night of sex. Colin Myler ran the story on the cover of the paper, and ordered video footage of Sophie snorting cocaine to be shown on our website. The clip had the largest number of hits since our website was launched.

The day after the story appeared, Sophie was axed from a £100,000-a-year contract as the face of Fake Bake, a tanning product. A friend of hers rang me to tell me that although Sophie was distraught after being exposed, the story had renewed her determination to kick her drug addiction, and that Sophie had checked into another rehab clinic, committed to beating her demons.

Sophie Anderton wasn't the only supermodel who sold cocaine to the Sheik.

Squeaky-clean Jodie Kidd, who plays polo with Prince Charles and was the face of the Marks & Spencer credit card, was secretly peddling the drug out of her designer handbag at highbrow parties. The darling of Middle England handed over three grams of cocaine and said, 'You wanted three [grams]. It's a ton fifty, right. [£150]. Ok, there's three.' She gave my sidekick three small wraps of white powder neatly packaged in an old Asda bag. 'I do it, I do it. I'm not going to do shit', she said bragging about the quality of her drugs. 'It's not the best, but it's what we can do at half past twelve at night.'

Coming so soon after Kate Moss had been exposed for her drug addiction in September 2005, I anticipated it would be difficult to stand up the tip that Jodie was a coke dealer. I thought it would take several meetings to gain her trust before she would even confess to taking cocaine, but I was wrong. It only took one dinner date with the model and she happily supplied the drug for the Sheik.

Jodie, who besides modelling is a racing driver, TV presenter, and has played polo for England, turned up at the Sheik's rented Mayfair pad with her brother Jack. Jack, a professional polo player who taught Princess Beatrice to ride, also confessed to being a drug user and pusher.

As the pair cosied up to the Sheik, they suggested we crack open a bottle of champagne and toast their divorces. For a moment I thought that cost-cutting measures might have blown my cover, as I had to make do with a young female reporter playing the part of a waitress.

The nervous trainee dropped a champagne flute as she served Jack completely soaking his trousers with bubbly, but he laughed it off.

'My dad, Jodie, and myself got divorced within four months of each other,' announced Jack. Jodie divorced Irish professional gambler Aidan Butler in August 2007 after an 18-month marriage. The pair had met at the Gumball Rally cross-country motor-racing event in 2004, which Jodie had described as 'love at first sight'; they were married a year later at a lavish ceremony in West Sussex, the occasion shared with her army of fans through the pages of *Hello!* magazine. Jack had just separated from his wife, American heiress Be Kemeny, after he admitted repeatedly cheating on her during their six-year marriage. The couple have four children all under the age of six.

I had been looking forward to meeting Jodie, who I felt I sort of knew from seeing her so often on TV and billboards and reading about her life in magazines. It would certainly impress my mates; however, I was disappointed as she came across as a foul-mouthed girl full of herself; Jodie, who was wearing a skimpy cream top and black trousers spent the evening bragging about her illustrious career and slagging off a long list of celebrities.

'I did my polo, got to win the women's championships within two years and then I decided I wanted to try motor racing,' boasted Jodie, who represented England in the Women's World Polo Championships.

Jack added: 'At 16 she was headhunted as a model and was the only person ever to have two Chanel contracts running at the same time.'

The 6ft 1in model's first big break was a fragrance campaign that she took over from Linda Evangelista, followed by a trip to New York for the Isaac Mizrahi and Marc Jacobs shows. Jodie, who is the face of LG Electronics, is the great-granddaughter of press baron Lord Beaverbrook. Her older sister Jemma, a highly successful make-up artiste, is married to the Duke of Wellington.

Even though she had only just met me, Jodie confided secrets about her celebrity pals and launched a vicious attack on her rivals. First the two-faced model had a swipe at her supposed friend Victoria Beckham. 'I've known the Beckhams and I go to all their World Cup parties up at their house, and I know them quite well. It's very strange going out with them. That's why I know David so well, it's through Victoria when she started getting into fashion many years ago. She was working with a good friend of mine. I did a show with her and she kind of attached herself,' bitched Jodie.

When the Sheik innocently asked if Victoria was a model, Jodie replied: 'No, of course she's not. She's certainly not a model. To me after a couple of bottles [she's attractive], whisky, definitely! She modelled, did a catwalk and got very into this fashion kind of thing.'

Jodie claimed Victoria has no fashion sense. 'Can you imagine her [in lingerie],' she said. 'If you have a look in magazines now it's her new perfume and there's a picture of her. Urrgh … and the glitz of David who is gorgeous! He's very nice and you know, you can see she wears the pants! And she's "great me!"' Jodie clicked her fingers to demonstrate Victoria's dominating nature. 'She wears the pants, which is amazing because he is the one who could have anyone in the whole entire world. He's petrified of her, of the consequences!'

Next, Jodie had a jab at fellow supermodel Caprice. 'I don't know why, I just don't trust women with fake boobs,' she said. 'She's fake. HMS *Titanic*.' Jack then chipped in with wild and untrue sexual allegations about Caprice as Jodie dished out even more vile slurs. 'She came over to England and reinvented herself and did everything that she needed to do to make herself beautiful,' said Jack.

When I mentioned that I had met Naomi Campbell, Jodie gave a big sigh and said: 'Oh god!' She went on to explain: 'We did have a fight. It was my first season in New York, I was 15 and I was sitting backstage, I had Christy Turlington and all the girls. I was sitting there going "oh my god" then there was "Go you pick up my bag!" I didn't actually know who she really was. I thought she was like a hairdresser. "Pick it up yourself!" Someone overheard this and she was completely in shock,' said

Jodie. Asked what Naomi is really like, Jodie replied: 'She's a fucking monster!'

However, she said that Naomi could curb her aggressive nature and turn on the charm when she had to. 'If there is something that she can get out of you, if you are a client, she's a darling, she's lovely! But the thing is that I'm very much [of the opinion] that everyone should be treated the same, no one is any different. And she will treat anyone that isn't going to pay her and give her nice boats or diamonds or whatever she wants, she'll just treat them like rubbish and I can't bear that.'

Jack added: 'She's arrogant for no reason.' Jodie claimed that Naomi is unattractive. 'She wears really weird contact lenses. They kind of look like, what's that, you know the yellow one, the really scary one, Lil' Kim. These eyes, and these extensions everywhere!'

Then she moved onto her pal Kate Moss. 'Kate was very cool but she got a bit affected. They get very affected by stardom. It goes to their head. She just loves to really hardcore party, hardcore. We all love to party but that's scary, addicts. They go dark, darkness.'

Even model-turned-actress Liz Hurley came in for a bashing. Jodie said that she is 'very difficult to work with' and claimed that her day had come and gone. 'She's at my agency,' said Jodie. 'I know Hugh more, but she's with my agency. She did the Monsoon campaign after I did the Monsoon campaign. One employer was like "she's a nightmare." She wants to control everything. She is very, very, controlling, very controlling!'

The pair, who were seeking a financial backer for a series of international polo events and fashion shows, believed that the Sheik might bankroll their project. Trying to tempt me to invest they made it clear that I too would be able to rub shoulders with stars and Royalty if I forked out the money for their scheme. 'It's an elitest world that people just love to buy into,' claimed toff Jodie. 'Top players will come through our names. I've done enough favours for people. Prince Harry is very good. I'll try and speak to Harry about it.'

Jodie boasted how both she and her father Johnny played polo with Prince Charles. 'My father, I don't know if you remember years ago when he [Prince Charles] broke his arm, dad was playing with him. Then I came with him in an exhibition. I played with him. I know them all quite well,' bragged Jodie. 'I play with Prince Charles, and I play number one which is the attacker and he always plays the back. So we were together, because the back is always with the attacker. He came in and rode me off and I rode him off like this and his horse slipped and he fell off. I was like "aaaargh, my god, I'm so sorry, I've killed the King!" There was mayhem and cars came in every direction. I was like "Oh shit I'm so sorry!" He was winded on the floor!'

At one stage, talking about Princes William and Harry, Jack added: 'They're nice. They are real boys. If we get this polo thing going, it's only a matter of time before they come along and play it.'

Jodie boasted how her friendship with rugby ace Mike Tindall could help the project. 'Mikey, who's probably one of my closest friends, is probably going to marry Zara [Princess Anne's daughter Zara Phillips]. So, I mean, Zara loves coming to events like that.' Jack branded Prince Andrew as 'Airmiles Andy' while Jodie described Camilla as 'normal' adding: 'She probably tells Prince Charles what to do.' She also described Prince Philip as 'mad'.

Over dinner, as Jodie tucked into her favourite spaghetti bolognaise washed down with a glass of red Merlot wine, conversation soon turned to drugs. I had been told about her secret drug sideline by someone in her own network of friends who claimed that the brother and sister supplied to well-known figures in both the polo and modelling worlds. Jodie claimed: 'I live in the country, I'm really boring, I don't fall out of nightclubs off my head. I'm off my head at home!'

She then explained the laws relating to drugs in Britain and gave me – a visiting Sheik from the Middle East – a bit of legal advice. 'Skunk is now Class A. You don't want to smoke cannabis in the street,' advised Jodie. But she explained that a small quantity of cocaine would be ok. Asked how much constituted a 'small amount' both brother and sister piped up in unison: 'Three grams!'

'They're looking to bust the people that are selling it,' said Jack. 'Keep one in the top pocket, one in the bottom pocket!' Jodie said: 'If you have it you could say, I'm not sure about coke, but you're not going to get arrested, you might get a fine for carrying anything more than three grams. Pot's alright to a certain amount.'

Jack continued: 'You could have a quarter and get away with it. But police aren't looking for trouble, there's so many people having fun now.' 'Everyone!' exclaimed Jodie. 'Personal is fine! As long as you're not flashing it about everywhere or smoking a spliff in a nightclub.'

Jodie, who grew up in Barbados, explained how the idyllic island has become the main staging post for cocaine en-route to Britain. The pair said that dealers diluted cocaine by the time it reaches England.

When I casually claimed that cocaine was expensive in Britain, Jack replied: 'You must be meeting the wrong people!' 'We certainly know many providers!' offered Jodie, who admitted cocaine abuse was rife in the modelling world. 'Do you know how many dealers I know in a little town called Billingshurst? There are two not far from my house.'

Jack, who claimed that he knew the person who gave Prince Harry a spliff at the time of his drugs shame, then detailed the delights of a new type of Ecstasy pill. 'It makes you dance a lot, smile, and want to kiss loads of girls!'

Jodie howled with laughter as she told how Jack had once spiked a rum punch at her birthday party making unsuspecting elderly relatives high. 'I had my 90-year-old grannie going "oooh",' screamed Jodie. 'Everyone was like "Aunty I love you!" Jemma and me were on the dance floor at 6am the next morning going "Oh my god!" Then we found out about the rum punch!'

Jodie claimed that a member of the Royal family takes drugs. Over a latte, Jack pulled out his mobile phone and read out a text from the Royal.

I'd got more than enough evidence that the Kidds were heavily involved in the drug scene, so I told them that I was about to head off to a casino. By this time Jodie was convinced that I was both a drug user and a potential customer. She brazenly asked my assistant Alex: 'If you want something there's certainly no one going to say anything with us lot ... Does he want some [gear] for tonight? We know ten people now that we can go to.'

Jodie then reached for her mobile phone and called one of her suppliers, Frank. Speaking in code on the phone she placed her order: 'I am in London but I'm wondering if you might come and pay us a visit. I'm going to be at Jack's at Windsor in 40 minutes. And how many do we want? Three. Can we get three? It's £50. I can get it for £40 but ... three [grams] £150,' she demanded.

She asked Alex to accompany her to Jack's home near Windsor where she was staying after her divorce. Jack assured him that it would be worth the trip and the drugs would be 'good quality'. Jodie added: 'I do it, I do it. I'm not going to do shit! It's fine, it'll do its job!'

As she pulled into the long gravel drive behind the electronic gates at the imposing old manor house, Jodie invited our reporter inside to meet unsuspecting England polo team captain Henry Brett who was also living at Jack's. Moments later a flash car pulled into the drive and Jodie rushed past a horse in the front garden to speak to her supplier, Frank. She took the crisp notes from Alex and handed him three small wraps of cocaine.

Jack advised: 'Next time you come give us some warning. We will get a load for you. Take it one bag at a time.'

There was no next time. Following publication of my story, M&S announced that they would not be renewing Jodie's £250,000 contract. As Jodie headed to the family home in Barbados to consider her future, M&S issued a clear statement saying: 'M&S doesn't do drugs. Period.' The BBC dropped her from a show and she was also barred from taking part in the Alfred Dunhill Links Championship at St Andrews where she was due to play golf with stars including Samuel L. Jackson. Not surprisingly, she pulled out of a fashion show too – hosted by Naomi Campbell!

CHAPTER 13

PARENTING: FROM LAS VEGAS TO LAHORE

Britney Spears's ex-husband Kevin Federline – known as K-Fed – counts the Fake Sheik as one of his friends; I'd be honoured except that his closest friend is a cocaine-peddling madam called Angelina Michaels. Our friendship began after I partied the night away with the pair of them at the Tao nightclub at the Venetian hotel and casino in Las Vegas. By the end of the evening, our relationship had developed so well that Kevin arranged a supply of cocaine for me as well as three hookers. Like Sophie Anderton, he had some demons to beat.

Kevin arranged to meet the Fake Sheik shortly after he was dumped by pop princess Britney. His motive was simple; it looked as if his supply of money was about to be curtailed and he urgently needed to find a financer to maintain the lifestyle he had become accustomed to, as well a backer for his new career as a rap singer. My motive was simple too. I'd been asked to establish once and for all whether Kevin had actually made any sex tapes with Britney.

After being quizzed by immigration officers for four hours at Las Vegas airport – largely because of my Muslim name – I finally rolled up at my palatial suite at the Venetian hotel; the Italian-themed hotel, complete with canals and gondolas, has 4,000 luxury suites. Kevin joined me for a drink together with his manager, Dan Dymtrow, and a team of minders including the aptly nicknamed Big Mike, a 6ft 6in black man with a crushing handshake.

I would normally have had my very own imposing minder, Jaws, with his full deck of gold teeth with diamonds embedded on display. However, Jaws's career had tragically been cut short after he was involved in a horrific motorway crash on the M6, just before we made this trip. He fought for his life in intensive care on a ventilator for several weeks; he survived but after a year in hospital was left permanently paralysed from the neck down. It was a real blow to the whole team as he had played a vital role in numerous investigations. What made it all the more tragic was that he was the most active and physically fit among us and would train for an hour in the gym and jog three miles every morning before breakfast. It was an emotional time. On more than one occasion I inadvertently called photographer Rob Todd, who stood in as a minder at the last minute, Jaws.

There was a sombre mood as we tried to carry on without Jaws. Kevin was also feeling a bit down having just been ditched by Britney via text message. I was the perfect shoulder for him to cry on.

Britney had caught Kevin with another woman in a hotel bedroom, but he claimed he was surprised when his superstar wife slapped divorce papers on him citing 'irreconcilable differences'. 'It's crazy. It wasn't expected. I haven't done anything wrong,' he said. 'I'm being portrayed as the villain.' Kevin tried his best to persuade me that he was a nice guy – and he was quite convincing. He wanted me to bankroll his concert tour, a new clothing line and even discussed a deal to publish his autobiography.

After 9/11 it had become a nightmare to bring ready-made covert video equipment into the States. Conrad, who was doubling up as my butler, had spent the night building a hidden camera system from scratch. He installed a pinhole camera inside an ice-bucket which would go unnoticed in the hotel room. The ice-bucket cam worked a treat and captured Kevin as he blamed the public for causing the split from his wife: 'They see me as the person who took the pop princess of the world away, all the jealousy factors and that stuff. Britney is America's queen, I'm the dude from the fucking slums that came along with my baggy pants and whatever and corrupted her. I'm the bad boy. I'm not the one that's fit to be with her. They want the all-American buttoned-up type,' said Kevin as he poured his heart out to the Sheik. 'I still love Britney, always will.'

Now that I'd got his trust, I hit him with the question I'd flown 5,000 miles to ask. Had he filmed Britney and himself having sex, as all the papers around the world had alleged? The denial was categorical and I believed him. 'It's shit. There is no sex tape, there's none of that. It's all media. Everybody makes up stories about my life. We never made a tape.'

I immediately went to the toilet and called the editor who was planning to splash on the story that weekend. I told him there was no sex video; Andy Coulson was disappointed because his over-enthusiastic news editor had assured him that there definitely was a sex video and that the Sheik would be able to buy it. I went back into the suite to rejoin Kevin.

A few months earlier I had been tipped off that Kevin was heavily involved with drugs and prostitutes, and so I decided to see if those allegations were equally false. By now Kevin was complaining about the way Britney was using their children, Sean Preston and Jayden James, to get back at him. 'That's the hard part to deal with, it's tough. With me and Britney, we're battling it out right now. It's one of those things where me and her are butting heads right now but she knows the only way to get to me is through the children.'

He said that Britney was being led astray by her army of lawyers and advisors. 'That's how it's always been. That's part of the problem; she can hire as many people as she wants. Whatever we do, we can both butt heads but we're both going to wind up with the same time and custody of the children. We're going to battle it out, for the next six months it's going to be crazy. Here a divorce doesn't go through for six months, even if everything is agreed on. If you have children together then you're tied to that person forever so eventually we're going to have to get along. The best thing I have is that my children were born in California and they have the strongest laws in California about protecting the children, and the mother and father being there.

'I've got four kids, I've got two from a previous. I'm done. My family is there already, I don't need a wife ever now. I'll be the bachelor.'

Kevin wanted to write a book about his life. He insisted it would not attack Britney but would just seek to set the record straight. 'It's just so people know who I am for me, instead of who I am that married this girl, the pop princess. This woman fell in love with me for who I am. In order for you to accept me you need to know who I am.'

Kevin admitted sales of his rap album had been poor and that he was struggling to promote the record across America; he put that down to his failed relationship with Britney. 'People don't know who I am; they believe what they read. They see me as the person who took the pop princess of the world away.' He claimed that several radio stations refused point blank to play his music. 'The radio out here doesn't want to play me because they read the tabloids, because her label has the radio. There's so much shit working against me out here. They're completely victimizing me.'

Bizarrely Kevin claimed that his marriage had been detrimental to his career and in fact had 'killed it completely'. 'If I'd got to do a rap album and show all the bullshit I went through in my lifetime, all the drugs shit, I went through all of it, but people don't know that. They think he got lucky, he married her,' said Kevin. As he sipped a glass of champagne he told how he met Britney and how it was the star who proposed to him – and he had turned her down: 'She proposed to me and I refused. I think I was playing around,' he said. 'I said I'm not going to say yes. You've got to let me propose to you. It was a weird situation.'

'We've been together for nearly three years, married for two,' said Kevin who was born in Fresno, California. 'We crossed paths a couple of times when I came to LA and started dancing. I danced for all kind of artistes, Michael Jackson, everybody. And we were in a club one night and that was it. We'd met each other three or four times over the years and it was just that one moment. You know, when you look that look in your eye and damn, it happens.'

The couple got together in 2004 after Spears's two-day marriage to a childhood friend. They married in September that year in a Kabbalah-influenced ceremony. She apparently told Kevin that she liked him, 'because he's not a shallow motherfucker Hollywood actor-guy.'

'If I did a book and I put my life with her in there and the way we talked about it, it would make people so sad that we are not together anymore. That's the way I bet it would be perceived.' Asked if there was any scope for a reconciliation, Kevin said: 'I don't know. I couldn't say yes, I couldn't say no. I still love her, always,' he said. 'Me and her were the most sought-after couple.'

When I asked him: 'Then why are you blowing it?' Kevin replied, animated: 'I'm not the one blowing it!'

Kevin went on to predict that, while his music career would rocket, Britney's pop career was on a downward spiral. 'Britney at the moment she's up here, one day Britney will be right there [signalling to the ground]. She will always be marketed to the teenage girl and then you got the guys that love her. With my wife they found a face, she got put in a room with somebody who makes hit music and they put it out. She was manufactured,' he bitched. 'She was 16 years old when she signed a contract to do eight albums.'

I felt as if I'd turned on a tap labelled 'Moan' and it wouldn't stop; Kevin wouldn't stop. 'Britney is America's queen, she can do no wrong, even if she's driving round with my fucking kid in the front seat of the car with no seatbelt on. Because of her stature in America, they'll get onto her for a second then they'll forget about it and move on. I come along and they fucking look at me, and it's jealousy: "He's not right for her. And since she's our queen we get to decide whether you get to be with her or not." That's the type of situation it is, exactly. And I'm glad to be getting out of it.' Kevin claimed his relationship with Britney had been stormy and that she suffered from severe mood swings. 'Nobody knows what I've gone through for the last few years,' he said.

Las Vegas was Kevin's kind of town, he described it as his home away from home, but he said that he wasn't able to go out to enjoy local strip clubs dotted around Vegas because of the press. 'We're here a lot. All my friends leave me in the room and go out and do what they gotta do. Because if I'm caught out with you it'll be on every fucking magazine.' However he offered to arrange in-room entertainment for his newfound friend the Sheik. 'I can work that out. I'll put you in connection with my security. Big Mike, he is Mr Vegas,' he promised.

Before he got up to leave, Kevin insisted I join him at the Tao nightclub where he was making a personal appearance. At the door of the suite Kevin paused briefly and enquired what champagne we'd served him as it was the finest he'd ever tasted. I asked my butler – Conrad, of course – which bottle he'd cracked open; I had to stop myself from laughing when Conrad whispered that it was Asti Spumante, the cheapest sparkling wine the casino had on offer. It costs £3.62 a bottle from Tesco's. I told Kevin I'd have a case sent to his room!

In the nightclub, Kevin lapped up the attention of hoards of female fans who flocked to see the man dubbed

> **'He [Kevin F] wanted me to bankroll his concert tour, a new clothing line and even discussed a deal to publish his autobiography.'**

Fed Ex. In between chatting to a bevy of stunning girls, Kevin introduced my assistant Alex to Big Mike, and Angelina, who was to 'make arrangements' for the Sheik. 'Angelina will look after you, she will get you as many girls as you want,' Kevin assured.

Angelina was a madam in her thirties; she described Kevin as being 'like a brother' and said: 'I look after him when he's in Vegas. I get all his party supplies [meaning cocaine]. What do you want? Is it just girls or would you like some party supplies as well?' She picked up her mobile and texted; within minutes she had lined up three very attractive prostitutes, two blondes and one brunette, and ushered them up to my hotel suite. 'They're $2,000 each for the night,' she said. In the suite Angelina opened her handbag and offered a wrap of cocaine. 'I've got this for you as well, it's free.' Alex declined the offer of drugs and I feigned an over-indulgence in Kevin's favourite champagne to send the girls packing.

The following morning Alex called Kevin to thank him for arranging the drugs and hookers. Talking about his best friend, the madam, he said: 'She's great, man. She's very trustworthy and very discreet.' Kevin felt the same way about me, as, without the alleged sex tape, there was no story, so nothing ever appeared in the paper. If the Sheik popped up again in his life, he'd be happy to see him.

It was hard to believe that a man that so readily laid on drugs and hookers would be regarded as a parent fit to have sole custody of his children. In a bizarre twist Kevin Federline was voted 'Father of the Year' in 2008 by *Details* magazine in the United States. Accepting the accolade, K-Fed said: 'I'm going to be the best role model for my kids. And if that example helps other young, single dads who might be going through the same experiences that I am right now, it would be a great compliment.'

The 'superdad' was the same guy who dumped his pregnant girl-friend, Shar Jackson, to be with Britney, and the same guy who the *News of the World* had revealed had spent two days locked in a hotel room in Arizona with a string of hookers and cocaine. Federline had won full custody of the children after Britney went into meltdown, shaving off her hair, going on drink and drug benders and checking herself in and out of rehab clinics.

I have had a unique insight into the troubled life of Britney, because one of her closest confidantes is a good family friend of mine. It's an awkward situation, because a lot of the private conversations that I have had would make great front-page stories for the *News of the World*, but I am duty-bound not to betray confidences. However, one story that Britney insisted I publish was about her battle to gain access to her children. She wanted the world to know that she cared for her kids and felt that K-Fed was using them simply as a tool to sponge more money off her. She asked 'a close friend' to tell me: 'Britney is a caring, devoted mum, despite her crazy lifestyle. The kids mean the world to her.' In an emotional phone call, I could hear Britney sobbing in the background as her friend told me of the heartbreak the star had suffered when K-Fed barred her from attending her two sons' birthday party. Britney's sister and her parents had all been invited to the party at a children's themed restaurant in Los Angeles. To add to Britney's frustration, her mother was siding with Federline in the bitter child custody battle.

Britney was keen to reveal that she had spent Jayden James's second birthday alone at home crying rather than drowning her sorrows in a nightclub; she knew that her ex-husband had hired a private detective, Aaron Cohen, who had spent months compiling a damning dossier on the star. Britney feared that the revelations would mean that she would never have unsupervised access to her children again.

Britney said, through her friend, that she felt 'really angry' at herself for 'messing up' and wanted everyone to know that she was going to change her ways and prove herself to be a worthy mother. Britney was happy with my sympathetic story and thought she had found in the *News of the World* a strong ally in her public battle against Federline. In fact, she was so happy that I flew to New York to meet her, as she was considering giving me a world exclusive interview with her side of the story.

But our blossoming relationship was nipped in the bud. The very next weekend we published sensational revelations by Britney's ex-bodyguard, Tony Barretto, how Britney was 'out of control' and 'needs help'. Barretto claimed: 'I have done this for her children. She's not a good mother. She has mental problems. With her drug and booze issues, her home is no place for kids to be raised.' It was a view shared by the courts; Federline was given full custody of the kids after Britney staged a stand-off with police, emergency services, and childcare experts when she refused to hand over her sons after a scheduled visit in January 2008.

But as her relationship with Federline improved, he allowed her more access to the children, sending Sean Preston and Jayden James to spend the day with Britney on Mother's Day, which made her really happy. I sent Britney a message wishing her well, and asking her if she would like to tell our readers about the way she had begun to turn her life around in a bid to become 'mum of the year'. She sent a swift response: 'No thanks.'

In 2001, it was another child custody battle that took me halfway across the world to Pakistan. In the scorching heat of midday, a short figure wearing a black burka with only piercing blue eyes visible, stood amidst the stench of an open sewer, peering down an alleyway in the village of Gujranwala.

But this was no local woman forced to wear the Islamic outfit to ward off the lustful glances of men in the village – it was Conrad Brown on an undercover surveillance operation. Dressed as a Pakistani woman he was keeping watch on a house owned by a heavyweight wrestling champion, who was believed to be hiding Zira, an eight-year-old girl kidnapped from Manchester.

Zira had been taken from her English mother by her father Sajid; the couple had separated and it was Sajid's turn to look after his daughter for the weekend. He had promised to take an excited Zira to Disneyland in Paris; but instead of a short flight to Paris, she was taken on a plane by Sajid's brother to Pakistan. Vicky called the police and Sajid was arrested. He was later convicted of kidnapping Zira and imprisoned for four years.

Despite Sajid's sentence, Zira was not returned to her mother in Britain. A distraught Vicky feared she'd never see her daughter again, and tried every possible avenue including approaches to the Foreign Office, local MPs, and had even written to Prime Minister Tony Blair. Nobody was able to help. A regular *News of the World* reader, Vicky called me to plead for my assistance to find her daughter who she hadn't seen for three years. I went to visit her at her three-bedroom semi in Leigh, Manchester, where the whole family gathered round and tearfully showed me photos of Zira. Vicky told me how she had fallen in love with handsome Sajid and married him, and that Zira was born soon after, but the relationship ended after three years when Sajid confessed to an affair. The close-knit family saw me as a beacon

Princess and the Cats

◆ Hard to believe that she was so easily taken in by the Fake Sheik but she really was – the Princess wanted to sell me her house, and the fact that I was prepared to keep her cat-flaps clinched the deal as far as she was concerned. To get to her lovely country home, I took a helicopter flight – but the chopper's blades nearly did for my disguise.

Michelle Collins
and The Sheik

◆ At a *News of the World* party, Michelle Collins said she couldn't believe people fell for my act. Only a little while later, I was proving to her that it was very easy to fall for it – but I wished she hadn't fallen for her abusive Italian boyfriend.

Kidnap Attempt
on Beckhams

◆ The police told me I'd just have to indicate that the gang who we knew were planning to kidnap David Beckham's wife and children had turned up to sell objects stolen from Sotheby's. But they hadn't told me I would be treated like one of the villains when they swooped in to arrest them. So here I am lying in the dirt, a sight I'm sure my many enemies will enjoy.

Working undercover

◆ The UK Press Gazette published this cartoon about me when my count of successful prosecutions topped 100. To date, it stands at over 230 villains nabbed.

'Split – it's Mazher Mahmood!'

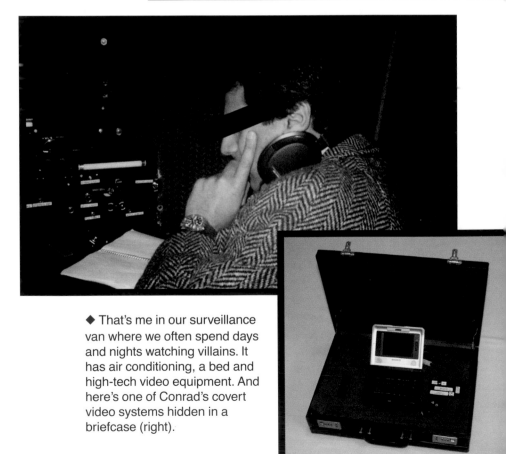

◆ That's me in our surveillance van where we often spend days and nights watching villains. It has air conditioning, a bed and high-tech video equipment. And here's one of Conrad's covert video systems hidden in a briefcase (right).

◆ James Nesbitt was shocked but completely open when I caught him sleeping with a 17-year-old girl. 'I'm stupid. I need to grow up,' he told me.

Honest James

s for Naomi Campbell, this tograph of us at dinner, tegically placed in our rented e, helped convince Sven I was a mover and sheiker.

Harry's Man:
The Cunning Docto

◆ Harry (left) is one of my minders, his imposing build making him the perfect bodyguard when the Sheik meets celebrities. Called 'fat man' by Dr Rangwani (above) who hired me to kill his mistress, the doctor sat in his cunning disguise – a hat and coat – in our hotel room (inset), and later in court tried to pretend he'd been drugged.

me of the people me across had redeeming tures at all. The edophiles, the ople-smugglers, drug-dealers – as proud to ose every one hem.

The Faces of Evil

▲ Smirking Terry Valvona and his wife Rosemary Iredale were an evil pair who abused the children placed in their care. Once Valvona knew I'd got hold of one of his sickening videotapes, he sent men with shotguns after me.

◆ Clifford Davis enticed children into his squalid home with puppies like these, and then photographed them and tried to prostitute the girls to me. He seemed more concerned about the welfare of his dogs than his daughter.

◆ Thomas O'Carroll appeared a happy man at the nudist camp in the south of France, but he was less happy when we exposed him as a dangerous paedophile.

Claire Kent offered to sell her 13-year-old ughter's virginity for £30,000. She even ered to join in – but wanted someone to ysit her young son at the same time.

Marriage Scams

◆ Paul Singh (above right) went to jail for five years, and the judge said, 'This sort of investigative journalism is in the best traditions.'

◆ Ismail Pirbhai (right) had stolen a woman's identity and used that to arrange marriages for £8,000 a time, to enable illegal immigrants to stay in the country.

◆ Priest Adeola Magbagebeola (bottom) married dozens and dozens of people illegally, even marrying the same woman – in the same dress – to two different men the same day.

of hope and I simply couldn't let them down; I vowed to bring Zira back home. The *News of the World* immediately swung into action; the paper paid for Vicky and her mum Sue to fly to Pakistan, and provided a bodyguard – Jaws.

One of the advantages and disadvantages of working in Asia and the Far East is that anything is possible if you have the right contacts or enough money to smooth your path; on arriving in my parents' birthplace Lahore, I called in favours from several family friends including a judge and police chief. I quickly established that Zira was living in a village some two hours away with her uncle, a wrestler called Shahid Butt, a tough man feared locally.

We needed to go to the village to snatch back Zira. However, it was the kind of place where everyone knows everyone and if I was seen lurking around, tongues would soon start wagging. Conrad volunteered to keep watch on the house; we needed to be certain that Zira was there before charging in, otherwise we would blow our one and only chance to rescue her.

The police chief's wife lent him her full-length burka as a disguise, and completed Conrad's transformation into a Muslim woman by carefully applying make-up and mascara to his face. He installed a video camera into a handbag, as we needed to get some footage of Zira for her mum to confirm her identity.

It was the first time I had seen Vicky smile; we were all cracking up with laughter as Conrad slipped on some high-heels, grabbed his handbag and made his way to the village. But it wasn't really all that funny, because if Conrad had been caught by villagers cross-dressing as a burka-clad Muslim woman, he would be looking at a serious kicking at best.

But within a couple of hours Conrad returned; through his veil he had seen a young girl coming back from school. The fuzzy picture on his covert video led to floods of tears from Vicky who was convinced it was her little baby girl.

Conrad got changed and we rushed to the police station. The Superintendent rounded up dozens of officers, many of them from the elite

Punjab anti-terrorist squad. After a quick briefing, the heavily armed policemen clambered into the back of three police jeeps; just as we were about to leave, however, the police chief called me over and told me there was a slight problem. 'Sir, I'm afraid there isn't enough petrol in the vehicles to get us there and back. Will you be able to pay for the petrol?' he asked. I wearily agreed to pay the £6 petrol bill and climbed into the back of one of the vehicles alongside the men. As we drove along pot-holed dirt tracks towards the village, the officers kept staring at Conrad and whispering among themselves. Eventually one of them plucked up the courage to ask me in Urdu: 'Is your white friend gay?' I wondered what he was talking about, and turned to look at Conrad – who'd only forgotten to take off the bloody mascara.

By the time we arrived at the house it was getting dark. A plain-clothes officer knocked on the door and, as soon as it was opened, dozens of armed cops with their fingers on the triggers of semi-automatic rifles stormed in. They searched every nook and cranny of the squalid three-storey house, but Zira was nowhere to be found. Shahid Butt and his family told the police that Zira didn't live there, but a six-year-old boy told another officer that Zira had gone to play at a friend's house.

We knew that the failed raid meant the family would hide Zira and we may never get to see her. 'Don't worry, get a court order and we will arrest every member of the family if we have to, including all the women,' promised our police chief. 'Sooner or later they will have to obey the law and hand over the girl to her mother.'

We took the case to the Pakistan High Court in Lahore where a female judge, Nasira Iqbal, ordered Zira's uncles to give her up. But when the brothers heard the ruling they issued a statement from their bolt-hole: 'We are currently in Afghanistan where we are planning to fight the *jihad*. We do not accept the judgement of any court. Zira is with us. The Taliban are the only true guardians of Islam and we will live according to their laws.' Their view was that Zira was a Muslim girl and they did not want her to be brought up by her Christian mother in Britain.

The judge ordered a nationwide search for Zira with all ports put on alert. After three months in hiding, Shahid Butt was finally captured – but Zira wasn't with him. The *News of the World* then funded a protracted and expensive legal battle in the Pakistani courts to get Zira brought back. After several court hearings, Judge Nasira Iqbal told Butt that he faced jail unless Zira was produced in court; outside court during one hearing, Butt's men threatened us – one of them even tried to intimidate us by flashing a ferocious-looking hunting knife with a serrated blade, but we were not going to be deterred.

Eventually, Zira was brought down from the mountains. A tearful reunion with her mother took place on the courtroom steps. I acted as interpreter as Zira – who hadn't seen her mum for three years – had forgotten English. Zira did remember her bedroom, her nursery school, her pink bicycle, and her *Lion King* video. We were all wiping tears from our eyes by this point.

As soon as the judge ordered that Zira could go home with her mum, we sped off to a safe-house where armed security guards kept 24-hour watch. The British consul in Lahore, Stephen Rapp, expedited her emergency passport and we all flew home. I drove Zira and Vicky back to their home in Leigh, where the whole neighbourhood had turned out to greet her. I was overwhelmed by our reception, and when time came to say goodbye, both Vicky and Zira gave me a big hug. 'We had honestly given up all hope of ever seeing Zira again,' said Vicky with tears of joy rolling down her cheeks. 'The first thing Zira will do as soon as she learns to write is send you a big thank you note.'

CHAPTER 14

'EXPOSED BY THE MOST FAMOUS JOURNALIST IN BRITAIN'

Psychologists have identified as natural human responses to grief four emotional stages of denial, anger, bargaining, and acceptance. Over the years I have discovered that the responses to being confronted by a _News of the World_ reporter fall within the same categories. Journalistic ethics dictate that once we have gathered our evidence we have to approach the subjects prior to publication and put our allegations to them, thus granting them a right to reply; the ensuing confrontations are known in the industry as 'showdowns'.

Showdowns can be quite eventful, not surprising perhaps when you consider that a person's secrets are about to be laid bare in front of some 12 million readers. It is common to be threatened or even physically attacked, but you also get people who offer you bribes, break down and cry, or even confess to things that you had no idea about.

A classic case of denial involved a judge whose job it was to evaluate evidence on a daily basis before passing sentence. His Honour Anthony Thornton QC paid £200 in September 1995 to two hookers in a seedy south London flat for his entertainment. The Old Etonian judge smoked a cannabis- and cocaine-laced cigarette before he stripped the tarts naked and spanked their bottoms. He then produced a bottle of Chablis wine from his briefcase, which he poured on the girls' feet before he sucked their toes. What followed we would summarize in the paper as 'far too disgusting to detail in a family newspaper'.

I had been sitting outside the flat with a photographer and we snapped the judge as he entered and left. The antics inside the flat were also captured on film – the hookers were my informants and had allowed me to install a covert video camera, so it was an open and shut case. But when I confronted the judge he at first completely denied any involvement with prostitutes or drugs. He said that he had spent the night in question at his own flat. However, when I presented my strong case to him, the judge changed his submission. 'I entirely accept I went there. I went to meet a friend of mine. So far as I'm concerned I don't know that she works as a prostitute. I didn't have any sex with anyone. I certainly didn't pay her for sexual intercourse. I didn't pay her at all,' he claimed.

The story appeared on the cover of the paper, but the judge continued to deny the allegations. Through his solicitor, well-known libel expert Peter Carter-Ruck, he fired off a threatening legal letter saying that there was no truth in our story. It was a foolish thing for a guilty man to do, for the following week, the judge was on the cover of the paper again under the headline: 'The Proof M'Lud!' Under the sub-heading 'Sex, Lies And Videotape' we published embarrassing photos of him taken from our covert video which showed him taking drugs and having sex with the hookers.

The most famous case of self-denial following a classic Fake Sheik sting involved actor John Alford, star of the hit TV series *London's Burning*. I had been tipped off by a celebrity that Alford – real name John James Shannon – was a drug dealer who sold gear to friends; a girl who knew Alford well also told me how she and her boyfriend often went round to his home to pick up drugs from the star. The only way to establish whether this was true would be through an undercover sting.

In the summer of 1997 I invited Alford to see the Sheik at London's Savoy hotel on the pretence that I wanted to open a nightclub in Dubai and wanted him to be involved in the project. I greeted him in my flowing robes, complete with mangled English and servile retinue. I liked Alford; he had a cheeky boyish charm, was down to earth and funny, he could easily have been in my circle of friends – were he not involved in drugs. During the conversation in the grand suite, I asked him about drugs. He was quick to brag: 'I could make one phone call and if it's there, it's only fifteen minutes away. I take cannabis all the time. I can't live without my smoke … I can get drugs, cocaine, nuggets.'

Alford went into one of the most detailed descriptions of cocaine taking I had heard to date. 'The powder's no good,' he insisted. 'You get nuggets [compacted cocaine] and you smash them. It's pure cocaine, they wash it and it comes back in a rock. To get crack they mix it with something else, that's what makes crack highly addictive. Pure cocaine, you can crush it up and snort it, or put it in a joint or whatever. There was some I was getting before which was in a bottle, called cocaine hydrochloride and it's 100 per cent pure. You very rarely get this, maybe 80 per cent, which is still good. You put it on your hand and it's like a snowflake. You watch it and it just evaporates. I wouldn't recommend snorting it, to be honest, because it's very pure.'

Alford was a drug connoisseur and told me about the different varieties of cocaine produced around the world. During dinner with the Sheik, Alford called his supplier, arranging to pick up drugs; he went off with my driver Alan Smith and returned an hour later. Back in the suite Alford offered a money-back guarantee on his drugs. 'Try one and if there's a problem I'll take it straight back, no problem at all,' he said as he puffed on a cannabis joint. Alford delivered three wraps of cocaine and a chunk of cannabis for £300.

Even though the deal had been captured on video, Alford didn't want to come clean. When I confronted him before publishing the story, he denied selling me drugs. Alford pleaded not guilty at the subsequent trial, arguing that it was me who was guilty of entrapment. I have never understood the feeble defence of entrapment put forward by villains who are caught red handed; the vast majority of people, if invited by a rich Sheik or anybody else to supply cocaine, would never do so. They wouldn't know where to get their hands on drugs and neither would they want to.

Southwark Crown Court agreed, after viewing our damning videos. After a lengthy legal argument, Alford pleaded guilty but in a bizarre speech to the court insisted, rather confusingly: 'The only reason I am pleading guilty is I know deep down in my heart I'm not guilty.' But a few days later, Detective Sergeant Keith Giles, who led the police inquiry, phoned me to tell me that after three days behind bars, Alford had changed his mind and opted to plead not guilty. DS Giles, a highly experienced officer based at Holborn police station, agreed that it was a bad decision as the evidence against Alford was overwhelming.

If Alford had put his hands up and admitted his drug problems, he might have avoided a prison sentence. He could also have kept his job – as other actors have managed to do after being caught taking drugs – by volunteering to go into rehab. Instead, Alford tried every trick in the book to escape justice; he even tried to bribe my driver Alan Smith, who had chauffeured him to the Savoy in a Rolls Royce. Some of Alford's loyal non-celebrity friends also subjected me to extreme intimidation throughout the trial, shouting abuse from the public gallery.

Self-righteous Alford returned to court in defiant mood, having sacked his defence barrister in favour of representing himself. His impressive acting talent came to the fore as he took on the role of defence barrister; his courtroom performance was sharp and polished, as good as many qualified barristers I have faced. Alford's celebrity supporters who attended court to offer moral support included actor Ray Winstone and ex-boxer Terry Marsh. Twice during the ten-day trial, Alford tried to get an order from the judge to force me to disclose my source. I told the judge that I would rather go to jail than reveal my confidential source. All journalists are morally bound to protect the identities of confidential informants, but for investigative reporters it is rule number one. Nobody would ever come forward with information about serious criminals if there was any risk of their name being revealed.

In his impassioned closing speech, Alford declared: 'I stand before you an innocent man. I am not a drug dealer, I was the victim of journalistic efforts which belong in the Dark Ages.' He told the jury: 'When the law and justice conflict, justice must prevail. Please follow your conscience.'

The jurors did. They took 4? hours to convict him by a 10–2 majority. Judge Stephen Robbins told the actor: 'You were undoubtedly motivated by the desire to earn even more money than you were earning as a successful actor.' He was sentenced to nine months imprisonment on two counts of supplying drugs, with the terms to run concurrently. He was also ordered to pay £3,000 towards the cost of the prosecution and a confiscation order was made for £300. But Alford remained in denial, launching an appeal against the verdict, claiming that his trial had been unfair and that he had been the victim of entrapment. At the Court of Appeal Lord Justice Potter upheld Judge Robbins's original finding and said that Alford had 'voluntarily and readily' applied himself to getting the drugs for me. He noted Alford's 'obvious familiarity with the current price of cocaine and in his ready advice as to obtaining it in the quantity and quality required, he displayed a familiarity with the dealing scene which itself suggested a predisposition to be part of it'. The judges, who said Alford had received a lenient sentence, also rejected Alford's claims to have been pressurized. After watching our videos they concluded that there was 'no basis for any such feelings of pressure other than the anxiety he might have felt to please the company in which he found himself'.

The judges dismissed Alford's application to take the case to the House of Lords and awarded the *News of the World*, which had contested the appeal, legal costs from central funds. But Alford still wouldn't accept his wrongdoing. He went bleating to the European Court of Human Rights arguing that he was the victim of entrapment, and that the British courts should have made me name my informant.

DS Giles, who closely monitored the landmark case, telephoned me again. I thought he was ringing to tell me that I was about be hauled up before the European legal eagles, but the call was simply to congratulate me on the result. The European court sitting in Strasbourg had agreed with our courts. They reminded Alford: 'The trial judge concluded that the applicant had not been entrapped into committing an offence but had volunteered, offered, and agreed to supply drugs without being subjected to pressure.' The European court also agreed that it was 'neither relevant nor necessary' to order the identity of my informant to be disclosed.

Another bizarre game of denial was played by footballer John Fashanu after I exposed him for fixing football matches for cash. The footballer turned TV star was one of the most corrupt men I had encountered. He came to meet the Sheik for a meal in 2003 at the Bombay Brasserie in south Kensington, to discuss organizing a football match in the Middle East. Fashanu insisted I send a limo to ferry him and his 'legal advisor' Delapo Awosike, a make-up artist who was his secret mistress.

'I am a statesman of football,' said the head of the Nigerian Football Association and chairman of Welsh Premier League champions Barry Town. 'All the footballers are my friends.' He had been accused of fixing games before in the well-publicized Bruce Grobbelaar match-fixing scandal, but was cleared by the Courts. However, Mr Justice McCullough told Fashanu he had to pay his own £650,000 legal fees because his 'conduct had brought suspicion on himself.' Fashanu, who went on to become a TV presenter alongside Ulrika Jonsson on the popular *Gladiators*, always pleaded his innocence; but in a series of sensational meetings with me and my team he reeled off a list of Premiership players and international stars he claimed were corrupt and on his payroll.

Fashanu admitted: fixing a huge match when victory for the underdogs would have embarrassed the losing manager; making £1.5 million working for a Far Eastern betting syndicate; fiddling his own charity for African children to line his pockets with tax-free payments; and pocketing a £5 million insurance payout after retiring early from the game with a knee injury that had him laughing.

His 'legal advisor' Dee didn't bat an eyelid as Fashanu readily agreed to fix a football match for the Sheik. 'It happens all the time in football,' said Fashanu. 'I tell him [the player] that this has got to happen. This is the situation. We cannot win, there are no ifs or buts, we have to lose. The goalkeeper goes to catch the ball, he hits someone's head, he falls over and – Oh, it's a goal. Even if it's 0–0, or 1–1 or even if it's 1–0, when I've got the goalkeeper in my pocket even if he has to push somebody he'll give a penalty.' I felt I was having dinner with any run-of-the mill Nigerian fraudster, as Fashanu said the rigged match would cost me £40,000 per man to play the match, plus a £30,000 bung to three players to make sure they lost.

At another dinner meeting, this time at a Chinese restaurant in Baker Street, Fashanu tried to convince me of his influence over players. He phoned his friend, ex-Manchester United goalie, Mark Bosnich and asked him to join us for dinner. Bosnich, who later became a close friend of mine, looked totally bemused as Fashanu told him of his plan and asked him if he would throw a game. Bosnich then became furious and said he had never played in a rigged match and never would. But as Bosnich left, bent Fashanu insisted that he would be able to persuade him.

Fashanu's match rigging services didn't come cheap. He said I would have to pay him £40,000, buy him a new Mercedes 4X4, and make another hefty payment to him through his charity. 'I need a couple of laptops straight away. There's a lot of typing to be done.' And he wanted money immediately – a £20,000 down payment. When I told him that even Sheiks didn't carry that kind of loose change in their pocket, he asked: 'What about later on tonight?' As he left the Chinese restaurant, Fashanu insisted on taking the left-over food home in a doggy bag and even ordered an additional large takeaway to be added to my bill.

Fashanu demanded at least some of the cash be handed over on the spot as a show of good faith. After a couple of discreet calls from the toilet to editor Andy Coulson and our legal manger Tom Crone, it was agreed that I could hand over a £5,000 deposit to Fashanu. It would provide further evidence – not that Tom felt it was needed – that he was taking bungs to fix football matches. The bribe was handed over to him by the Sheik's assistant at Fashanu's flat in Chiswick, west London. The soccer ace spread the crisp £50 notes on his king-size bed and counted them carefully. The scene was captured beautifully by our covert video camera. He was, as my story proclaimed, 'bung to rights!'

But in a ludicrous denial Fashanu claimed he had played along with the Fake Sheik in a reverse sting to gather evidence on me to take to the police. In a Sky TV interview straight after our story broke, he said: 'They gave me £5,000. I did the right thing. I took it straight to the police station. I told police I wanted them investigated and arrested. I'm glad I gave them a full statement and didn't take one penny.'

Later we asked the cops for our money back, but they said that Fashanu had lied; he had pocketed the cash. Chief Superintendent Jeff Harris, of Hounslow police, told news editor Greg Miskiw: 'The £5,000 has not been taken into police possession but was retained by Mr Fashanu.' We threatened to sue the lying soccer idol to get our money back. It was only then, two months later, Fash gave us the cash.

Eccentric boxer Chris Eubank tried to deny that he had exposed himself to a pretty blonde salesgirl in the stairwell of the Thistle hotel in Brighton in early 2002. An informant had handed me video footage showing the ex-world champ, who loves to parade as a true English gent in riding outfits and a monocle, pleasuring himself in the hotel's fire exit. The footage showed how the married star stroked his genitals as he asked the shocked girl to touch him. She refused, saying, 'It's cheap and nasty!' but Eubank replied, 'Cheap and nasty is fun. I've got to take the opportunities when they arise. Dirty is nice. Right now I need you to be dirty. How about a quick one?' But despite his member being captured on camera, Eubank bluntly denied the allegations. After we published our story, complete with a picture taken from the video, other women rang in saying they too had been his victims. It must have taken Eubank onto the next stage of the psychologist's model – anger.

Some of the most unlikely subjects can resort to violence: in 1994, when I confronted married

Reverend Barry Smart from Abingdon, Oxfordshire about his gay sex experiences with a 17-year-old boy, I got more than I bargained for. I approached him as he left the young lad's home at around 2am one rainy night; the vicar screamed at me, 'You are a fucking bastard, get out of my way!' He then jumped in his Mini Metro and drove straight at me. I leapt onto the bonnet, holding onto the wipers for a few seconds before being flung onto the road. He left me lying bruised in the middle of the road. The following day with my arm in a sling I turned up at his church and confronted the vicar again while he stood at the altar. Nursing my wounds overnight in the hotel bed, I had studied the Gideons Bible and shocked him by reciting from Luke 12:2: *'There is nothing concealed that will not be disclosed, or hidden that will not be made known. What you have said in the dark will be heard in the daylight, and what you have whispered in the ear in the inner rooms will be proclaimed from the roofs.'* Rev. Smart broke down sobbing and confessed: 'I knew this would come out one day. I should never have got involved with him.'

After being run over by a vicar I soon learned that anything is possible, and I have learned to prepare for the worst-case scenario every time. And after being struck by several vice girls' high heels, handbags, and having wine glasses hurled at me, I now resort to confronting them on the phone; it's a prudent safety precaution.

One memorable angry showdown involved a waif-like 15-year-old schoolboy from Bradford, Yorkshire in October 1998. He was selling drugs to other school kids and pimping two hookers in the city's notorious red-light district, one of them only fourteen years old. The Asian boy sold me crack cocaine, heroin, amphetamines, and cannabis – the widest range of drugs I had bought from any dealer. He bought one of his girls (who he referred to as his 'bitches') to my hotel. I chatted to her about her drug problem, paid her cab fare and sent her packing; but moments later, the schoolboy pimp, still wearing his school sweater, stormed into my hotel room demanding I pay the £100 escorting fee. 'You've fucked me about here. I've already given that bitch a rock of crack. I've got to make the money for that,' he shouted.

I refused to hand over any more money and politely asked the kid to leave the room. He refused. In the hope that it would scare him and encourage him to leave, I told the boy that I was a reporter from the *News of the World* and pointed out that he was being videoed. This didn't work. 'I can get shooters. Don't mess with me!' he threatened. As I gently guided him towards the door, the boy lashed out at me, punching me in the face. The kid could punch; I was dazed and seeing stars. I could also see myself making the front page of the Bradford *Telegraph and Argus*. It had all the ingredients for a front-page splash: a London 'businessman' in a hotel room with a stash of Class A drugs, an underage hooker, and a fight with a school kid – it would have taken a few days at the local police station to talk my way out of that one. A great story for a younger version of myself to write, though. Fortunately my minder Jaws, who was standing outside the hotel room, rushed to my aid. He calmed the schoolboy's tantrum and took him home; the boy lived with his father, a retired accountant, and schoolteacher mum.

One of the classic exponents of anger is rock star Mick Jagger, who was furious when he found out I had rumbled his secret sexy rendezvous in October 1996, especially since he'd gone to extraordinary lengths to make sure he wasn't caught.

Jagger had booked two rooms in the name of Mr Philips, at the Halycon hotel in Notting Hill Gate, a small boutique hotel famed for its absolute discretion. The plan was that the model he was meeting would check into one of the rooms and then slip next door to spend the night with Jagger. Not even the hotel staff would suspect. I had been tipped off about Jagger's cunning plan by one of his closest friends, whose sympathy lay with Jagger's long-suffering partner, Jerry Hall. I checked into the room next door to 'Mr Philips' just as Jagger, in a rudimentary disguise of a pair of sunglasses, walked past me as I went to my door.

Jagger ordered a bottle of chilled champagne to be sent up. I squinted through the spyhole and saw an attractive 23-year-old curvy beauty walk past my room as she headed to Jagger's room. Grandad Jagger had done well to pull her, I thought.

Throughout the night I could hear the couple giggling. As morning dawned, Jagger's secret date discreetly left the hotel. At around noon, Jagger must have been burdened by a guilty conscience, for he called reception to ask staff to look outside to see if there were any photographers lurking outside the hotel. Meanwhile, a blue Mercedes with blacked-out windows drove twice round the block, with the chauffeur taking instructions on a mobile phone.

> **'A girl who knew Alford told me how she and her boyfriend often went round to his home to pick up drugs from the star.'**

When Jagger was convinced the coast was clear he made a furtive dash for the car from a rear exit – just where I was standing in wait. I politely asked him how he was and then how Jerry was keeping. But tight-lipped Jagger didn't reply. So I confronted him: 'You just spent the night shagging a young blonde. Is Jerry not giving you satisfaction anymore then Mick?'

He waved his fists at me as he launched a tirade of abuse, the most valuable quotes included: 'Fuck off. You can't fucking prove anything. I didn't shag her!' He climbed into his car and rang his friend and continued screaming: 'Mahmood is the most horrible fucking reporter I've ever met. He just asked me if I'm not getting no more satisfaction from Jerry! He is frightening. This could be not funny. He hasn't got a photo of me with the girl though. He was asking about Jerry, but she's in France so she won't read it. But they can't prove I fucked her.'

He was right. Our lawyer Tom Crone agreed with Jagger, I had no proof he had committed adultery. 'All you can say is that he spent most of the night with a girl in a hotel room. You cannot say they had sex or he will sue. He has already denied having sex with her,' cautioned Tom. I thought that wasn't a bad story in itself. Jagger smuggled a girl into his hotel room and then didn't have sex with her. I wrote a piece saying he was 'Top Of the Flops' and hadn't been able to rise to the occasion; I heard later that Jagger was fuming when he read the piece, as his virility had been called into question – he'd rather have been exposed for bonking the girl all night.

Bargaining is often the most sensible option for people who are caught red handed. The same advice would cost a fortune if dispensed by public relations firms and solicitors keen to cash in on fallen celebrities. Whenever a tabloid story headline contains the words 'Confession', 'My Shame' or 'My Hell', it invariably means that a secret deal has been done to bury the real story. Soccer's Mr Clean, John Barnes, cut a deal after he was caught cheating on his wife, Suzy, with a pretty time-share rep, Pippa Hall.

Barnes, a former Liverpool star, met Pippa in Spain in early 1996 as he enjoyed an off-season break. With Pippa onside, I had full details of his love match complete with tape recordings of his nightly dirty phone calls, and covert videos of his marathon sex sessions; he enjoyed giving dirty running commentaries to his lovers as he had sex with them – but Barnes certainly didn't lack stamina. One liaison with Pippa lasted so long that I fell asleep while monitoring his performance in the back of a surveillance van.

When I confronted Barnes, he put his hands up and pleaded with me to leave out some of the details of his adulterous sessions, as his trusting wife of fifteen years, Suzy, was pregnant with their fourth child at the time. Barnes sobbed that he didn't want to upset his poor wife, but his pleadings had little effect on me, and I asked him why he hadn't thought of his wife's feelings before he fell for Pippa's unquestionable charms. I remember Barnes tearfully pledging never to play away from home again. 'I promise you, you'll never catch me fucking around again. I know I did wrong,' he'd reassured me. 'I know I've made a mistake, one that I will regret for the rest of my life. I have no excuse for my stupid behaviour. Please you've got to help me!'

Determined to soften the blow, Barnes then tried bargaining with editor Rebekah Wade – and it worked. Eventually it was agreed that we would make it look as if it was a one-off session. It is often advantageous to strike deals with celebs like Barnes; we still get our story and the subjects feel indebted to us for leaving out some of the more damaging and embarrassing details. A few people I have exposed have felt so grateful that they have since become invaluable informants.

But Barnes's friendly relationship with the *News of the World* was nipped in the bud, when just eight months later I received a phone call from Zena Reid who worked at the *Financial Times* as a secretary. She wanted to sell a straight kiss-and-tell story about her affair with the soccer idol. I can't imagine what effect the story had on his poor wife, Suzy, but I know that I was personally disappointed that Barnes had broken his promise to stay on the straight and narrow.

This time there were no more deals on the table, and we went to town on him. He'd made the same smutty phone calls to Zena, the same demands for sordid threesomes, and indulged in the same perverted sex acts as he had with Pippa. I discovered that Barnes had even been sleeping with Pippa at the same time as he was bedding Zena; again I was impressed by his stamina but saddened by his disloyalty to Suzy, who was now mother to their four children. I rang Barnes and asked him if he remembered me, and the promise he had made to me. I told him if he didn't, I would be happy to play the tape back to him. Speechless, Barnes simply managed to croak out, 'Oh no! Oh no!' before he hung up the phone.

One of Britain's best-loved entertainers, Lionel Blair broke down and cried when I caught him cheating on his wife with a secret lover. He was regarded as a family man and had recently posed for photos with his wife Sue, and their three grown-up children at his home in Barnes, south-west London for a *Hello!* magazine spread. A kiss-and-tell queen had targeted Lionel, who was performing in a play at the Devonshire

Park theatre in Eastbourne in August 1999; he'd succumbed to her charms and invited her back to his room at the Grand hotel. In turn she'd phoned me and invited me to the hotel too – to get proof of her tryst with a celebrity and discuss a hefty fee.

Lionel was devastated. I was embarrassed as hotel guests stared as Lionel sat sobbing in the lounge, pleading with me not to publish details of his one-night stand. During a long stroll on the seafront, Lionel opened his heart to me; I felt like a psychiatrist as I listened to him talk about his loneliness and the pressures he faced to live up to his 'goody-two shoes' image.

We agreed that I would write a story about Lionel's secret double life, and how he had enjoyed a few one-night stands. I was happy to do it, as I share the contempt that most of the public have for women who make a living out of targeting footballers and celebrities for sleazy kiss-and-tells. By 2am, Lionel and I had written the story that he was happy with, and he finally went to his room. With a throbbing headache and hunger kicking in, Conrad and I jumped into a mini-cab to go and get a kebab. As we climbed into the old Toyota saloon, a tall lanky figure came running towards us and knocked on the rear passenger window. It was Lionel, he said he couldn't sleep and wanted to know where we were going. I told him, and he insisted on joining us, as he'd never eaten a kebab.

At the takeaway, drunken youths mobbed Lionel. He happily posed for snaps and signed their kebab boxes, and was thrilled as they chanted: 'Go Lionel Go! We love you!'

But at 6am I was woken by Lionel knocking on my hotel room door, concerned that I wouldn't honour the deal we'd struck. 'I've made a few phone calls to my agent and friends and I have found out who you are. You are ruthless and you have ended a lot of people's careers,' he said shaking nervously. 'How can I trust you?' It was not a nice wake-up call, but

202 CONFESSIONS OF A FAKE SHEIK

nevertheless I did my best to reassure him. I rang editor Phil Hall who spoke to Lionel and calmed him down again.

But with a whole day to go before publication, and a seaside photo-shoot lined up for the afternoon, I needed back-up. Our showbiz correspondent Jon Barnsley was despatched to help keep both Lionel and myself from having a nervous breakdown. When the first edition of the paper was handed to Lionel and he read the story, it was word for word as he had dictated. He literally danced around the room with joy holding the paper. 'I really didn't believe that tabloid journalists told the truth. You have restored my faith!' he told me.

But one form of bargaining I wouldn't advocate is straight bribery. That's what Labour MP Mohammed Sarwar's aides tried after their pal was exposed by the *News of the World* for allegedly trying to bribe an election rival, after the Labour Party came to power in the 1997 elections. His sidekicks wanted to buy our evidence, a damning dossier including tapes, which they thought could end Sarwar's political career. Millionaire businessman Maqbool Rasul and local Labour branch treasurer Hanif Rajah flew down from Glasgow to meet me at Heathrow airport, thinking they were talking to a bent legal assistant who worked in the *News of the World*'s legal team. They'd found me by contacting a London-based interpreter who they knew had translated the Sarwar tapes. 'We need the tapes by hook or by crook. Money does not matter,' Rajah explained to me. 'We need to know everything before Sawar is interviewed by the police. He cannot remember exactly what he said in the conversations. We need to buy the whole material.'

Rasul, who was not only one of the richest Asians in the country (his £30 million fortune had come from his chain of video shops) but also a Justice of the Peace, added: 'Nobody will know we have obtained anything from you, it will be secret. Help us and we help you, we are men of means, we will look after you. We have got to help Mr Sarwar in any way we can. As Muslim brothers this is our duty.' The pair then slagged me off to my face. Rasul warned: 'There is a Pakistani reporter working at the *News of the World* called Mazher Mahmood. Have you ever met him? Be careful of that bastard. He is a fucking traitor to Asians and Muslims in particular.' Unbeknown to them they were talking direct to the Muslim Judas.

A few days later, the pair met me at Glasgow's Forte Posthouse hotel where I turned up clutching a bundle of tapes and documents. Rajah wanted to make sure that I wasn't a *News of the World* plant and insisted on taking me to the toilet to frisk me for recording devices. Luckily, I'd anticipated he might want to pat me down, so I'd hidden the recorder and microphone in the one place I knew he wouldn't want to touch.

'You know we are in the same position as Sarwar if we get caught. We are in the same shit,' warned Rajah. 'We are business people not cowboys. This man Rasul is number 13th richest Asian in Britain. He has been in the *Sunday Times* Rich List.' Rasul agreed to pay me £2,000 as an initial fee for my work, and in the lobby lounge of the hotel, he handed me a £500 deposit in a small wad of notes. As he did so we went into action; our photographers banged off photos of the bent businessmen, and I revealed my true identity. They both flew into a rage. 'I haven't given you anything,' yelled Rajah, maintaining that fine Asian tradition of lying when caught. Meanwhile his millionaire pal simply pushed and shoved me before storming out of the hotel.

A full-page photograph of the men handing over the cash to me was published on the cover of the paper under the headline: 'This Is Bung MP's Pals Trying To Buy Our Evidence.' It was one deal the businessmen hadn't bargained for.

Housewives' favourite, Radio Two presenter Johnnie Walker epitomized the psychologist's stage of acceptance – and it worked a treat for him. Walker too was invited to meet the Sheik at the Grosvenor House hotel in Park Lane to discuss a radio deal for the Middle East. Thanks to some penny-pinching in the budget I was given to work with, it nearly went wrong, too.

It was summer 1999, I'd been tipped off by one of his BBC colleagues that Walker's cocaine addiction was out of control, and that he was brazenly supplying the drug to colleagues around the studios.

The veteran DJ was escorted to a suite by the Sheik's grey-haired assistant, journalist Gerry Brown; as soon as Walker entered, he was intrigued by the sight of the Sheik dressed in his robes, smoking his Arabic sheesha pipe. 'It smells very sweet, what is that?' inquired Walker, as the smoke from my pipe wafted towards him.

He asked if he could try the sheesha and soon relaxed in the Sheik's company as he shared his pipe. Inevitably, the chat soon turned to drugs. 'What do you like, hash or grass?' asked smooth-voiced Walker. He told the Sheik how it was easy to obtain drugs in Britain if you had connections. 'It's knowing the right people, really, there is dodgy stuff around, they cut it,' he explained. 'If you take a line of so-called cocaine and the first thing you do is go to the toilet, that's because they put laxative in it. They chop that up and mix it in. You were born too late. You should have been here in the 1960s, then you'd have had too much of everything. Do you like a little cocaine?' When I asked him if he had any contacts to obtain the drug, myself, Gerry and Conrad – who was monitoring the conversation next door – were all taken aback by his candid response. 'Well I've got some in my pocket.'

It normally takes more than a few minutes for the Sheik to gain someone's trust before they confess to criminal activity, but Walker not only discussed his cocaine habit but also dished out advice on quality control. 'The only way to tell is by taking it. If it's in a big lump of rock then you know you've got some good stuff. It should be £60 a gram,' he said.

He then asked if it was ok to use the table, as he pulled out a wrap of cocaine from his trouser pocket. He poured out the white powder onto the glass tabletop and divided it up into neat lines with his gold credit card. Walker invited me to snort a line with him, but I quickly made an excuse saying I never took coke before dinner. 'I'll leave it there for you. We can call it pudding,' replied Walker, as I hurriedly escorted him downstairs for a meal at the hotel restaurant.

I really enjoyed Walker's company. He was a great dinner guest and his anecdotes about pop stars and tales of his *Top Of The Pops* days kept us all entertained. It was only after our meal, as Walker and the

Sheik headed back to the suite, that things came close to going pear-shaped. In the lift we bumped into a madam who I had arranged to meet later – she had turned up early.

In a bid to save costs, my bosses had decreed that I should use the same suite for two different stories. It was fine except that the woman in the lift didn't know me as an Arab who could barely speak English, but as an Indian chauffeur with a Cockney accent called Perry. She was coming round to introduce me – posing as a fixer for my Indian diplomat boss – to hookers who would escort him to Wimbledon. Her package included lunch with John McEnroe and Pat Cash, seats in the Royal box on Centre Court, and the company of cocaine-snorting tarts.

I tried my best to stare at the floor and hide behind my burly minder, but the eagle-eyed madam sidled up to me in the lift and said loudly: 'Hi Perry.' As she stared at me up and down and looked bemused, I quickly whispered in her ear: 'Not now, not now! I'll be free in half an hour, wait in the bar darlin!' As we got out of the lift, Walker asked me if I knew the woman. I told him she had obviously mistaken me for someone else. (Luckily she believed me, and we ended up on Centre Court with two cocaine-peddling hookers.)

The chance meeting in the lift with the madam could easily have cost me both jobs and the firm a few quid. But fortunately, Walker wasn't suspicious, he was too busy thinking about the 'pudding' he had already laid out on the table. As soon as he returned to the suite he produced a £20 note that he rolled up into a straw. 'Do you want a little livener?' he asked me. 'Nobody will know, nobody will know.' I made another excuse but the DJ snorted lines of cocaine off the table. He was recorded hoovering up every last speck of the powder by our covert video cameras.

After the story appeared on the cover, I was preparing for the same old entrapment arguments to be hurled at me yet again; but I was wrong. Walker gallantly put his hands up, and although the BBC suspended the star, he checked himself into guitar legend Eric Clapton's rehab clinic on the Caribbean island of Antigua in a bid to get his life back together. In court, Walker pleaded guilty to possession of cocaine and was fined £2,000. His determination to kick drugs won the sympathy of the court and his eight million listeners a week. He was soon back on the airwaves wooing his audience. I was really pleased for him. In his autobiography, Walker thanked me for exposing him and rescuing him from his drugs hell. He said he was 'grateful' for his brush with the Fake Sheik, as it was just what he needed to go and seek help and kick the habit for good.

Another satisfied customer who accepted his fate when I confronted him was actor James Nesbitt. I suppose he had little choice as I handed him back his green Paul Smith boxer shorts, which he had left behind after spending a night in early 2004 with a seventeen-year-old hooker. The married star of the TV series *Cold Feet* said: 'Thanks for my underpants. It's a fair cop and I suppose it's a great honour to be exposed by the most famous journalist in Britain.'

I found Nesbitt to be a likeable down-to-earth man brimming with Irish charm. Over a coffee, he openly confided that he struggled to fight off the temptations of alcohol and female fans that throw themselves at stars. Nesbitt's genuine remorse at his drunken antics at the Dartford Bridge Hilton led me to rewrite the piece. Rather than a hard exposé of the adulterous boozed-up star who paid a teenage hooker, it was a sympathetic confession of a man who had erred under the influence of drink. I thought his truthful admission would win over most of our male readers who would sympathize with, if not envy his plight. Then he worked on winning over our female readers, including his loyal wife Sonia, mother of their two children. 'I'm a responsible father and husband most of the time, but I have a self-destruct button. I've had affairs before and I know I haven't behaved well before. And I know I keep saying it, I don't want this to happen again. I have a really happy life. I love my job, and my home life, and my kids. I've humiliated myself and my family. I'm stupid. I need to grow up.'

It was a sentiment shared by footballer Ian Wright when I confronted him over his affair. Arsenal and England striker Wright was known to be a devoted family man, married to Deborah. He had even been quoted saying: 'Deborah knows the kind of guy I am. I never had girlfriends all over the place. I've only had about five in my whole life. She knew I wasn't the type to mess around.'

Wright had chosen the wrong time to top up his girlfriend count. I was tipped off by a waiter at the TGIF burger restaurant in Mill Hill, north London, that the soccer star had become besotted with a waitress called Tina Hodgson after she had served him one afternoon. Wright had become a regular visitor to the burger restaurant; the pair would leave together after Tina's shift finished. Together with a surveillance team, I spent day and night keeping watch on the pair, and ate my way through the entire menu at the restaurant. I even had to spend Christmas and New Year's Eve 1996 at the restaurant to try and gather evidence of their relationship. After weeks of work we caught Wright at the restaurant and followed him as he drove to Tina's home nearby.

It still wasn't enough to accuse the football hero of having an affair. So I confronted Tina in the restaurant and told her I knew all about her relationship and that we were going to publish the story that weekend. I told her that she might as well come onside and help me fill in the small gaps in return for money – of course the 'gaps' were yawning chasms. Tina knew her romance was doomed. 'I know I have no future with Ian, and that while I am with him I'll never be able to have a relationship with anyone else,' she said. So she spilled the beans, giving me all the sordid details, complete with love notes from Wright, and photographs of the couple together. When I confronted Wright, I was expecting him to deny it or refer me to his solicitors. But he took it squarely on the chin. He said: 'It happened, I hold my hands up, I did sleep with her but it was just a few times. And it was me who wanted to end the relationship.'

Wright asked me: 'Please will you not tell my wife. Give me a few minutes to tell her myself. I've got to apologize and explain it to her.' Later his wife Debbie spoke to me too and told me how their marriage had been in crisis for some time. Sadly the marriage didn't survive and the couple later divorced.

One outcome I never anticipated was when I confronted Lord Laidlaw over parties with £3,000-a-night prostitutes that he was hosting at a luxurious hotel in Monaco. Lord Laidlaw, worth £730 million and one of the biggest donors to the Conservative Party, could easily afford the most eminent legal minds in the land and we thought that it would be an instinctive response for him to try and avoid being exposed in the paper. Our evidence was strong as it included secretly videoed admissions by the madam who had supplied girls and young men to entertain 'the lusty Lord', as the paper christened him, at his latest party, where the guest list included a dominatrix he'd specially flown in from New York. A 'trilingual bisexual' model-cum-hooker who had attended the function had also talked to me.

However, no sooner had I left messages for the 'happily married' Lord to discuss a 'private matter', that I received a phone call from news editor Ian Edmondson. 'You are not going to believe this, Lord Laidlaw's people have been on. He has put his hands up and is giving us a statement confessing that he is a sex addict and he's checking himself in for treatment in a clinic,' announced Edmondson with his trademark mischievous chuckle. 'Fucking unbelievable result. And guess what, he's donating a million quid to charity, but he wants the money to go to a sex clinic to help other sufferers.'

He also gave us a statement: 'I have been fighting sexual addiction for my whole adult life. There is no cure for it, and self-help is rarely successful. But having an addiction is no excuse for my behaviour. I have been in therapy a number of times, but I have not worked hard enough or continuously enough on this. I should have been stronger in resisting temptations … I am also planning to make a £1 million donation to a UK addiction charity to help others in similar circumstances fight their addiction. I hope that, in time, people will be able to understand and forgive me as I fight this difficult personal battle.'

It was an honourable and heartfelt admission, and as a result we left out most of the details of his sexual antics, as well as turning away a line-up of hookers who rang in trying to sell lurid tales of their romps with the Lord. Here was a remorseful man who had acknowledged his deviant behaviour and was willing to seek help.

One of the most amusing showdowns came when I confronted *Sharpe* star, Sean Bean. The swashbuckling hero was having an affair with actress Abigail Cruttenden, who played his wife in the hit TV series set in the Napoleonic wars. I only found out by sheer coincidence, as I was staying at the same hotel in Bradford as them; Sean was staying in the room next door to mine. He returned to his room with pretty Abigail, wearing tight black jeans and a figure-hugging black top, in tow.

Sean was still married to his wife, former *Bread* star Melanie Hill. I instructed photographer Bradley Page to follow the couple, while Jaws was tasked with befriending the film crew, who were also staying at the same hotel, as they filmed scenes in the Yorkshire moors.

We managed to get video footage of the lovebirds enjoying a romantic meal at a restaurant, as well as some grainy shots of the couple smooching in the bar. I confronted Sean as he was having a quiet drink in the bar with Jaws, chatting about his favourite football team Sheffield United. Having introduced myself, I put it to him that he was having an affair with Abigail. Sean smiled broadly and said to me: 'Do you blame me Maz? Just look at her!' I did, and he was right. I didn't blame him. She was absolutely gorgeous.

'Write what you want but don't make it look like I've said anything,' he said. 'I'm seeing her and it could be serious. Don't blow it for me!' I asked him if he would pose for a photograph with his new love, but he said Abigail wanted to keep the relationship quiet. However, Sean tipped me off that he would be leaving the hotel in an hour, and we could secretly bang off a picture then. He came out on cue, proudly holding her hand for our 'secret' photograph. Sean married Abigail a year later and I sent the couple a big bunch of flowers.

CHAPTER 15

SVEN SAILS INTO A STORM

W.C. Fields spelled out the golden rule of showbiz by warning actors: 'Never work with children or animals.' Well I can reveal that the golden rule that applies to Fake Sheiks is 'never work with yachts or helicopters' as your Arab headdress is bound to fly off.

It was something that wise old England manager Sven-Goran Eriksson clearly understood well. As we sailed off the coast of Dubai, aboard the £2 million yacht *Eternity*, I presented him with a gift from the Fake Sheik, a designer Arab outfit complete with red chequered headdress with gold piping and black supporting rings. I'd bought it from a market stall near the gold souk for £18 and the box claimed it was made by Christian Doir (sic). I thought it would be appropriate to give him – a fake 'Fake Sheik' outfit.

Sven appeared thrilled with the gift and thanked me as I handed it over. I desperately wanted him to try on the headdress as it would make a fantastic picture that I knew would go round the world. But he wouldn't. 'Mohammed if I wear it, it will blow off. It's too windy. I will wear it at home,' he promised me.

He was right. I was struggling to control mine and the hairpins my mother had used to secure the cloth to my head were giving way. I must have gone to the toilet a dozen times during the trip to reposition the damn thing.

The historic yacht trip in the run-up to the World Cup 2006 was to mark the end of Sven's career as England coach. His meeting with the Sheik infuriated fans and his FA bosses alike; at a time when his mind should have been firmly focused on helping get our boys through the tournament, here he was in Dubai trying to persuade me to buy a football club and to give him and his daughter jobs.

I'd approached Sven with a simple proposal, after we'd heard that he was trying to line up another job for himself. The Sheik wanted to establish a footballing academy of excellence in the desert to train players from around the world, and I needed a man of Sven's calibre to head the organization. I approached Jürgen Klinsmann, the German coach, with the same proposal, but the crafty German had done the honourable thing and told me that he wouldn't consider any employment proposals prior to the World Cup.

But Sven, we were told, loved the idea and was keen to initiate talks immediately. Following a couple of phone calls to Sven's agent Athole Still, 'legal advisor' Richard Des Voeux was despatched to meet my people in London. My colleague Alex D'Souza tried his best to steer him towards dinner at a plush restaurant but Des Voeux was adamant that he wanted to visit our offices, so we quickly conjured up an office in Tenterden Street off London's Hanover Square, hired for a couple of hours to help convince him. We had one small room in the serviced office block but we had to be out by 5.30pm when the building would be locked up; things got a little hairy, though, as Des Voeux was running late, and the job would collapse if the manageress of the office knocked on our door and told us to get out, as our time was up.

Des Voeux turned up just in the nick of time and was greeted downstairs by our secretary, an aspiring actress drafted in for the meeting. She hurriedly escorted him up to the office, where Alex had strategically placed some framed photos of me to make it look as if I used the office normally – one of me with Naomi Campbell, and another with my nephews when they were very young – on the desk and a pile of Arab magazines on the coffee table.

During the short meeting, another one of our planted secretaries entered the room to ask Mr D'Souza to sign her holiday form to make it look like it really was the bustling headquarters of a multi-million pound business. As Alex grabbed his coat, Des Voeux said he'd join him for a drink, but not right away: 'Mind if I have a quick look round?'

214 CONFESSIONS OF A FAKE SHEIK

It was downright rude. A real jobsworth, with an amazing memory and ability to reel off every statistic under the sun, Des Voeux was one of those people that instantly irritates you. He walked round the office saying hello to a couple of the genuine – and surprised – secretaries in the office, before Alex managed to lure him out of the building.

But we seemed to have satisfied his curiosity, as later over drinks he said that he would talk to his boss Athole and try and fix a date for Sven to fly to Dubai to meet the Sheik. We offered to pay for first class flights and accommodation for Sven and Athole, hoping that Des Voeux – who we nicknamed Sherlock – would not tag along.

But we were out of luck. Athole asked if Des Voeux could come along too. He said he'd pay his own airfare and could doss down in the hotel bedroom we would arrange for Athole. I headed out to Dubai with my crew a few days earlier to make preparations for our VIP guests; but two days before Sven was due to fly out, I received a phone call from a police officer telling me that I must return to Britain immediately, as I was required to give evidence in a court case. He warned that if I didn't attend I would be guilty of contempt and could be banged up. I asked Alex to call Athole and break the news that the Sheik had to cancel the meeting for personal reasons. I was gutted, but not as much as Des Voeux who had purchased a non-refundable airline ticket.

The postponement of the Sven meeting only served to add to our credentials; after all, no reporter in the world would cancel a meeting with the England manager – it meant I had to be a real Sheik.

I re-booked Sven into the world's only seven-star hotel, the iconic Burj Al-Arab, in a £1,500-a-night suite. To keep costs down, I arranged for Athole and his sidekick Des Voeux to stay in the five-star Hyatt Grand in the centre of Dubai. Costs were shaved even further as, together with my team, I was staying at the less than luxurious three-star Al-Khaleej hotel, in Al-Nasser Square, a budget-priced favourite of back-packers.

By greasing a few palms I had arranged for Sven to be greeted on the tarmac as his plane landed and chauffeured over to a private terminal reserved only for visiting Royalty and dignitaries. He was also spared the usual immigration and customs checks. He and Athole were whisked to the Burj in a new Rolls Royce Phantom. I think this would have convinced even me I was in the presence of a real Sheik, if someone had laid all this on for me.

Alex showed him to his luxurious suite, number 1103, dripping with gold and marble and reeking with opulence; I thought that he would be used to such splendour but Sven was overwhelmed by the luxurious surroundings. As his personal butler showed him the bedroom, Sven, with a huge grin, commented on the large mirror above his super-king-sized bed. 'It's such a shame to be here alone.'

As Sven and Athole enjoyed lunch at the Al-Muntaha restaurant on the top floor with startling views of the Arabian coastline, our old friend Des Voeux was en-route too. He'd forked out again for another cut-price flight, landing in Abu Dhabi, about an hour's drive from Dubai. He would be coming over to join his colleagues by bus. From our previous encounter with Des Voeux, I knew that he could be a problem and would be on the lookout for any cracks in our façade; it is always annoying when agents and hangers-on insist on tagging along with the Sheik's guests.

Because Sven was bringing two of his sidekicks with him, I had to make sure I wasn't outnumbered, so along with my minders I had recruited Aseem Kazi, a Pakistani freelancer based in London, to fly over and join the Sheik's team of lackeys, alongside Alex.

I wasn't going to let Des Voeux disrupt my meeting with Sven and decided that the Sheik would just ignore him. I made my usual grand entrance spinning my worry beads in my hands while I was escorted to the bar at the Burj. Sven sat there wearing a smart suit next to Athole – a portly man who had negotiated his £8 million England contract – and Des Voeux.

Fortunately Des Voeux was severely jet-lagged and was almost nodding off. I took some pleasure in asking him how his journey had been, knowing full well that he'd endured a long and tiring economy class trip by plane and bus to get to the Burj. I asked him if he wanted to go to the room and go to sleep. He was very apologetic, bowing before me and calling me Sir.

We headed to the simulated underwater restaurant in the basement, the Al-Mahara, where we had booked an impressive private dining room. The conversation that unfolded over dinner surprised me and our army of football-loving readers; Sven hardly mentioned my supposed football academy, instead he was more interested in persuading me to bankroll a takeover of Aston Villa, and installing him as the new manager.

Sven and Athole ordered two bottles of vintage wine, Gaja & Rey 1999, costing a staggering £969 in total. As Sven tucked into crab cakes and a £138 rock lobster, he got down to business. Within an hour of meeting him, Sven brought up the idea of buying a club.

'You never thought about buying a club? Aston Villa is for sale,' said Sven. Together with Athole, he pointed out that the club was an excellent target for a takeover because its Chairman, Doug Ellis was elderly and in poor health. 'The Chairman is an old man today. He is sick,' said Sven. Athole claimed it would cost £25 million to get a controlling interest in the club and added, 'He is 83. He wants to go.' When I asked Sven if I would able to prise him away from England, he laughed and said: 'Everything is possible, but only at the end of the season.'

I asked Sven again if he was seriously interested in ditching the England job to take over Villa. I wanted to make sure that nothing was lost in translation, with his less than perfect English and my 'Arabic' accented English. But Sven was unequivocal; 'I'm not joking,' he said. 'You will not win the league in the first year but you will have to spend hundreds of millions,' he said. Some of his FA bosses, he said, didn't like foreigners. 'He's not English, he's earning too much money, he has too many scandals.' His England contract was supposed to last another two years but he added: 'After five and a half years ... it's a long time to be England manager. I always say, if it's coming a big club, a big club for me there are very few. Then I should like to go back to club football. But if you come in with a project, which is to be a big club, that is as interesting as a great club.'

It was hard to imagine that the mild-mannered Swede sat in front of me was revered as a sex god having bedded the likes of Ulrika Jonsson and Faria Alam. In case I didn't know about his sexual prowess, Sven almost proudly slipped in how the press had caught him cheating on his long-term lover Nancy Del'Olio. 'The problem is with the ladies. They sell the stories,' he complained. 'Women today they want to be married. And when you tell them no, that's not the meaning by this ...'

I was surprised that Sven, who seemed a cool calculating man, went on to make a series of indiscreet comments about players and managers to someone who may or may not have been a Sheik – but was certainly a complete stranger. I asked him about Sir Alex Ferguson who he said was good but would not get another job if he left Manchester United.

'It is difficult with Ferguson because the day he leaves Manchester United I don't think he can go anywhere else. I think when I came to England he has had maybe two or three teams since that time, he had good players. Butt and Scholes and Beckham ... a lot of English players. They came through the system but even when they became 25 he treated them like children.' Sven said that he thought Ferguson should have resigned after winning the treble. 'In one way it was a pity, after winning, he should have resigned and said goodbye. Because it must go down after that.'

We soon became good friends over the £1,714.73 meal, and Sven believed that he had found a wealthy future employer in me. After dinner I asked him if he wanted to enjoy the nightlife in Dubai, but he was tired and said he would have a quiet drink at the bar and go to sleep. Later it was reported that during the 'quiet drink in the bar', Sven had befriended Romanian cabaret singer Ruxandra Galeriu, who went on to become another of his stunning sexual conquests.

But I was not interested in his uncontrollable lust for beautiful women; we'd already filled enough pages of the paper with lurid details of his sex life. What was of concern was his shameless betrayal of the England team. I rang Andy Coulson, firstly to alert him to the massive bill that was heading his way for entertaining Sven, and to discuss a budget for lunch the next day. Andy suggested that I take Sven and his cronies for a Bedouin picnic in the desert, which would be relatively cheap, but I argued that it would be far more impressive if we took him on a yacht trip. Andy agreed, and put aside £2,000 for the yacht and £400 for the meal. So while Sven lay beneath his full-length mirror, we raced to Dubai marina and booked up the luxury 72-ft yacht *Eternity*, and ordered an Arabic lunch to be delivered on board by chefs at the Burj.

The following morning, exhausted by my night's work, I again donned my Arab robes and jumped aboard the yacht in time to greet Sven who arrived casually dressed for the boat trip. Athole was clutching his swimming trunks in a carrier bag, and Des Voeux had a broad grin on his face. He apologized once again for rudely nodding off during the dinner the night before. Sven headed for the bedroom below deck and changed into his shorts and blue England T-shirt.

We relaxed on the deck of the luxury yacht, Alex clutching a briefcase containing a concealed video camera that he positioned on the table opposite Sven. However, we hadn't anticipated that the sound of the yacht's noisy engine would be so loud that our tape recorders wouldn't pick up a thing. I asked the captain, who thought I really was a Sheik too, to turn off the motors and instructed Conrad to make sure the catering team from the Burj, who were to deliver our luncheon and drinks to the yacht, took their time. Otherwise we would have spent a fortune to record nothing but the droning of a diesel engine.

The delay in setting sail gave Sven a chance to discuss his terms for working for me; overnight, Sven had clearly been lying in bed thinking not only about Ruxandra, but his future career as a Premiership manager working for me. 'I have two more years with the FA and there I have £3 million net per year, plus bonuses. Now if I leave the FA, I should like to have a contract of three years.'

He explained that he wanted a three-year deal that would match Jose Mourinho's £5 million-a-year at Chelsea. He also wanted to bring along his Swedish pal Tord Grip, who he said was on £300,000 a year. When asked about annual bonuses, he suggested £200,000 to £300,000 a year for players if cups were won. For himself? 'A little larger than that.'

Then Sven promised to tap up David Beckham and bring him back to England as a Premiership captain. 'I'll phone Beckham,' he said. 'Beckham and I, we have a relationship like that [he crossed his fingers], we are friends, but a lot of respect.'

'Aston Villa will sell more shirts in one week than they did for the last ten years. And you are taking the captain of England back to England.' Underlining his own commitment to walk out on England and take over Villa, Sven added: 'If you have a very good project then he will be the first player we will take. I think so.'

Even with my limited knowledge of football, I realized that news that Beckham wanted to leave Real Madrid in Spain and come back to play in Britain would make headlines in sports pages and TV bulletins up

> **'Sven, with a huge grin, commented on the large mirror above his super-king-sized bed, "It's such a shame to be here alone."**

and down the country. So I quizzed Sven about it further. 'I know for sure he wants to come back to England,' he told me. 'If it is a London club, he will come back tomorrow. And it's up to me to convince him that Birmingham is the right place to be. That would be a good start for you. Monday I spoke to him, and I spoke to him about this. Not about Aston Villa.'

I asked why Beckham was so keen to get back to Britain. 'Because it is his third season never winning anything. And he can't see things going to be better. Some of the big stars are getting older, like Roberto

Carlos and Zidane, and he has had five managers in three and a half years. He went there to win. He wants to come to England because he is a bit frustrated. If you buy the club and the first signing is David Beckham … he will finish his career in Aston Villa.'

In another exchange Sven revealed his massive personal admiration for Beckham. He said: 'You know that David Beckham is very, very special. He's a nice boy, he's always shy. Probably very nice looking, according to all the ladies. Every age with the ladies, they can be 70 or 17, it doesn't matter. So when we go around with England and Beckham is not there everything is quiet.' Sven sounded a little wistful, as if he personally missed the furore Beckham created wherever he went. 'I'm not talking in the team but around the team, outside the hotel and things. No one is coming. If Beckham is there, thousands and thousands.'

As the food from the Burj turned up, Sven sensationally claimed top Premiership clubs were riddled with corruption. He named several managers who he alleged were taking bungs in player transfer scams.

When the yacht finally sailed, Sven headed to the top deck to take in views of the Dubai coastline. Athole, a former professional swimmer, put on his swimming trunks and dived into the warm Gulf waters.

Meanwhile Sven continued to spill the secrets of Britain's top players as he tried to curry favour with me. He claimed Wayne Rooney had a temper. 'He's coming from a poor family, a very rough area. His father was a boxer, he could have been a boxer as well.' He went on to claim that Rio Ferdinand was 'not in good shape', Chelsea had 'paid too much' for Shaun Wright-Phillips, Ryan Giggs 'wished he could have played for England', and that Michael Owen was 'not happy' playing for Newcastle United but had gone there 'simply for the money'.

As he ranted on, I was thinking the two-faced football coach would have to ring a lot of people to apologize once my story was published. But at least I spared him the ear bashing he would have got back home from his long-suffering partner Nancy Del'Olio by not mentioning Ruxandra or revealing that he told me he would never marry Nancy. Sven described his lawyer girlfriend – who stood by him despite flings with Ulrika Jonsson and FA secretary Faria Alam – as 'a fiery Italian' and claimed she was 'very jealous.' As he lounged on the top deck and ate the Arabian mezze, I asked if Nancy was understanding. He replied: 'No she's not! She's Italian!'

He said that she kept a close eye on him since he had been caught with his pants down. 'But she's the kind of woman, she's learned marking, it's man to man. It's tight,' he said describing her revised game plan. Asked if he would ever consider marrying her, Sven said: 'No I tried it once. Never again.' As the yacht sailed on, I pointed out the gold souk and asked him if he wanted to buy a gift from Dubai to take back for Nancy. Sven said: 'No. Just gave her for Christmas, that's enough now. She knows how to shop by herself. She has everything. The dressing room, you should see it.'

I reminded him that Dubai was a tax-free haven where gold jewellery was particularly cheap and I could show him round if he wanted anything for Nancy. 'No absolutely none! All over!' he said. It would have been fine if he'd said yes, as I could easily have laid on a trip round the souk with a limo and driver; I have a family friend who owns a shopping mall there and I could have called in a favour and made it look as if it were my own mall, if necessary. But Sven had had enough of spending money. He told me how Nancy had inherited her shopping gene from her grandmother who had recently died at the age of 102 years old. 'Even when she was 100, every day, she has high heels shoes,' said Sven. '100 years old. Shopping bag there, and some mascara.' I told him that to be well presented was very much an Italian trait, to which he replied: 'But the woman I have is the most Italian of every Italian you can find.'

As bottles of Dom Perignon were cracked open, Sven asked me for a personal favour. He wanted me to give his daughter a job with my company in Dubai; I thought to myself, he'll be looking for a job himself after I had finished my piece. Ironically he told me how Prime Minister Tony Blair had joked with him about how long Sven would keep his job as England coach. 'The first time I met him was about six months after I took the job, and he said, "Welcome to England. Shall we take a bet?" "On what?" "Who is going to keep the job the longest time – you or me?"' laughed Sven. 'He said we have two impossible jobs! When we qualified for the World Cup, and before that when we lost against Northern Ireland, all the shit came out about my private life. So when we qualified, on my desk was a long, handwritten letter from Tony Blair.'

He also mentioned his connection with Prince William, the President of the Football Association, and reminded me that he is an Aston Villa fan. 'He came into the office a couple of months ago. You will see, he is very nice. And he is an Aston Villa fan.'

Before leaving, Sven arranged to meet me for further secret talks in London the following week. As the vessel returned to Dubai marina, Conrad stood at the shore discreetly taking photographs as Sven shook my hand before he disembarked. As soon as Sven was whisked away in a waiting limo, Conrad jumped on board and asked: 'How did it go?'

I told him that we had got some amazing quotes from Sven. Conrad replied: 'No I meant, did you manage to survive the trip without your headdress falling off!'

I'd forgotten all about that in the midst of Sven's amazing indiscretions.

I headed back to the Burj to settle the bill, and to pick up the expensive aftershaves and creams that are left for guests in every suite. But to my surprise the chambermaid told me: 'Your guest has taken everything. He's even taken all the pens!'

Back in London, Andy faced a difficult editorial decision over my Sven exposé. If our tone wasn't right, we would offend England fans and infuriate readers. It would look as if we were undermining our national side in the run-up to the World Cup. We rang Athole to break the news to him that I was the Fake Sheik and the Aston Villa deal was off. Shocked, Athole told our sports editor Mike Dunn: 'It's such a shame because we all had such a lovely weekend in Dubai!'

In the end, the vast majority of our readers and sports commentators agreed that Sven had proven to be so devious and treacherous that he warranted being exposed. The article also resulted in an urgent FA inquiry into the alleged corrupt managers that Sven had mentioned. In a television interview after his sacking, Sven blamed me for ending his England managerial career. I was happy to take full responsibility; England's legions of loyal fans had the right to expect the man in charge to put his heart and soul into the job!

But Sven's name was never far from the front page of the *News of the World*, especially when I exposed his former lover, Bangladeshi beauty Faria Alam, as a £8,000-a-night hooker.

I first met Faria in May 2005 in New York, almost a year after the original Svengate scandal, in which details of her three-month affair with the England coach emerged, netting her over £500,000. Now she claimed that Sven, who was touring the States with the England team, had phoned her asking if he could meet her while he was in New York. Sven knew her kiss-and-tell history, and this was at a time when Faria was suing the FA for unfair dismissal and sexual harassment; it meant that either Sven was madly in love with her, or simply barking mad. In the end Sven thought better of it and didn't show up to meet Faria. I wrote a story about the aborted secret tryst and Faria's undying love for the slippery Swede. It was a strange but highly lucrative kind of love, considering she had been sleeping with FA boss Mark Palios as well as Sven.

Faria was extremely attractive for her age and had a sense of humour to match; I could see how her twinkling Eastern eyes would easily seduce men. Over lunch at a café in downtown Manhattan – where she was working for a fashion label – we were constantly interrupted by phone calls on both of her US mobile phones. She would excuse herself and walk away, but I could hear her purring down the phone to callers in an artificial husky voice calling them all 'Darling'. I saw her jotting down addresses in her small notebook.

I'd seen this behaviour before, and I was pretty sure I knew what it meant. Either she'd suddenly become a high-powered executive in the States, or she was on the game.

I reported my suspicions to deputy editor Neil Wallis. Northerner Wallis had joined the *News of the World* after a stint as editor of the *People*. A hardcore newsman through and through, the type that has no care for political correctness, Neil is loud, blunt but invariably right. Through his sources Neil too had heard that Faria was working as a high-class hooker; but she was a friend of the paper, knew a lot of the reporters and executives, and would be a hard case to crack.

It was the kind of challenge I welcomed. I instructed Alex to contact Faria posing as a TV executive interested in signing her up as a presenter (she'd already done a Princess Diana-style interview on Sky TV about her relationship with Sven, and appeared in *Celebrity Big Brother* alongside George "Pussycat" Galloway). She appeared to love fame and bright lights almost as much as she loved money.

Faria went for dinner with Alex at the Jumeria Carlton Tower hotel in Knightsbridge. At the end of the dinner, the head of the fictitious TV empire, American Tommy Bryant – another undercover reporter – made a cameo appearance. As he left, Alex told her that millionaire Tommy was an international playboy whose life revolved around high-class escorts and casinos. Her ears pricked up and she casually asked how much he usually paid for liaisons with his female friends.

Later Alex told her that Tommy wanted to spend a night with her and asked her if she would be interested. She was. Another dinner was arranged at the Bombay Brasserie in south Kensington, where Faria got straight down to business and shocked diners on nearby tables as she spoke loudly about her sexual services. She bragged about her 'party trick', an oral sex technique she had perfected by practising on a candle, which she said had received full endorsement from Sven. As well as detailing her lesbian experiences, she also confessed to having taken cocaine.

I was waiting in our surveillance van outside as Faria turned up at our £600-a-night apartment in Knightsbridge to meet Tommy; I sat watching the scenes taking place in the luxury apartment on a small TV monitor. First, Faria demanded Alex pay her £8,000 fee in cash. 'I'm pretty good at what I do. It's business darling I tell you,' she said as she counted the money before stuffing the notes into her designer handbag. She promised a wild sex session including spanking.

As Tommy arrived, and Alex left, Faria sipped a glass of Joseph Perrier Cuvée Brut champagne and then headed to the bedroom. There she took off her black jeans and black sequined Indian top to reveal a designer cream bra and knickers. Tommy walked into the bedroom, made the traditional *News of the World* excuse, and sent Faria packing.

I rang to confront her the following day as she attended a celebrity bash at the Hilton hotel in Park Lane. I was not surprised when she upheld that old Asian tradition and denied the allegations completely. 'Maz, you and I are friends, I wouldn't lie to you. You have got to help me. Someone is obviously trying to make some cheap money here,' she said.

She tried to convince me that she'd spent the night at home, but when I told there was audio and visual evidence that proved otherwise, she suddenly remembered that she had gone to see a 'friend' at an apartment in Mayfair but continued to deny that she had been paid £8,000 for sex.

The story marked the end of her reign as a kiss-and-tell celebrity.

CHAPTER 16

THE PRINCESS AND THE CAT FLAPS

The dark green Twin Squirrel helicopter gently touched down on the grass landing pad in the quaint parish of Bisley-with-Lypiatt, Gloucestershire, in the grounds of a 17th-century manor house. Out stepped the dashing Arab Sheik, resplendent in his white robes and head-scarf, accompanied by two personal assistants and a bodyguard. A beautiful princess was staring out of an upstairs bedroom window, eagerly waiting for the Sheik to arrive. She had handpicked her favourite yellow rose to present to him as he entered the wrought-iron gates of her mansion.

It could well have been the start of a romantic novel, except that I was the Sheik, and my grand entrance was marred by the downdraft from the huge rotor blades of the chartered helicopter, which sent my headscarf flying. As my bodyguard, a former police officer, reached into the small baggage hold to retrieve a briefcase containing a hidden video camera, my 'assistant' Aseem Kazi unceremoniously dragged me out of view to the back of the chopper. 'Your headscarf is all over the place. You walk in like that and she'll suss you in seconds,' warned Aseem. It took what seemed like an eternity to re-adjust the small cap underneath my red chequered headscarf and to firmly clamp it to my head with the black rings.

The housekeeper, David, approached our helicopter and shook hands with my assistant Alex and greeted William Duckworth-Chad, the estate agent showing the home who had flown with us. In a display of appropriate Sheik-like arrogance – one of the great things about being the Sheik is that you can use the haughtiness people expect you to have to get through almost any social situation – I barely acknowledged the servant and simply strolled behind him towards the imposing property.

It was Nether Lypiatt, the country home of Prince and Princess Michael of Kent, which had been on the market for several months for £6 million but hadn't attracted any buyers. A couple of phone calls and emails to Duckworth-Chad of the Country Department of top estate agents Savills is all it took to arrange a viewing. This was a massive security blunder; even though I was using a false name, Sheik Mohammed Al-Rashid, and claimed to own a completely fictitious company, the Al-Jamal group in Dubai, I was invited not just to rub shoulders with senior members of the Royal family but to visit them in their own home.

The Princess was so excited at the prospect of a wealthy Sheik buying her home at an over-inflated price, that she'd asked Duckworth-Chad if I'd like to join her and her husband for a spot of tea when I visited. It was an invitation that I wouldn't miss for the world, and it didn't disappoint; but like most jobs that seem easy, it wasn't without its unique complications. A few months earlier I'd had dinner with her son Lord Frederick Windsor at the Savoy. It was part of an ongoing inquiry into a VIP concierge service set up by Ben Elliot, nephew of Camilla, Duchess of Cornwall. The private members club, Quintessentially, was run by Britain's new-generation aristocracy, with Tom Parker Bowles and Zac Goldsmith helping to provide an 'efficient and discreet service' to their clients. They claimed to have airlifted elm tea bags to Madonna and found a dozen albino peacocks for a Jennifer Lopez party.

I'd been tipped off that one of their account managers, Aurelien Goldstein, was taking Quintessentially's pledge 'to provide just about anything for their members' a little too far, as he was supplying cocaine at £100 a gram to his upper-crust clients. Besides breaking the law he was ripping them off to boot, as the going rate for coke was £50 a gram.

It was a classic *News of the World* story, made even better by the fact that Freddie Windsor was working for the company run by his pals. I invited him to dinner posing as the Sheik, to discuss signing up to the concierge service. He was a very pleasant, well-mannered young man, who belied his reputation as a wayward Royal seen leaving nightclubs looking the worse for wear. Old Etonian Freddie was regarded as a bad influence on his friend Prince William after he had confessed to taking cocaine. 'I admit it is true. It is very difficult to avoid getting into this sort of thing when you move in these circles. But I don't blame anyone else for the incident,' admitted Freddie, after being caught sniffing lines of white powder off a magazine.

> ❛It had been like having high tea with Del Boy and the Princess had tried to flog me everything including the kitchen sink and a white tiger!❜

Freddie, who was wearing a bespoke pin-stripe suit and a tie with a giant knot, told me how he had put his wild days behind him and was concentrating on studying towards a career in the legal profession. 'I have now rejected that side of life and I'm going to commit myself to my studies.' After the meeting I concentrated my efforts on trying to persuade my bosses to part with the £24,000 joining fee to have my own dedicated 24-hour concierge who would cater for all my needs around the world. It was purely a business decision for editor Andy Coulson and managing editor Stuart Kuttner. It would cost over £30,000 to pick up the tabs for hotel suites, flights, and the Sheik's entourage, to investigate my tip-off.

There was of course the possibility that the allegations would prove unfounded, and even if true, unless Freddie himself was involved in drug dealing – something I knew after that dinner he would never do – the story wouldn't warrant the front page. The job was put on hold and eager Quintessentially staff were getting impatient as my assistant Alex fobbed them off. It turned to suspicion as Harry Becher, who worked for the company and who'd attended my dinner with Freddie, approached our accommodation address in Piccadilly and called our rented office in Dubai to try and track down the Sheik.

A short while later my colleagues at the *Sunday Times* carried out their own investigation into Quintessentially. They'd taken advantage of the cut-price 'dedicated service' costing a mere £2,500 a year and got alongside Aurelien Goldstein at the Cannes film festival. He offered to supply their undercover reporter 30 grams of cocaine for a party as well as prostitutes. It was a great story, and I was pleased to see it out there.

So as I stood in the courtyard of his home beside the ornate fountain, I knew there was a chance that I would bump into Freddie. As a prospective buyer, I would be shown around the whole house. As I twirled my worry beads, I pondered what would be more humiliating, my Arab headscarf falling off or being recognized by Freddie.

I was shown round the eight-bedroom Cotswolds manor house – set in 36 acres, complete with outhouses and stables – by a cheerful Duckworth-Chad. The house was littered with antiques, paintings, ornaments, and family photographs of the Royals. There was a photo of Prince Michael together with the Pope and Princess Diana on a side table in the main living room. Duckworth-Chad showed me the Princess's personal office, which had wall-to-wall bookshelves and an assortment of framed cartoons. We walked up a magnificent William and Mary staircase, to Princess Michael's bedroom, which was pan-elled in oak and had a four-poster bed as its centrepiece.

My heart was beating fast as the moment arrived when I was led across the paved courtyard past a gazebo to Freddie's quarters in an annex. Princess Michael had moved him out of the house 'because his music was too loud,' as she told me later. I asked Alex and Aseem to lead the way, while I strategically lagged behind admiring a portrait on the wall. 'It's clear,' whispered Alex. 'He's not here!'

Relieved, I strolled into the self-contained apartment, which had a small study on the ground floor, while upstairs was a spacious lounge, with Freddie's CDs stacked up on shelves next to a piano. Above his bed in the wooden-beamed loft bedroom was his collection of model planes.

Outside, we strolled on beautiful manicured lawns, and came across Princess Michael, dressed in a simple red frock, in the rose garden pruning the roses. 'How do you do? It's a pleasure to meet you,' she said as she took off her gardening gloves and shook my hand and greeted my entourage.

I told her it was a lovely house and asked her why she was selling it. 'It's because we can't afford two houses. We live in Kensington Palace, we're only here at weekends. My husband doesn't get paid anything for doing all the work that he does. We simply can't do it anymore. Most weekends in the summer months we have to do Royal duties, you know,' she said.

I expressed my surprise that a member of the Royal family should be so hard up, particularly since I knew the Queen had granted her rooms at Kensington Palace to the tune of £120,000 a year. 'The Queen is very rich but my husband is a second son. That doesn't occur in your part of the world. In England when you are a second son, you get nothing. And we're getting older.' The Princess – dubbed 'Princess Pushy' because of her rampant ego – carried on: 'You have to work very hard, you know, because you get nothing in England. It's the custom. The government doesn't pay a penny. We do all our own charity work on our own expense. You know, I just can't do it anymore. The children have grown up and we've both got bad backs. Gardening doesn't help. So we can't ride anymore really. I love the horses. I'm going to give them all away.'

The sale of the Grade I listed building that she bought for £300,000 in 1981 and was seeking to flog to me for a cool £6 million would certainly help fill her coffers. 'I love this house. It's been my passion for 25 years. Before I married I was an interior designer, and when I married they said it's not appropriate for a Royal Princess to be in trade. And so I had to give it up and I could only do my own house. But this was a ruin when we got it,' she said.

She pointed out that Prince Charles was in nearby Highgrove and Princess Anne in Gatcombe Park. 'We make a triangle you see. We're very close to Highgrove and to Gatcombe. It's ten miles each way, and we would see a lot of one another obviously. I adore Princess Anne and Prince Charles, our children get on very well; we do live rather close to each other. But all of us live in the Palace. Princess Anne has an apartment at Buckingham Palace, Prince Charles has his at Clarence House, the Queen Mother's place. We live in Kensington Palace, we have one little bit of Kensington Palace, next door to Diana.' But the visiting had come to an end: 'We just can't do it anymore. We're getting on you know, we're getting on. We're Old Age Pensioners now.'

I looked at Alex and Aseem in disbelief. We'd simply come to look round the house and here was a member of the Royal family whinging like a grumpy pensioner to complete strangers.

Then she leaned over, cut a yellow rose and handed it to me. 'This is the Princess Michael of Kent Rose, there you are. And it says in the catalogue that Princess Michael of Kent resists black spot and mildew,' she told me proudly. She told me she used to breed racehorses and had once been invited by Sheik Maktoum to attend the Gold Cup in Dubai. She asked me if, like my fellow Sheiks, I was involved in racing. 'Yes but only camels!' I told her, hoping to hide my ignorance about the sport. But she was delighted with the news: 'My husband owns a racing camel!' I prayed the topic wouldn't come up over tea, as I knew even less about camel racing.

After a stroll around the extensive gardens, we entered the impressive breakfast room where Prince Michael warmly greeted us. He was casually dressed in a blue shirt and trousers. 'I'm pleased that you're able to come. I know your part of the world but I haven't been to Dubai for many years,' said the Prince. We sat down at the small round dining table. Princess Michael gave me a book, *The Royal Homes In Gloucestershire*, which had a chapter dedicated to the history of Nether Lypiatt – an attempt to pass off her home as a Royal residence on a par with Highgrove and Gatcombe.

Over tea and homemade cake, Princess Michael was as indiscreet as I'd hoped for. I feigned a lack of knowledge about the royals and asked if she thought Charles had loved Diana or not. She told me how

Charles was under pressure to find a wife. This is how the taped conversation went – eight years to the day since Diana died.

> **PRINCESS:** 'He was under pressure from the press, pressure from the public. He had to have an heir. He couldn't marry the woman that he wanted to marry so he married, what Napoleon said when he married Marie Louise, he married a womb.'
>
> **SHEIK (in a puzzled tone):** 'He married a … womb?'
>
> **PRINCESS:** 'A womb. In other words, somebody to give him children. You see in the past that would have been all right. That's what people did. She was in love with him. But his heart was somewhere else. And so unfortunately, this broke Diana's heart and made her strange. If she had been loved I believe she would have been a different woman, not the woman she became through bitterness.'

We all sipped our tea while I absorbed her revelations. The Princess put her cup down and told me how she knew for sure that Diana had discovered Charles's infidelity on their honeymoon.

> **PRINCESS:** 'He didn't love her and she loved him. When you're a young girl and you marry a man for love and you discover on the honeymoon he's talking to the other woman on the phone, and saying, "No matter what, I will always love you" to Camilla. And Diana picked up an extension and heard that. And Diana thought because she's young and beautiful he will forget about Camilla and love her, but he didn't.'
>
> **SHEIK:** 'He was cruel?'
>
> **PRINCESS:** 'No. He was very sweet with her. But she was nasty because she found out. Her attitude was, "The whole world loves me, why don't you?" He was jealous of her success, you see. She was like … superstar.'

I said I'd heard Camilla was nice.

PRINCESS: 'My mother used to say to me, nice is very easy. It's easy to be nice. I mean "you" might be horrible, but you're being nice to me.' She went on, 'Women don't understand how men think. I don't understand it because I thought she [Diana] was wonderful. I was very close to her. Life moves on, Camilla will be our Queen and that's the way it will be,' she stated. 'It was difficult for her [the Queen] to accept this marriage, it is still difficult.'

What the Princess, though, had forgotten to say about her relationship with the Royal family was that while it was true that Anne and Charles both lived within ten miles of the Kents' estate, Charles was furious when he discovered the Kents were buying a property near Highgrove – because he can't stand her. And it seemed to have slipped her mind that Anne has never been known to visit Nether Lypiatt and is credited with inventing the 'Princess Pushy' tag.

But most surprising was her sales pitch: only her cut-glass Royal accent stopped her from sounding like Del Boy from *Only Fools and Horses*, as she tried to sell me the furniture in the mansion, redecorate the place for me, open a supermarket in Dubai and even do a lecture tour to earn a few quid. And just when I thought she'd run out of things to sell me the Princess tried to knock out a rare white tiger.

'I'd even sell the furniture; we can leave an awful lot, 90 per cent, I think. But obviously you would have to come to an arrangement about how to buy the things I leave.' She offered to throw in tea services and bed linen if I bought the place, saying that she would help me replace anything she took – but only if I employed her to do it: 'What we don't leave I'd be prepared to replace for you in my taste. I know where to get everything so you're walking into a house fully furnished.'

Looking around the room she pointed at some plates on the wall. 'I mean, for example, here is an early 18th-century dinner service. It's particularly beautiful. But does it stay or does it go? Do you know what I mean? I mean, things like bedclothes, which are such a bore to get. You could employ me to get it all for you. We're not shy to talk about money!' laughed the Princess. She was dead right about that.

Princess Michael also promoted herself as a writer, claiming to be 'hugely successful in France' and a lecturer. She offered to do a lecture tour of Dubai for the Sheik. 'I write books and give lectures; I'm a professional lecturer. I should come and lecture in Dubai. I lecture all over the world. I'm lecturing in Russia next month which I've done before.' She asked me to look at her website and browse though the forty-seven lectures listed. 'It's a one-hour, one-woman show but I'm very good, as you can imagine,' she boasted.

'I can write anything. I don't usually discuss fees. But it's £25,000 to speak. Is that not enough? Shall I do more? And expenses? Well you have to get me out there and my lady-in-waiting. And you'll have to house me comfortably.' She added, 'You know, times have changed and I know exactly that we're worth a lot but I don't want to be greedy either. That's why I haven't put my fees up as a lecturer.'

Meanwhile her husband Prince Michael spent his time moaning to Aseem how Royals are no longer respected. 'Not only the deference has very much gone, the whole thing of tradition and history – all the things that we grew up to think were the right priorities – have all been dismissed as of no importance,' he sighed.

The Princess quickly popped out and returned clutching a copy of her latest book to prove she was an established writer. She signed a copy of the book, *The Serpent and The Moon*. 'The British Royal family only sign with their first name, because that's our legal signature,' she said, as she signed her name Marie Christine.

And when I offered her the chance to do interior design on the Sheik's hotel complex in Sri Lanka, the Princess said she'd give it the royal stamp of approval. I asked her if I would be able to say in publicity that the premises had been designed by Her Royal Highness. She said: 'Absolutely, absolutely!' And then the Princess started angling for a cut-price Middle East palace. 'I don't want to be here in the winter any more. Maybe you can find me a nice little, not too expensive, residence in Dubai?' she asked.

She also tried to interest me in buying an exotic pet – offering to get me a white tiger from showbiz pals Siegfried and Roy, who used the animals in shows at the Mirage casino in Las Vegas. 'They sell, you know. I could introduce you to them easily,' promised Princess Michael. 'I've got photographs of myself feeding little white tiger kittens. I can email them to you,' she said.

Before I left, the Princess had another gift for me – two pots of the homemade raspberry jam we'd enjoyed at tea; later I gave them to Andy Coulson. But as she handed them over, she had another dig at Prince Charles, criticizing his range of organic foods. The Prince is one of the biggest producers in the country with his Duchy Originals range, but the Princess sniffed: 'This is made with my own raspberries. He doesn't make it himself; he's got factories doing it. It's just got his name on it!'

Clutching my pots of Royal jam, and on my way back to the helicopter, I looked at Alex and we both burst out in a fit of laughter. But I had to control my giggles (as well as my headscarf) as Duckworth-Chad climbed on board with us. The Prince and Princess waved us off as I hovered over their country estate in my chopper. As soon as I landed at Elstree aerodrome, I phoned Andy Coulson, who was keen to know how the meeting had gone. I told him that it had been like having high tea with Del Boy and that the Princess had tried to flog me everything including the kitchen sink and a white tiger! He thought I was joking, however, by the time I reached the office, a polite email, addressed to one of the many dummy accounts we have set up, had landed in my inbox from the Princess, saying how pleased she had been to meet me. A photograph of her with a white tiger cub was attached.

Keen to clinch the property deal with the Sheik, she emailed me again a couple of days later and suggested meeting for dinner or drinks in London. Her email read:

'I am leaving for Budapest on Saturday morning and on to Madrid on Monday morning for the rest of the week. My husband is not travelling with me and will be in London, but should you wish to meet with us both before the week after next, can I suggest tomorrow, Friday evening for drinks or dinner? My husband was planning to leave for

Nether Lypiatt on Saturday morning after dropping me at Northolt airport.

With very best wishes, Princess Michael

PS I have sent an email to Siegfried and Roy to ask about a white tiger. Where would Mr Al-Rashid plan to house it? I know Siegfried and Roy always ask for these details. Once they reply I will put you in touch direct.'

I arranged to meet her again for dinner at Claridge's. The Royal couple drove from Kensington Palace in their black Bentley Armitage. The Prince, wearing a blue double-breasted suit with a blue tie and the Princess, in a beige designer dress complete with pearl necklace, were ushered up to my lavish penthouse suite. She was disappointed that I wasn't wearing my 'romantic' Arab robes and had opted for a more traditional Gieves and Hawkes suit instead (my own, of course, not bought on expenses). 'Women have a thing about uniforms,' she explained. 'You look very romantic in your Arab robes.'

The Princess ordered seared foie gras with Charentais melon followed by roast halibut with Swiss chard, caper and raisin emulsion. He ate creamed sweet shallot soup with blue cheese crouton followed by the halibut.

Over dinner, conversation again turned to other Royals. She leapt to the defence of Prince Harry who had been photographed wearing a swastika at a fancy dress party.

The Princess, whose father Baron Günther von Reibnitz was a Nazi, said, 'He will never live it down. But I believe if he had been wearing the hammer and sickle there wouldn't have been so much fuss made. And yet what does a hammer and sickle stand for? Russia, Stalin.'

After dinner, in the lounge, Princess Michael served the Sheik coffee: 'I'll be mother,' she said as she passed round a tray of biscuits. She discussed Mohamed Al-Fayed's campaign accusing the Royal family of colluding with MI6 to murder Diana and his son Dodi. 'I'm very fond of him, it's very sad. But I think his grief drove him to say foolish things,' she said. In her case it was purely greed that drove her to say foolish things.

My story appeared over five pages headlined: *Pushy Sells Out Royals – Fake Sheik Strikes Again*. It must have caused the already unpopular Princess gross embarrassment. In an interview in the *Observer* a few weeks later Princess Michael was asked about the Fake Sheik. She said: 'He was so, so charming. Absolutely delightful.' Asked if she could see the funny side of it, she replied: 'I think I might find it funny in a few years time. The thing was it was so sad because they were just the perfect buyers. He didn't want to change a thing. There are people who have come to look who say, "Ooh, all the doors are crooked". Well, you want to point out, it's a 17th-century house. But it was wonderful to have this gentleman say how much he loved all my decoration. I asked: will you keep the cat flaps? And yes! He loved cats!'

CHAPTER 17

AN ETIQUETTE LESSON

The men's toilets on the mezzanine floor of the world's most luxurious hotel, the Burj Al-Arab, are very nice. They ooze opulence with gold taps, an ornate Italian marble floor, and gold embroidered hand towels. A pleasant fruity fragrance is pumped into the air, while in between the Roman pillars are two seascapes made from a mosaic of tiny marble tiles that would not look out of place in an art gallery. But there's only so long that a Sheik and his minders can hide in any toilet no matter how luxurious. After 25 minutes of nipping in and out of the cubicle every time somebody came into the toilet, my patience was wearing thin.

Former Royal butler Paul Burrell was on his way down from his £1,500-a-night suite to join me for dinner at the hotel's Al-Mahara seafood restaurant. As the Sheik I wanted to make a grand entrance, I didn't want to be sitting in the bar or at the restaurant table waiting for a butler. Since I was claiming to live in Dubai I wouldn't have a room at the Burj myself – not that the *News of the World*'s budget would allow it, anyway.

And there was one other complication. The head concierge Olivier Raveyre, who had been extremely helpful in arranging limos and a yacht during my Sven-Goran Eriksson exposé a few months earlier, now knew I was the Fake Sheik. The Frenchman, who was a big football fan, was roaming around the hotel and would recognize me. He could easily blow my cover if he spotted me. I had to stay low.

My minder, former Scots Guard John Miller, left the toilet and returned a few minutes later: 'You won't believe this, Burrell is all over a gay Filipino guy that works at the hotel. He's been standing there chatting him up for the last ten minutes. He's telling him all about how he worked with Diana.' I sent Alex to nip the flirting in the bud and to escort him to the underwater restaurant.

Burrell was smartly dressed in a grey Savile Row suit and hand-made shirt, complete with cuff links he claimed had been given to him by Princess Diana. 'She said, "whenever you're on duty and you think you're representing me, you wear them." They're just plain silver and enamel with her initial. I always wear them when I'm on duty. She had them made at Asprey.' He tried to sound casual, but he immediately struck me as a pompous man with an ego far bigger than any of the Royals he had served, more royal than the Royals. 'I'm unique, there's only one of me in the world. I'm the living Jeeves,' he said. 'No one can touch me. I feel invincible.'

I had invited Burrell to Dubai following a tip from a reliable Royal source, as I was told that Princes William and Harry were outraged that Burrell was continuing to betray Diana's memory. It was also alleged that he was selling some of the Princess's personal posses-sions to wealthy collectors (although in 2002 he had been acquitted of stealing 310 items from her personal estate).

My colleague Alex had first met Burrell as he stood smiling behind a small table in an aisle in a supermarket in St Petersburg, Florida, pro-moting his new range of cheap wines, 'The Royal Butler Collection'. A scruffy American lad dressed as a beefeater, bizarrely wearing a bearskin, stood beside him as Burrell handed out free samples of his wine to elderly shoppers.

Burrell has two sons, Alexander and Nicholas, who are being edu-cated at American universities, and lives between his two luxurious homes. He owns a quaint Georgian cottage in Farndon, Cheshire where his wife Maria lives; he also has a lavish five-bedroom home in Florida complete with swimming pool, hot-spa, and Cadillac with per-sonalized 'PB' number plates in the drive. He has penned two books about Diana. *A Royal Duty* made him an overnight millionaire gross-ing around £8 million, while *The Way We Were – Remembering Diana*, is estimated to have earned him at least another million. He also pocketed £50,000 from Diana's will after her death and has continually topped up his earnings with lucrative media deals, including an appearance in *I'm a Celebrity … Get Me Out Of Here!*

After his first book, Princes William and Harry pleaded with Burrell to end his betrayal. Prince William made a formal statement: 'We cannot believe that Paul, who was entrusted with so much, could abuse his position in such a cold and overt betrayal. It is not only deeply painful for the two of us but also for everyone else affected and it would mortify our mother if she were alive today. If we may say so, we feel we are more able to speak for our mother than Paul. We ask Paul, please to bring these revelations to an end.'

But those pleas fell on deaf ears, as the butler was still eager to make more cash. When Alex told Burrell that he worked for a wealthy Middle Eastern investor, his eyes lit up at the prospect of swelling his fortune even further. He readily accepted my invitation to fly to Dubai to discuss various business projects accompanied by his agent Chris Kirby. Within seconds of meeting him Burrell boasted about his Royal connections, claiming he would be attending the Kentucky Derby the following month where the Queen would also be present.

As aperitifs were served at the restaurant, Burrell carried on talking about Diana: 'She called me her rock. She said: "Paul you are the only man I have ever trusted." I'm finding ten years on, we're entering the tenth anniversary year of her death, August is the tenth anniversary, and I find that it's taken me ten years to come to this place and this time to be able to say this is me, and this is what I'm doing, and I'm very happy to do it.'

Burrell claimed that he had shared a very close relationship with the Princes when they were children: 'I was a surrogate father. I was a surrogate uncle, whatever you like to call it.' Burrell branded Prince Charles as being 'mentally dysfunctional' and criticized his parenting skills. 'Charles is a bully. In his world, remember, in his world he is god and no one says no. Everyone says yes. He has a man every morning squeeze his toothpaste onto his brush,' he said. 'The Queen is grounded and she doesn't understand where her son has gone wrong.'

He said that Prince Charles hadn't been able to give his sons love in the way that Princess Diana did, with Harry particularly suffering. 'Harry had to go through it alone, because his father isn't tactile. He doesn't touch them, he doesn't love them, he doesn't put his arms around them and smother them with kisses ... but then that's his upbringing, he's been brought up that way. He was born to be King and perhaps that's the one title that will elude him. Isn't that ironic?'

Burrell claimed that William and Harry had both been 'brainwashed' by the Royal family: 'They live in their father's world now and they have to accept their father's rules. Their mother's world disappeared on 31 August 1997 and everyone in it. People within the Royal family say you have to follow the rulebook, you have to follow the guidelines, you cannot waver from the path. This is the way it's always been, this is the way it will always be. Don't step out of line. Now they are brainwashing William and Harry in that way, well especially William. He cannot step out of line, he never steps out of line. His brother does, but he doesn't, he can't, because the health, the longevity of the Royal family depends on an heir, and the heir is William, and he has to stand strong. He has little to do with Camilla, very little to do with Camilla, but he has to toe the party line.'

As the waiter brought a basket of bread to the table, Burrell demonstrated the correct way to tear a bread roll and butter it. His free masterclass in bread-eating protocol was welcome, as guests attending one of his etiquette weekends to learn airs and graces from Burrell were charged £279 each for the privilege.

Burrell moved on to lobster for his main course, while he elaborated on his earlier remarks about Prince Charles. 'I don't think we are ever going to see King Charles and Queen Camilla. I think behind closed doors some agreement was reached because there is no way the Queen is going to leave the throne to Charles and Camilla, no way. So I think they came to an agreement; Charles said he wanted to marry Camilla, the Queen and the Duke of Edinburgh said to him "that's fine". The Queen would say "well that's fine, so when I die ..."

and she will die Queen, "when I die then you will say you renounce your rights to the throne in favour of your son." There will be no abdication, Charles will just say I'm too old, and he will be seventy-something.'

Burrell said he had been driven to exhaustion by Prince Charles's bizarre demands when he worked for him. 'He's been treated like a god and he expects it. The Prince of Wales rang his bell one day and I walked in the room, he was sat at his desk and he said to me [*impersonating Prince Charles's accent and mannerisms*] "Er Paul, er, er, a letter from my mother seems to have fallen in my waste-paper bin, could you fish it out." His waste-paper bin is there, he rang his bell and asked me to pick it up.'

He told how he had ended up in hospital suffering from exhaustion after looking after Prince Charles when he broke his arm in a riding accident. 'He went to hospital. I worked for five weeks every single day from six in the morning until midnight without a day off looking after him. Backwards and forwards from hospital. Taking his food daily, his china, his crystal, with his silver, absolutely every meal, taking paintings for the walls, his favourite paintings hanging on the walls of the hospital,' said Burrell. 'At the end of five weeks I collapsed. They took me to hospital and the doctor said I should report him. "You are exhausted, you are going to stay here for two weeks, sheer exhaustion".'

Despite the fact that he was on the committee that chose the design, Burrell then had a go at the fountain erected as a memorial to Princess Diana in Kensington Gardens. 'It looks like a toilet. And they dedicated this to the memory of the Princess.' He also criticized the decision by the Queen to hold a private memorial service for Princess Diana on her tenth death anniversary, to be attended by Charles and Camilla. 'How can Camilla stand in the house of god and praise the life of someone whom she helped to destroy?' He returned to talking about Prince Charles: 'He used her [Diana] and abused her. Mentally abused her, not physically. Mentally tore her apart. And that's why him and Camilla between them set her down the road to bulimia and anorexia and all those nervous conditions. He was jealous of her and her popularity and her presence.' The conversation then took a bizarre turn:

> **BURRELL:** 'Charles could never marry Camilla if she had been alive. That is fact and more.'
> **SHEIK:** 'Really?'
> **BURRELL:** 'No.'
> **SHEIK:** 'So, in a way, he was …'
> **BURRELL:** 'As heir to the throne of England, he could not have married Camilla with the Princess alive. It had to take her death. She had to be dead. He had to be a widower, to marry as heir to the throne of England.'
> **SHEIK:** 'So he'd be celebrating then really?'
> **BURRELL:** 'Yes.'

Despite what he'd just blurted out, Burrell then insisted the Queen trusted him. 'The Queen recognized the fact and said to me no one has ever been in your position. I mean not since John Brown, Queen Victoria's servant was called John Brown, and he was very close to the Queen. It will never happen again. I am a special case on the side because the Queen said to me, "No one", her words, "No one, Paul, has been as close to a member of my family as you have." And that is a very difficult thing for me to carry. And I didn't understand at the time but I do now. But she awarded me her private order, she decorated me at Buckingham Palace and I am the only man on this planet to be awarded the Queen's personal order for services to Diana. I'm not knighted. Who knows? Wouldn't it be fun to go to Buckingham Palace for the Queen's Award to Industry, because every year, she nominates, the government nominate a hundred industries, a hundred companies who have given significant contribution to industry.'

Burrell interrupted himself, as if he realized he'd been claiming a little too much: 'I never want to be accused of exploiting the memory [of Diana] because if people realize who I am they'll understand exactly where I come from and what I've done.' But he has made exploiting

Diana's memory his lucrative trademark. He earns a very healthy living by using his Royal association to flog everything from Burrell teddy bears, dinner plates, salad dishes, cups and saucers, crystal wine glasses, and champagne flutes all under his seal of 'Royal Butler'. Then of course there is his range of cheap plonk on sale in America, not forgetting the new furniture range including a Princess bed, and a range of rugs – all the time still denying that he is cashing in on Diana's memory. And still the revelations poured out.

William and Harry would never articulate their true feelings about their new stepmother, Burrell claimed. 'Remember the boys are standing by and doing nothing, because they live in their father's world. And they're told ... William will be King one day. He cannot, there cannot be dissent in the ranks, the Queen won't have it. The Queen will not have a destructive force within the family. She won't have it. She knows it's there but she won't let it breathe. It will not grow. She's in charge of it. It will not grow. Can you imagine, it would destroy the Royal family.'

He compared things to how they'd been in the days of the Queen Mother. 'She lived in a very privileged world, she thought everything cost two shillings. Even to her death, she didn't know she was £5 million overdrawn at Coutts, because she lived a lifestyle that never changed. There was always champagne, there was always fresh lobster and caviar around. She lived that elegant lifestyle.'

I was flattered when Burrell momentarily paused from his Royal disclosures and noticed my own 'elegant lifestyle,' spotting the two gleaming diamond rings on my finger, the kind of bling that wouldn't look out of place on a rapper's hand. 'I love your ring. It's very beautiful. And the Cartier one too. You see when I meet ladies I usually say what beautiful jewellery; I've done a quick appraisal. I know exactly what it's worth,' he said admiringly. I looked at Alex and we couldn't help bursting into laughter. Burrell had no clue how much they were worth, but Alex did, as he was with me when I picked up the tacky rings off a market stall in an alleyway in the gold souk for just £18 for the pair. I joked with Burrell that my rings had cost a bargain £18. He joined in the laughter.

When the giggling had ceased, Burrell declared Prince William would marry Kate Middleton. 'He will be King one day, and he has to take very good care of himself and his reputation. He's only ever had one girlfriend, Kate, and he will marry Kate. I dare bet you everything I have he will marry Kate. William is safe. You have to put your chips on someone that's safe and William is safe.' The butler then began criticizing Prince Harry. 'He is a wild card. He's off to war, he's going to fight for his Queen and country in the Iraq war. He won't be on the front line, but he's in the armed forces and his brigade has been detached to Iraq, he has to go with them. But they'll take great care of him. Actually it'll take more security looking after him, he's a liability. They will have to be very, *very* careful with him in Iraq. He'll be more difficult to guard there than he is here. So it's going to cost the taxpayers a lot of money to send him safely to Iraq.'

> **Burrell: "I'm unique, there's only one of me in the whole world. I'm the living Jeeves ... No one can touch me. I feel invincible."**

'He chose that course and his regiment has to go, so it would be very difficult for him not to go because his men would say, just a minute you are in charge of us, why are you not showing leadership skills and taking us to the war? So he has to go. And the Queen would say fine, let him go but keep him somewhere safe.' Asked if Harry going to Iraq was worthwhile, Burrell replied: 'No. It's not. No. It's just a PR exercise.'

The comments infuriated 2nd Lieutenant Prince Harry who later served on the front line for ten weeks with his regiment in Afghanistan, sharing the privations and dangers his men faced as they fought the Taliban.

I told Burrell that I was planning to open a new concierge service and had considered employing the Duchess of York, Sarah Ferguson. He became very animated, saying that she wouldn't be interested in 'our' business venture: 'She's too concerned with being Royal and not upsetting the Royal family. She is no longer a member of the Royal family, but her daughters are Princesses. She's a Duchess and she's not a Royal Duchess, she's a Duchess. This is a strange woman. She has a reputation of pimping her daughters into social situations, which isn't very helpful. Let me just put it in a nutshell, and to be kind, she is a survivor, and she has learned how to survive by going to America. Me too, I'm a survivor and I've learned how to do it by going to America, because America is more embracing than England. Sarah, she was a little girl, a farmer's daughter, I'm being kind, brought into the Royal family, like a little girl brought into a sweet shop and told she could have anything she wanted. And she did, she had everything, not just one thing, she had the lot. Absolutely. Abused everything and had everything she could possibly, gorged herself. I saw it.'

Mention of Sarah Ferguson always put me in mind of her ex-lover, Johnny Bryan, who I'd exposed when he arranged hookers and cocaine for the Fake Sheik in the Beverly Hills Hilton. He'd told me his wild sex with Fergie was 'the best I've ever had,' and reminisced, 'she's unbelievable in bed. The first time, you just can't believe it … it's unimaginable. You know what they say about red-heads, well she's on fire in bed!'

By the time desert arrived, I was hoping that blabbermouth Burrell would shut up. I knew that I would have to go back to my hotel room and listen to the tapes and laboriously transcribe every word he'd uttered; I was in for a long night. The following day I invited Burrell and his sidekick Chris Kirby on board the Sheik's luxury yacht, the *Dominator*, for a tour of the Dubai coastline. Colin Myler and I had planned this, and allowed for the £2,000 it was going to cost in the overall budget for the operation.

The butler seemed to be out of practice as he arrived at the marina wearing an un-ironed shirt. However no sooner had we set sail, than Burrell launched into a tirade of even more derogatory remarks and accusations about his former employers. He started talking about Prince Charles's relationship with Camilla. 'He never wanted a lover, he wanted a mother. She's not attractive, but then he was never looking for, he never wanted the physical presence of a beautiful woman, he wanted someone that would look after him. Would you cross over the road to see Camilla?' he sneered. 'She's not one of the most attractive of women. I am being kind!' I said to Burrell that Prince Charles did have a caring streak and appeared to show great affection towards Camilla. Burrell retorted: 'Yeah. Well he likes horses! He plays polo … I'm saying she runs at 3.30 at Kempton!'

He claimed that Prince Charles had simply used Diana. 'Well he had to marry someone to provide him an heir and a spare. He had to have children and she was a young filly with no history and safe. Good breeding. She was good breeding and would provide, would provide good heirs for Prince Charles. So she was used in a way. And he said to her in later life, "I never loved you. I only married you to have children,"' he claimed. 'She was constantly undermined behind closed doors and she would come downstairs looking absolutely stunning and he'd tell her "you look like an air stewardess, go back upstairs and change." So she'd go back upstairs and change and I'd follow her and she'd be in a heap in the corner weeping and I'd say come on pull yourself together you look fantastic. You know you look great, it's just him. It's his problem not yours.'

His callous betrayal of their private secrets, to a complete stranger such as myself, shocked me; but the two-faced servant, busy making a fortune out of his Royal role, then turned on Prince Charles, cheekily criticizing him for making money, claiming that Charles was mean to farmers who lease his land. 'The land has been passed down from heir to heir to heir, always belongs to the Prince of Wales who is Duke of Cornwall. They pay him £4 million a year for their rent for nothing, to farm the land, and they are trying to make ends meet, but they still have to pay rent to farm the land. Now wouldn't you think one year he would turn round and say I am rich enough, I have more money than god, this year you'll pay no rent and to give you a start, all you farmers who work hard on the land, a start in life,' he suggested. He also swiped at Charles's organic food products, suggesting that the money went towards cosmetic surgery for Camilla. 'Jam and biscuits, purely business. It pays for Camilla's surgery. Have you not seen the improvement? Look at her, there is an improvement. She's had a little few things done. If you see a picture of her fifteen years ago and you look at her now. She's not so many teeth now. I think she's had dental work done. She may have had a little bit of stretching.' Burrell summarized his view of the Charles–Camilla union by saying: 'I think it's be careful what you wish for, because you might get it.'

And he also had another go at business rival Fergie, who has also launched a line in bed linen. 'She's no longer part of the Royal family. She thinks she can be a commercial animal. What does a Royal Duchess know about linens, think about it! She's launched her linens, bed linens, but she's never made a bed in her life. She wouldn't know how to use it. What I do is I have a product and I show them how I use it in a Royal concept,' he explained. 'She's a lady that has her finger on the self-destruct button and she just keeps pressing it. She can't help it. She gets herself into situations. Well she's just been in the British press, pictures of her and her daughters surrounded by people smoking marijuana.'

Burrell paused only to hand me a copy of his latest book *The Way We Were*, which he signed for the Sheik. As he handed me the hardback, Burrell told me that Princess Diana would have loved to meet me, as the Fake Sheik was just her type! Lounging on the deck, Burrell confessed: 'When I first heard this proposal, I did wonder if I was being set up. Because, people have in the past, in my position been set up, by fake situations, by a sting. It would not be beyond the *News of the World* to go to this length. It's not a concern of mine now, but I have been at times, guarded … I mean, it's a great story, if you could turn someone inside out. And you could, really, really go to town with them.'

He was right, I thought, as I laughed inside – my expression gave away nothing, while he continued to provide me with more quotes than I could possibly squeeze into any newspaper article. For instance, Princess Diana's brother Earl Spencer came in for a Burrell battering. 'Well he is a hypocrite,' claimed Burrell. 'Because during her lifetime he never offered her assistance or help. And only in death did he come forward and claim her.' When I reminded him of the moving speech made by Earl Spencer at Diana's funeral which had touched the world, he replied: 'They did not know that during her lifetime he refused her assistance. Earl Spencer wrote to the Princess and said he wanted a tiara back, the tiara that she wore on her wedding day, the Spencer tiara, he said "I want it back because it was given to me by my grandfather and it's mine, I want my wife to wear it. I don't want you to wear it, it's mine." And she said "but I'm Princess of Wales and I get to wear it on state occasions when your wife could never wear it." Would she wear it around the house? Yeah so it was that bullishness of being the Earl and being in charge of the family. In death he claimed her. That's what families do, in death they claim their own, and he took her to Althorp, back to his family home, buried her on an island surrounded by water away from people. Isolated in death the way she was in life, think about it. How cold is that? I asked the Queen if she [Diana] could be buried in Westminster Abbey or somewhere in a public place and she said "Paul it's not my decision it's the Spencer family, the Spencer family." He took her and she was then a trophy in death that she couldn't be in life. So suddenly he was in control of her.'

Burrell also laid into Mohamed Al-Fayed, who he described as 'very vulgar' in the way he spoke to Princess Diana and branded him a 'liar'. Burrell, who in 2008 admitted lying and withholding evidence at the inquest into Diana's death, blamed Al-Fayed for the Princess's death. 'He has got a second agenda and people have forgotten about this,' said Burrell. He claimed that if it were shown that the cause of the death was a drunken driver and that a security guard had been changed at the last minute, then Al-Fayed would be 'ultimately responsible'. Burrell alleged that the theories put forward by Al-Fayed were a smokescreen full of 'myths, lies, and untruths. I think some of it is denial. But I think he is responsible,' he claimed.

Burrell then described the moment of Diana's death in Paris: 'Because they were chasing her on motorbikes, the car speeded up.

But what happened inside the car was I feel, Dodi was giving instructions overriding the security and saying "faster, faster, faster!" They were speeding.' He also suggested that Diana had believed Dodi was taking cocaine. 'They were on the boat in the Mediterranean and I rang her. And she said, "I'm so looking forward to coming home, it's freezing cold on the boat, and below decks." She said I'm crawling up walls. It's a small environment for her and I want to come home. He keeps going in to the bathroom. She said I keep losing him. He goes in the bathroom, locks the door. "What's he doing in there?" she said. I said, "You know what he's doing in there." She said, "Do you think he is?" I said, "Yes, he is." She was naive. She didn't do drugs.'

Back on dry land, Alex told Burrell that the Sheik was a huge Diana fan and would love to get hold of something that had belonged to her. Burrell didn't disappoint. 'I can get him something. It's going to have to be very discreet. And I know he's not going to be shouting about it. Let me find something that will surprise him,' promised Burrell.

The most poignant thing Burrell said during his weekend with the Sheik was that Diana once told him: 'I've been a bad picker of men!'

As I watched Burrell walk away, I thought her prophetic words applied perfectly to him too.

CHAPTER 18

A ROYAL ENDORSEMENT

Her Majesty The Queen was not amused. She read my exposé of her daughter-in-law, the Countess of Wessex and described it as 'an appalling piece of journalism!' I'd won Reporter of the Year, the newspaper industry's 'Oscar', and picked up several awards over the years, but this was my most cherished accolade. The image of the Queen spluttering over the *News of the World* in front of her boiled eggs and toast at Buckingham Palace was hilarious.

The Sophiegate exposé made headlines all over the world and led to an urgent review of the role of the Royal family; but it was a story that was nearly never published. It all began with a phone call from a disgruntled employee at RJH, a public relations firm that Sophie had set up in Mayfair with her partner Murray Harkin. The employee was Sri Lankan-born Kishan Athulathmudali who had read some of my previous investigations. Kishan felt that I had the right credentials to carry out an undercover sting on his boss. But during the brief phone call he didn't mention who his boss was, other than to say it was a 'high profile' individual with Royal connections.

I thought it might be a set-up, as over the years I have exposed so many villains that I sometimes get phone calls and emails from people trying to lure me out for meetings to 'discuss a story'; they are simply attempts to get their hands on me to settle old scores. But well-spoken Kishan sounded genuine and readily volunteered his home phone number, which I immediately checked out. Nevertheless, I took Harry along with me to the meeting at Trader Vics at the Hilton in Park Lane, to watch my back.

Kishan was a 32-year-old man who had been working as an account manager with RJH for some 18 months. As soon as he mentioned the name of the firm, I became very interested indeed; he complained that Sophie was shamelessly using her Royal status to drum up business for her firm, that clients were offered invites to Royal events and the company would even engineer photo opportunities with Royals.

She had become a 'Rent-A-Royal' who was also exposing herself to huge security risks. The company offices had even been visited by police officers investigating one of their clients who had dealings with the Countess, but later turned out to be a suspected criminal.

Kishan told me that as long as she felt there was money to be made, Sophie would accept virtually any client and help promote their businesses. Besides this, her business partner in the firm, Murray Harkin, was a cocaine user.

It provided the perfect background for a Fake Sheik sting. I approached RJH posing as Sheik Mohammed with a fictitious leisure complex in Dubai that I wanted them to promote. The only contact details for the Sheik's company I provided was a mobile telephone number, as I wanted to test their security arrangements. But that turned out to be more than enough; as soon as the account executive who answered the phone heard that he was talking to a Sheik, he put me straight through to the boss – Harkin.

On the 7 March 2001, I sat in a suite at the Hilton hotel in my Arab outfit, complete with a black robe with gold braiding. The editor of *Yoga* magazine, Ali Malik, posing as the Sheik's cousin, sat blowing smoke from an Arab sheesha pipe as Harkin turned up, accompanied by Kishan.

Harkin told us he had set up the PR firm five years ago with Sophie, who owned 60 per cent of the business while he owned the rest. In between discussing my business proposal, conversation turned to drugs. Harkin complained about the strict drug laws in Britain. 'It's crazy. We've got a client in Amsterdam; when people have been in coffee shops there they have to throw it all away, get rid of it before they get on a plane to come back to England. And the distance between here and there is nothing.' He also confessed to taking cocaine. 'I don't do lots of drugs, but you know, the odd line of coke I quite like.'

Harkin, who was openly gay, spoke of rumours about Prince Edward's sexuality. 'There have been rumours for years about Edward. I'm a great believer that there's no smoke without fire. He's not what you expect.'

I made it clear to Harkin that we wanted to sign up his firm simply because having the Queen's daughter-in-law associated with our project would be beneficial. Sophie had already caused controversy after she was pictured stroking the bonnet of the new Rover 75 at the 1999 Frankfurt Motor Show; this was seen as Royal endorsement. As a result, she'd promised the Queen that she would stay in the background. All new clients of her company had to sign a contract acknowledging that her name would not appear in any promotional material or invitations. Neither would she 'star' at any engagements where photographers would be present, and firms were not to publicize that they were employing RJH; strict conditions to hire a firm whose fees were up to £10,000 a month. But it soon became clear that the agreement wasn't worth the paper it was written on. Harkin was prepared to break the rules and dangled the Countess and Edward in front of us. Even though Prince Edward had distanced himself from Sophie's business, Harkin said that he would be prepared to come with her to visit our complex in the Middle East.

'Between you and me, they went to one of our clients ... they'd gone for the weekend. So again it's like she's bought into it and she's got Edward involved. And it was Dubai,' he said. 'It's the kind of thing that as the relationship grows, we'd get her out to Dubai as quickly as possible and when she sees it for herself, she buys into it, you know, it becomes a reality. There's potential for Edward as well. What's the TV network like in Dubai? You see they can both combine business and get a bit of pleasure at the same time, couldn't they?' At the time Edward was running the Ardent Television Production company.

Harkin promised that Sophie would attend the launch of our supposed holiday complex. 'If we do a launch party in Dubai and she's there and she's photographed, that's not a problem,' he explained. 'The fact that she would be involved would give the project profile in the media anyway.'

It looked as if Kishan was right and Sophie was using her Royal status to endorse her clients' businesses, though Harkin realized he had to be careful here, so he said: 'The thing is, it's just the word endorsement. It's just being clever about it. If, for instance, if the two of you were photographed together by the media in Dubai, it would not be a problem. Her doing a photoshoot would be. If it's a party or an event or she's there, it's not a problem. Staged photography is a problem.'

Harkin said that we would be able to announce that Sophie was handling our publicity. 'One easy way you may want to do that is to take over a press trip in which she takes the press, and at that point you make the announcement that she's going to look after your project. We do this all the time, Sophie and I.' Then he cut to the chase.

'You've recognized the fact by taking on her company that it's going to have an impact. There's no doubt that you're gonna ride off the back of it and you shouldn't be doing it,' he said as he laughed. 'If you said to her: "Would you give a speech?" she'd say "I couldn't, not at a do," but in the last five years, I've seen her give many speeches – and I think you'll find the more she buys into projects, the more she will … When she went over to India, there were all sorts of things she wasn't going to do and she ended up doing all of them.'

Sophie had been flown over to Delhi by an IT company called Mastek and was photographed with businessmen. Sophie also flew out to the Spanish resort of Sotogrande for another client and the pictures appeared in *Hello!* magazine. 'Anyway you can buy photographs of her meeting various people and you can do whatever you like with those. So in that sense you get endorsement from it.'

After meeting Harkin, I went to our office in Wapping and discussed the story with editor Rebekah Wade. I had expected her to be overjoyed at the prospect of exposing a rent-a-Royal scandal, but she wasn't. She argued that Royals earning a living, rather than off the civil list that was funded by the taxpayers, was admirable. Assistant news editor Neville Thurlbeck and I tried in vain to explain how we too were in favour of working Royals, but against them cashing in on their privileged status. That cocaine-snorting Harkin is Sophie's right-hand man is a big story, and the way he was shamelessly touting her Royal status to endorse projects through the back door was the icing on the cake – at least that was how I saw it. However Rebekah reminded us how a previous story about Sophie had backfired badly while she was working at our sister paper, the *Sun*. Editor David Yelland had published topless pictures of Sophie Rhys-Jones when she was about to marry Edward. The photos had been taken while she was holidaying in Spain with TV presenter Chris Tarrant and other Capital radio staff. Sophie worked as a public relations officer with the radio station.

> ❝Sophie: "It's a shame really because William is very intelligent … But he's got this awful kind of way he talks … he sounds like a puppet."❞

The Palace was furious and lodged a complaint to the Press Complaints Commission on the grounds of 'gross invasion of privacy'. The Palace described the publication as 'premeditated cruelty'. Even the Prime Minister Tony Blair had chipped in to condemn the *Sun*. 'The freedom of the press is important, but with that freedom comes responsibility, and it is important that when media exercise that freedom they show judgement.' Yelland was forced to publish a grovelling full-page apology to Sophie, and his tenure in charge of the country's best-selling daily newspaper came to an end soon afterwards.

Rebekah feared a similar fate. However, with Harkin having already arranged for the Sheik to meet Sophie, Rebekah agreed with me that the meeting should go ahead. On the 14 March I booked up the £1,500 Terrace suite at the Dorchester hotel, which had a balcony with panoramic views of Hyde Park, where Sophie was to join the Sheik for lunch. A menu had been faxed over to her office earlier and she'd already placed her order for a light lettuce salad. Sophie arrived promptly, having strolled over from her office in South Audley Street accompanied by Harkin, account director Brett Perkins, and a Royal Protection Officer. Waiting in the suite were myself, Malik as my cousin, and Conrad.

Normally we would have installed at least three covert video systems in the suite but as our guest was a member of the Royal family, we were worried that her security team might sweep the premises. Conrad had installed just one video camera concealed in a carriage clock that blended into the hotel décor, and would hopefully go unnoticed. We needn't have worried. Sophie's Royal Protection Officer seemed uninterested; meanwhile Sophie was so convinced that the Sheik was a potentate that she bowed in deference as she shook hands.

Sophie struck me as an extremely attractive woman, who bore a striking resemblance to Princess Diana. However any doubts that I may have had about the justification for the story were soon dispelled as Sophie herself cashed in on her Royal status to try and win the Sheik's contract.

'In some ways, being in the kind of business that I'm in does, it does cause some conflicts. So obviously with all clients, we are very straightforward and explain they must treat our company the same as they would treat another PR company,' she explained. 'I'm not there to endorse other people's products on a commercial basis, that's not what it's about. If anyone ever gets some kind of additional profile or benefit from being involved with us because of my situation, that's an unspoken benefit. It's not something that anybody promises, it's something that just occurs.'

She continued her sales pitch: 'Most of our clients do end up having extra mentions in the press, or you know, additional profile. For instance in your own country when people find we're working for you, the chances are you'll get people interested: "Oh gosh, they've employed the Countess of Wessex's PR company."'

Business out of the way, we moved to sit down at the table to eat. If I had thought Harkin had been open at our first meeting, I was amazed as Sophie was even more indiscreet; she regaled us with a series of revelations even though we had only just met. The unguarded comments recorded over the meal were to change her life forever:

> **SOPHIE:** 'When we got engaged, they were very, very keen to put me onto the empty pedestal that had been left by Princess Diana.'
> **SHEIK:** 'Make you the new Diana?'
> **SOPHIE:** 'And I don't think I could have coped with that level of pressure or expectation. Everyone said: "Gosh, doesn't she look like Diana?" Then they thought: "This isn't going to be much good because she's not going to be turning up every day in different outfits, opening children's homes," you know. I do some of that but not as much as they'd like.'
> **HARKIN:** 'Turning up at hospitals in the middle of the night with make-up on.'
> **SOPHIE:** 'Exactly, hospitals and that sort of thing.'

The chat moved on to sport, particularly shooting and bloodsports.

> **SHEIK:** 'It's not as if you're shooting tigers – what do you shoot here?'
> **SOPHIE:** 'Exactly. We shoot pheasant, grouse, partridge. It supports a whole industry. Of course there's a practical side to it as well, foxes are vermin and they have to be kept down … If you stop hunting the fox, the numbers will increase, they will spread further. Fox hunting is just vermin control but people think it's the aristocracy running round doing what the hell they like.'
> **SHEIK:** 'So there's a lot of ignorance in the anti lobby?'
> **SOPHIE:** 'That's why we've got problems with our Prime Minister, because he doesn't understand the countryside. He's ignorant of the countryside. His wife is even worse, she hates the countryside. She hates it! And because the popular vote is within the city, he's going to go with that. I mean, because of the foot-and-mouth situation they've been forced to take notice of the countryside.'
> **SHEIK:** 'She seems low-key.'

BRETT: 'She's a barrister.'

SOPHIE: 'She's an intelligent woman and I think she wanted to keep her hand in. Or maybe she didn't think her husband's government was going to last long so she'd have to go back to work anyway.'

SHEIK: 'Who is going to lose the election?'

HARKIN: 'The Tories.'

SOPHIE: 'I think the majority is too great. Labour will lose a lot of seats.'

HARKIN: 'Portillo seems nice. Has a bit of panache about him, a bit of style, which Hague doesn't seem to.'

SOPHIE: 'It's a shame really because William is very intelligent. I think he's got real vision. But he's got this awful kind of way he talks, like that all the time [mimics Hague]. He sounds like a puppet unfortunately. John Major had this real problem of being quite defensive at Prime Minister's question time. In front of a TV camera he came across as completely wooden. He was actually far too nice to be Prime Minister in some ways. I mean I have to say that I blame him, and a lot of people do for a number of things, and he used the Royal family badly to cover up a lot of things they were doing. The leaks that came from Downing Street were frightening. Now the thing with William Hague is he is very good at debating. After they finished delivering the Budget and William Hague got up to give his view he was brilliant. He totally took the Budget to pieces and showed it to be a nothing Budget. It really is. It's all for the election, that's all it is. It's a load of pap. It's all promises. And the increase in everybody's taxes is something frightening; since the Labour party came to power, the man in the street is paying something like an additional 40 per cent in tax. They've snuck in so much through the back door.'

SHEIK: 'But there's no chance of Hague being elected?'

SOPHIE: 'I don't think the general public like him very much. They don't understand him. I mean, just to give you an example, when Diana died Tony Blair came out and he gave this completely impassioned, supposedly off-the-cuff speech. I know it wasn't off-the-cuff at all because I know who wrote it. He almost did the Bill Clinton; we call him President Blair because he thinks he is. That's his style.'

HARKIN: 'Without the Monica!'

SOPHIE: 'Well, we don't know yet! And unfortunately William Hague, who they managed to find on his Yorkshire farm somewhere, stood and went Aye! [impersonation of Hague speaking in common accent]. It sounded so nothing, you know what I mean?'

Talk then turned to how Sophie deals with the public.

SOPHIE: 'I'd never be rude to anybody. But I think normally people do generally act the proper way when I'm wearing my Royal hat.'

MALIK (SHEIK 2): 'You have to wear a hat?'

SOPHIE: 'No no, I'm describing different hats that I put on different mornings, sort of, who am I today.'

BRETT: 'Did you see Prince Charles on the news last night? He did a tour of his charity, showing young boys how to DJ and scratch records.'

SHEIK: 'He's too formal, isn't he?'

SOPHIE: 'Actually he's always been, he likes formalities in life. But he's great fun, he really is. For instance, with William and Harry he's so laid-back, I mean what you don't see is when the Prince of Wales is messing around and being funny and silly, he's a different person, oh he really is. He's hysterical. And he plays around with the boys all the time, they mess around with each other. He'll always have a go at putting a wig on or doing something silly. He's a man who's always been ahead of his years all the way along: he was damned a complete quack, people laughed at him for his views on architecture, but now they're starting to take notice and have actually come to the same conclusions he drew 25 to 30 years ago.'

SHEIK: 'The Diana thing probably gave him a bad image.'

SOPHIE: 'It did but he's had people working for him. The Prince of Wales and Camilla were possibly number one on people's unpopular people list.'

SHEIK: 'He's now more likeable?'

SOPHIE: 'Oh yes, the thing is a lot of things came out after Diana's death about the way that she behaved. I think everybody realized that it takes two. You'll get the fanatical Diana diehards who'll always blame the Prince of Wales for everything, we can't do much about that.'

SHEIK 2: 'Have people accepted Camilla now?'

SOPHIE: 'It's a very difficult situation. On the one hand there's no reason why she shouldn't be accepted because he's divorced and she's divorced, but then again you've got issues of the monarch being the head of the Church. I think it's hard, especially while Queen Elizabeth is alive, the Queen Mother. It's very hard for anybody to publicly recognize Camilla. And it's not really fair any more to describe her as Prince Charles's mistress because I deem somebody a mistress if the man is already married. They are not married.'

SHEIK 2: 'Then why can't they marry?'

SOPHIE: 'There's no legal reason. They could marry. You can have a ceremony, it doesn't need to be in a register office, you can actually do them anywhere now. And they could have a church blessing, which would be different. But because he is going to be the head of the Church, when he actually succeeds to the throne, there's a difficulty there. I don't think a lot of people would want Camilla to be queen because of the history of the whole process. But then again I don't know, things change all the time. He said he doesn't want to get married.'

SHEIK: 'Will your children be called princes?'

SOPHIE: 'Well they can be, yes, it's up to us. The only reason we wouldn't want them to be Royal Highnesses, princes and princesses, is because of media attention. For instance, Zara and Peter Phillips, who are the children of the Princess Royal, they have a normal life. You're starting to hear more of Zara now because she's starting to get to that age now and everyone's taking notice in her life. She'll always have interest but on a daily basis she can do whatever she pleases. Beatrice and Eugenie, who are daughters of the Duchess of York, they will always have more of a problem because they will expect their

Royal Highnesses to work. Their name, wherever they go, will inevitably create interest. We would ask for our children to be addressed as viscount. However it would also be their right, if they wanted, to take their title. But if we changed what's written, we would be changing it for other people. Once Charles succeeded, Prince Harry, for example, would become a child of the monarch. If Harry married and had children, they could not be called Royal Highnesses [she means if Sophie and Edward had re-written parts of the Royal succession protocol] although they would really be entitled to it. So if we changed anything then it would have a knock-on effect.'

After dinner, Sophie happily posed for photographs with the Sheik and his cousin. The Sheik escorted the Princess out of the Dorchester and she walked back to her office. My driver Alan Smith chauffeured me back to my office. I rushed into see Rebekah again and played some of the tapes to her and told her how I had got Sophie bang to rights – but it wasn't enough. Rebekah told me that she felt that there simply wasn't enough justification for running the story, that Sophie was merely doing her job. Andy Coulson, her deputy, who was also in the meeting, agreed with me; as I left the office, deflated, Andy told me not to worry as he'd work on Rebekah and try and sort something out.

Rebekah decided to contact the Palace to try and sort something out with them. The Palace was plunged into panic. After seeking advice from the PCC, the Palace was informed that there were no grounds to claim we had entrapped Sophie. It had been a legitimate investigation instigated by information supplied by an employee of RJH. So next the Palace decided to gag Kishan by issuing a High Court injunction against him preventing him from revealing any business dealings at RJH.

I wrote a small piece about the injunction which served to set tongues wagging in media and Royal circles alike; there was clearly something to hide if the Palace had gone to the trouble of gagging an employee at Sophie's firm. A few days later Rebekah who had some 'good news' for me, as she put it, called me into the office. She told me how she had pulled off an amazing deal with the Palace. Their ill-conceived containment plan involved a simple swap – we hand them our tapes and photos, and they would offer us an exclusive interview with Sophie worthy of our front page. I have never been one for cutting deals, but Rebekah assured me that it was the best option.

Reporter Carole Aye Maung and photographer Martin Cullum were discreetly ushered into the Palace by a side entrance. Simon Walker, the Queen's Communications Secretary sat in on the interview. In the trade-off our tapes were handed over to Palace officials who were desperate to hear the full extent of Sophie's indiscretions. Rebekah had agreed to give the Palace editorial control in vetting the interview in advance of publication. It made it all the more shocking when I read our splash; I couldn't believe the Palace had sanctioned such an extraordinary interview.

Our front page headline read: 'Sophie: My Edward Is NOT Gay'. Sophie went on to make a series of demeaning comments which must have caused great embarrassment to her husband. Besides claiming she would not be part of a 'sham marriage', Sophie also discussed her fertility and said she would consider IVF treatment to have children. For a woman who was supposed to be head of a PR company, this verged on gross incompetence.

Just to annoy the Royals, Rebekah added my by-line in small print at the end of the interview, crediting me with 'additional reporting'. Rebekah thought she had pulled off a major coup – until the first edition of the *Mail on Sunday* landed.

After the gagging order had been imposed upon him, a worried Kishan had turned to PR guru Max Clifford for advice and told him about his dealings with me. Max had leaked details of the Sheik sting to the *Mail on Sunday*. Their front page read: 'Queen's Outrage At Sophie insults'. The story was an account of Sophie's meeting with me, riddled with inaccurate quotes attributed to Sophie about fellow members of the Royal family and politicians.

Senior executives were just as annoyed as me to have to read my exclusive scoop in a rival paper. In yet another spectacular error of judgement, Sophie fired off letters of apology to the people she had insulted during our meeting. Recipents included those not even mentioned in the *Mail on Sunday* piece, which only served to fan the flames. Other papers began reporting more alleged remarks that she'd made.

By the end of the week, so many inaccurate quotes had been attributed to Sophie that the Palace were almost relieved when we told them we were going to set the record straight. Over ten pages we ran full transcripts of Sophie's conversation: Buckingham Palace normally take two copies of the *News of the World*, but that weekend they ordered 100 copies.

In an unprecedented personal attack by the Monarch, Her Majesty The Queen issued a statement from Buckingham Palace in which she said she deplored 'the entrapment, subterfuge, innuendo, and untruths to which the Earl and Countess have been subjected in recent days'.

To add to her embarrassment in the days after the Fake Sheik scandal, Sophie went on an official tour with Prince Edward to Bahrain and Qatar where she mingled with real Sheiks. On her return she was forced to resign from RJH; in the wake of the scandal several of her big clients pulled out, and the company was eventually wound up.

The Queen ordered a review of the commercial affairs of working Royals, carried out by Lord Luce, head of the Royal household. The Queen agreed to pay Sophie and Edward £250,000-a-year to concentrate on official duties.

When former trade and industry secretary Stephen Byers appeared on the BBC's *Question Time* programme, he said: 'If a Sheik came to me with a glass of champagne, I would make my excuses and leave.'

Sophie must wish she'd done the same.

CHAPTER 19
<u>THOROUGHBREDS</u>

The world of Arab Sheiks and thoroughbred horse racing are intrinsically entwined. Sheik Mohammed bin Rashid Al Maktoum, ruler of Dubai, is the most powerful man in the world of horse racing. He has spent more than $1 billion on his stable of horses, has built for them their own 747, and won the biggest races worldwide.

So when in early 2004 a fax landed on Royal jockey Kieren Fallon's desk from Sheik Mansour – who claimed to run Cavalier Sports, part of the Al-Jamal Group – it wasn't out of the ordinary. It said that the Sheik wanted to stage six international races offering the highest prize money in the world, and he wanted Fallon on board as a consultant. I was on Fallon's case because associate editor, Gary Thompson, had received information that the jockey was passing tips on to big punters who were cashing in on the inside information. He'd asked me to get alongside Fallon to see if the allegations were true.

Fallon jumped at the opportunity and agreed to meet me for dinner, as long as I arranged a room for him to stay overnight in London. But as soon as Fallon checked into room 429 at the Dorchester hotel in Park Lane, he became suspicious, and he had good reason to be careful. 'I have a bird coming here. You know Sam? She's coming down,' he told his friend John who was in the room with him. The cunning jockey looked all round the hotel room trying to find hidden cameras or bugging devices, under the bed and behind a painting on the wall. Still feeling uncomfortable, Fallon rang the receptionist and said: 'I just need to change rooms, is that possible? It ends in 29 and 29 is an unlucky number for me. Number 29 has been terrible for my family.' The receptionist asked if he wanted to change 'both rooms' which made him all the more suspicious. 'He said you booked connecting rooms,' Fallon told John. 'Why would they book a connecting room?'

I was sitting in the room next door dressed in my Arab robes alongside Ali Malik and Alex and we could hear the conversation through the adjoining door. 'You never know what these guys are doing. You know, fucking camera, next thing you know you'll be fucking looking at pictures of it in the fucking *News of the World* wouldn't you? I know with these cunts because they're always on your back,' said Fallon. It looked like the canny jockey had made us fall at the first hurdle, as he grabbed his bags and moved to room 715.

I told my team that I wouldn't be joining Fallon for dinner at the restaurant downstairs because we had already been rumbled; I didn't want to give him the pleasure of humiliating me and unmasking the Fake Sheik. So I changed back into my suit and packed up my robes and sent Alex and Malik to the dinner. About fifteen minutes later Alex left the dinner table and excitedly rang me on the hotel house phone. 'It's alright, Malik has turned it round. Fallon is convinced we are genuine!' said Alex. 'You won't believe the dialogue Malik is coming out with.'

Malik had played an absolute blinder. Speaking in his naturally soft-spoken voice with a heavy Asian accent, one of the opening comments he made to Fallon was: 'So Mr Fallon, do you like horses? Which is the best horse?' No reporter would ever ask a stupid question like that. It was like asking Tiger Woods if he likes golf, or Michael Schumacher if he likes driving – or if I like Häagen Dazs ice cream. Fallon was dumbfounded, and to dispel any suspicions further, Malik asked him if he knew who had stolen Shergar. By the end of the dinner Fallon was on the hook. He gave his new friend tips on the following day's races and invited Malik to bring the Sheik to watch him race at Lingfield in Surrey.

Over the next few days, the jockey gave us tips on ten different races; one of the tips he provided to the Sheik landed him in hot water.

On 2 March 2004, three hours before the 3.30 at Lingfield, Fallon phoned Alex. This is how the conversation went:

> **ALEX:** 'You on the road?'
> **FALLON:** 'Yeah, I've got a few rides today. Theatre Lady will win today … then there's another race as well there – I'm actually down as the favourite. It's not very good. The horse of Jamie Osbourne's going to win the race. A horse called Rye. Have you got a paper? I ride Ballinger, the favourite.'
> **ALEX:** 'That's your 3.30.'
> **FALLON:** 'Yeah, but you see the horse trained by Jamie Osbourne in that race? Rye … that'll win.'
> **ALEX:** 'So, go heavy on that one you reckon?'
> **FALLON:** 'Rye and Theatre Lady, yeah both'll win.'

Before the race Fallon was telling us that despite being the book-maker's favourite, he would lose the race. And he was predicting the winner. His forecast proved accurate. During the televised race, Fallon was clear by a huge margin on the home straight. Then, he twice looked over his shoulder to check the following pack and eased up. Rye, ridden by unsuspecting Chris Catlin, came past to win. The crowd were incensed, and Fallon was mobbed as he dismounted and across the country appalled punters tore up their betting slips in disbelief. Fallon told a stewards' inquiry that he had given the horse 'a breather', being afraid that the horse might become 'legless'. The stewards found Fallon guilty of an error of judgement. He was later quoted in the racing press as saying: 'I read there were suspicious betting patterns, but I can assure anyone who thinks I'm linked with that sort of thing, that they're barking up the wrong tree.'

A few days after the race, we'd arranged to meet Fallon again, this time at the plush Marbella Club in Spain. He was still reeling from the criticism over his Ballinger Ridge ride, which meant that Fallon, who was accompanied by fellow jockey John Egan, would view his new friends with renewed caution. Once again I called upon the ever-resourceful Malik to help diffuse the tension. I asked Malik, a yoga expert, to strip to his pants and stand on his head. The unforgettable sight of Malik upside down in his baggy white Y-fronts was the spectacle that greeted the two jockeys as they entered the lounge of our sprawling Spanish villa; it was enough to quash any lingering suspicions.

Fallon, who was later arrested for race fixing, was acquitted at the Old Bailey.

While the Fake Sheik came close to being sussed by Fallon, on another story in May 2004 my three-year-old son almost blew my cover.

As I walked through the lobby towards my suite at the Hilton in Cologne accompanied by three prostitutes and my two minders, a toddler shouted: 'Daddy, daddy' and ran towards me. One of the hookers turned around and looked bemused. 'He can't be mine, I have four wives but none in Germany,' I joked. It was my son Danyal, who was sitting in the hotel lounge. I'd bought my wife and child along with me, as I hadn't seen them in weeks. I quickly said to Jaws in Urdu: 'Grab him or we're screwed!'

In a manoeuvre that would impress any rugby player, Jaws managed to intercept him before he could reach me and tug at my Arab robes. It could have been worse because Danyal's favourite greeting at the time was: 'My daddy is a reporter. He puts nasty men in the paper!'

Just a few weeks earlier the three women had filed rape charges against Leicester City footballers, Keith Gillespie, Frank Sinclair, and Paul Dickov. The Premiership stars had met the women at the Hyatt Regency hotel in Spain's La Manga resort, where the alleged rape was said to have taken place. The footballers, who denied the charges, faced up to twelve years' imprisonment if convicted. The women, Malawi-born Ruth Lourenco, and her Kenyan pals, Beatrice Wanjiro and Martha Wilbert, had repeatedly denied that they were vice girls. One girl had told the court she worked as a dancer; another claimed to be a businesswoman while the third said she worked in a chocolate factory.

But when approached by the Sheik in their hometown of Cologne, they readily admitted they were on the game demanding £3,300 each for a weekend of non-stop debauchery. My damning videos of the women stripping off and offering various sexual services cast severe doubts over their credibility. As a result of my story the rape case was dropped. The relieved players and Leicester City chief executive Tim Davies rang me to express their gratitude.

One story where I was found out – without the assistance of my son – followed a meeting with Prince Harry's pal Guy Pelly who I flew out to Las Vegas.

I'd first come across Pelly earlier, in 2002, when I exposed Prince Harry's drug taking. Together with my team we'd spent weeks carrying out a surveillance operation on the Rattlebone Inn pub in Sherston, near Highgrove. It was Harry's local where he enjoyed drinking while underage, and late night lock-ins with his best mate Pelly. They also experimented with smoking cannabis together in the pubs' run-down outbuilding, and even smoked joints at parties back at Highgrove. The tip had come from a member of the Royal family who was concerned about Harry's wild behaviour.

We kept watch on the goings-on at the pub and bought drugs from one of the dealers operating at the rough country pub. Prince Harry was involved in a fight that broke out during an out-of-hours drinking session and was temporarily barred from the Inn. The Prince was questioned by police following the scuffle between him and the two men, with whom he was playing pool. The Prince was said to have called a French employee a 'fucking Frog'.

Prince Charles and Royal courtiers were extremely concerned at the company Prince Harry was keeping; it was clear that Pelly, who had a conviction for drink driving, was the worst influence on the Prince. When confronted with our evidence, the Prince of Wales acted like any responsible parent; also because, as a patron of several drug charities, Prince Charles knew the devastation drugs can cause. He asked his son: 'Are these really the right people to be hanging round with? Are these really the right things for you to be doing in your position?' He arranged for him to spend a day with addicts at a drug rehabilitation centre called Featherstone Lodge, in Peckham, south London, which he had opened a few years earlier. The shock tactics worked and a day with smack addicts was enough to make Harry give up drugs. The Palace for once were grateful for our intervention and provided us with details of Charles's private chats with Harry and Prince William.

A senior aide to the Prince of Wales blamed Guy Pelly for leading the young Prince astray, telling us, 'Harry was mindful only to smoke in private with close friends in the local area, he never smoked cannabis inside Highgrove but in the grounds. But his friends, including Guy Pelly, did smoke there and that led to staff complaints, which in turn led to the Prince confronting his son.'

Pelly was ousted from the Royal circle, but soon managed to worm his way back in; in February 2006, he was caught again at the Tunnel House Inn, a pub in Gloucestershire, while he danced with Prince William and his girlfriend Kate Middleton. Pelly was apparently handed what he thought was a cigarette by a girl on the dance floor when it was in fact a cannabis joint. Despite Palace concerns, Pelly's friendship with both Princes Harry and William has grown even closer; he became a self-appointed court jester with a predilection for mooning and party tricks, which include impersonating the Queen.

Pelly currently works as 'marketing manager' at Mahiki, a trendy bar and nightclub in Mayfair, which has become a regular watering hole for his Royal pals. The Princes' visits to the Polynesian-themed club have become a headache for Royal courtiers, as there have been several incidents involving the Princes staggering drunkenly out of the club that have made headlines around the world.

We splashed on a story written by Rav Singh about a group including Prince William and Pelly, who 'drank the menu' at Mahiki, downing £4,700 worth of champagne and cocktails in a four-hour session. Going through the cocktail menu is known as 'doing the Mahiki Trail' and is based on a map; if guests can finish eighteen of the concoctions, costing from £9 to £50, they get the club's infamous Treasure Chest – a £100 cocktail for eight – for free.

The future King managed to win the free cocktail before he stumbled bleary-eyed into his car, flanked by Royal Protection Officers. It was after this binge session that a Royal source asked me to investigate serious allegations about Pelly and his undesirable association with the Princes.

Pelly accepted my invitation to meet the Sheik for dinner in Las Vegas to discuss setting up a new concierge service for VIPs; he brought along his 18-year-old aristocratic girlfriend, the beautiful and intelligent Susanna Warren.

I had booked into a luxurious suite at the Venetian hotel, dripping in gold and marble, crammed full with antique Italian furniture, Roman artefacts, and oil paintings. Even for someone used to visiting palaces, this suite was impressive. Pelly and Susanna seemed nervous as they entered; or maybe they were just startled by my outfit. I was wearing a bright white suit, turquoise tie and handkerchief, and tacky cream-coloured crocodile-skin shoes. I'd picked up the trendy Sheik's attire from a shop called Players in the nearby Boulevard Mall for $99. The outfit complemented my favourite bling – two fake diamond rings purchased from a souk in Dubai. Pelly was in jeans and a shirt, but Susanna looked stunning in a black designer dress.

As the Sheik's assistant served aperitifs, I helped ease the tension by offering to play my guests a tune on the imposing grand piano in the corner of the suite. My rendition of Mozart's Piano Sonata in C Major was well received by Pelly who applauded loudly. But Susanna, a music student, laughed as she realized that I was a fraud – the piano was computerized and I was only pretending to tinkle the ivories. Susanna then offered to show me how it should be done, playing beautifully while she sang her own composition, a romantic ballad. It was a performance that even Simon Cowell would struggle to criticize.

Over dinner Pelly tried to interest me in his own idea: 'Have you been to any of the strip clubs over here?' asked Pelly over the steak and wine, while the Sheik varied his choices from Bacardi and Coke – i.e. Coke – to vodka and orange – i.e. orange juice. 'Strip clubs haven't been changed for such a long time. I've tried to come up with something new and fresh. My idea is to have like fantasy rooms, or like a jungle room or even with girls going into water, do you know what I mean, now it's all about pole ...' he explained. 'Being an entrepreneur don't you think, it's all about looking at the future, how are things going to be in the future. Think about it, no one has tried to move the strip club industry more forward. You get essentially the top clubs – Stringfellows is still probably one of the top ones and it hasn't changed for several years.'

‘As the bubbly flowed, Pelly lived up to his hell-raising reputation by climbing onto a table and attempting to spray champagne on the strippers ...,

He continued: 'You have got to find a venue where you have got enough rooms to do something. I think those places still make money, you know, definitely make money. You know when I've been there, all the time, the kind of clientele you get in there spend a lot of money. If you're in a strip club you've generally got money to spend because you don't go in there just for no reason,' he said. I thought it was an embarrassing and inappropriate conversation to have in front of his teenage girlfriend, but Pelly reassured me that she was a fellow traveller. 'She's seen a few,' bragged Pelly. Susanna put her cutlery down to take a sip of wine and confirmed: 'I like it, I honestly don't mind at all. It doesn't bother me.' When I pointed out that many women find strip clubs degrading to womankind, Susanna replied: 'I have great fun there!'

Pelly added, 'Oh god yeah. Sue started university in Liverpool and I went up there last year. It was one of the first kind of nights we went out in Liverpool and we went clubbing and I said "let's go to a strip club" and she said "yeah ok", so we went to this one, god it was horrible. It was instead of being a nice table, there were no tables. There were blokes at the bar with a beer and things like this, and Sue and I thought, it's not quite what we were thinking of.'

I was surprised that Pelly's idea of a date with an English rose would be to drag her to a sleazy strip club, but it would surprise her parents more. Her father, John Warren, is the Queen's racing manager and bloodstock agent. He is one of only three people who are able to phone Her Majesty anytime – along with eldest granddaughter Zara Phillips and Prince William. Susanna's mother is Lady Carolyn Herbert, daughter of the Queen's former racing manager, the late Earl of Carnarvon. Lady Herbert, who dumped Prince Andrew for her husband, was a close pal of Princess Diana.

Pelly warned there would be a few problems that we would have to deal with to run a strip joint. 'I'd want to nick the team that are running one, because you are then involved with guys that know the underground slightly, meaning the underground gangsters,' he explained. 'For instance the girls they are all controlled like by guys. I'd be up for it but that's how I would do it. I'd want, you'd want to turn up and nick the guy that was managing somewhere that was successful and he'd have all the contacts and know who to deal with.'

Susanna excused herself from the dining table, and I asked Pelly again if it was ok to discuss opening a strip club in front of his young girlfriend. He laughed loudly and replied: 'No, no honestly. She'd be very raunchy. Honestly. Definitely. Honestly.' He claimed he'd taken her to a strip club in London a few days earlier.

Pelly, described as the leader of London's rich 'aristobrat' group, spoke enthusiastically about his business venture. 'I have this idea, you could possibly do it, some room that would have the girl and the pole going under water. So at least it's more showy. Water from the ceiling and the pole in the middle and it's lit up well, and it starts to shower on the girl, and it's kind of, things that are more theatrical rather than just the boring.' Pelly suggested a suitable venue in the West End that may already have a licence to run a strip club. However, he pointed out that he would have to stay in the background and couldn't publicly be linked to a strip club, as he obviously wouldn't want to embarrass his Royal pals or Susanna's dad.

The following night I was planning to join Pelly and Susanna at a nightclub to further our friendship. But after a quick look around the Tao and Jet nightclubs, Pelly insisted on going to a strip club. Pelly's penchant for strip clubs really wasn't the basis of my investigation, but more importantly I didn't want to be party to taking an underage girl into a strip club as anyone entering a lapdancing club in the state of Nevada must be over 21 years old and produce valid identity documents. I made an excuse and sent Alex along to keep an eye on Pelly's antics.

Pelly took Susanna to the Spearmint Rhino lapdancing club; he handed the receptionist a driving licence belonging to another blonde girl so that Susanna could claim to be over 21. Inside Pelly headed straight towards a VIP table behind a blue velvet rope and ordered a bottle of champagne. As the bubbly flowed, Pelly lived up to his hell-raising reputation by climbing onto a table and attempting to spray champagne on the strippers who danced provocatively around him, Susanna laughing at his antics. He bought $200 worth of 'Rhino chips' to pay for the lapdancers and summoned two gorgeous strippers over to entertain them. The girls writhed over Pelly and Susanna, allowing Pelly to grope the gyrating topless dancers as his girlfriend watched. At one point the strippers took it in turn to French kiss Susannah, while sliding their hands up her skirt. Pelly squealed with delight. The action hotted up, and Pelly invited two girls into a VIP champagne room away from the main dancing area of the club. The champagne rooms, where the dirty dancing gets even dirtier, are sectioned off from the rest of the club – and, with a burly security guard minding the doorway, punters with pockets bulging with Rhino chips are invited in.

The couple emerged from the room an hour later looking dishevelled and worse for wear; Pelly paid for the night's entertainment by credit card.

The following day Pelly reported to the Sheik's assistant that he wasn't very impressed with the club but had enjoyed the company of the dancers who he described as 'full on'. He was more eager than ever to interest the Sheik in opening a similar club in London, but reiterated that his name should not be directly connected to the enterprise.

Pelly's insistence on visiting the lapdancing club had meant that I didn't get the opportunity to substantiate the allegations that had been made against him by my Palace source. Therefore, I arranged to meet him again the following week in London. But Pelly was so excited at meeting the Sheik, he mentioned it to his boss, owner of Mahiki, Piers Adams. As Pelly reeled off details of his five-star visit to Las Vegas, it rang alarm bells with Piers, who counts several tabloid journalists and editors among his friends. Pelly described me and my crew. Piers made a couple of phone calls and was able to confirm that Pelly had been targeted in a Fake Sheik sting. I was rumbled.

Our investigation was aborted and we did not publish details about Pelly's antics in Vegas. However, worried that pictures of the couple cavorting in the club with strippers would be published, Pelly launched a damage limitation exercise. News of the failed operation was leaked to the *Mail on Sunday*, claiming that 'The sting looked to be the work of a tabloid newspaper.' The inaccurate story went on to suggest that we had lured Pelly out to Vegas pretending to discuss opening a US branch of Mahiki in a bid to get him to spill Royal secrets. The article revealed that Pelly's suspicions were confirmed when he 'saw a wire peeping out of a briefcase'.

I hadn't gone to the lapdancing club with Pelly, hadn't tried to get him to spill Royal secrets, hadn't mentioned a US branch of Mahiki, and there were no briefcases: the Sheik was shaken but not bowed.

CHAPTER 20

THE WORLD'S MOST EXPENSIVE HOOKER?

I sat with Jaws on a torn vinyl seat in the back of an American cab with my fist firmly clenched around the handle of a plastic carrier bag. I barely looked up as the Indian cabbie screeched to a halt to avoid going into the back of another driver who had cut him up. The turbaned man rocked on his beaded seat cover and cursed the other driver in his native Punjabi as he banged his hands on the steering wheel.

'Check nothing has fallen out of your bag,' Jaws whispered to me. He needn't have worried. My eyes remained fixed on the bag which contained a large brown A4-size envelope we'd just picked up from a branch of the Bank of America. Inside was $60,000 in bundles of crisp $100 bills.

I needed the money to pay the world's most expensive prostitute, an international supermodel and darling of the lad's mags. The model, Ms X – who can't be named for legal reasons – had demanded payment for just six hours of wild sex. The mindblowing fee – $10,000 an hour – meant she was definitely in the high rollers league. Even David Beckham's contract with L.A. Galaxy nets him a mere $6,000 an hour.

Historically vice stories have been one of the main ingredients of the success of the *News of the World*. It's true; sex sells. When I joined the paper our sensational and titillating exposés of hookers had earned us the nickname 'News of the Screws'. In those days pages were allocated every week for a vice story and all reporters were under pressure to deliver stories involving hookers, and I certainly did my bit for the cause.

For one investigation in which I exposed a chain of massage parlours frequented by policemen, I had seven separate hookers rubbing baby oil into my back in one day. I had the softest skin in Fleet Street for months. Prostitutes I have exposed have included everyone from British Airways stewardesses, a schoolteacher, nurses, a postmistress, a firefighter, a bus driver, a barrister, and even a WPC. There was also the cocaine-peddling hooker who was working as a barmaid in the House of Commons and was bedding retired Chief Superintendent, Baron MacKenzie of Framwellgate. My CV also lists an impressive line-up of celebrity hookers I have uncovered including supermodel Sophie Anderton, TV presenter Debbie Corrigan, actress Holly McGuire, WAG Linsey Dawn McKenzie, Sven-Goran Eriksson's lover Faria Alam, and endless Page Three models.

But in all my years I have never come across any hooker who had demanded $10,000 an hour with a minimum spend of $60,000. I scoured the Internet and looked up page after page of the supermodel's photographs, closely examining her in every pose and stage of undress. Purely in the interest of research, you understand. While the stunning model definitely had a lust-worthy figure and looked fabulous, I wondered who would pay $60k for a night to remember with her?

But there was a market out there for her, with multi-millionaire punters willing to cough up to enjoy a night of passion with the cover girl. I knew because I had been told by Bella, the plump Indian single mum who had a reputation as Britain's biggest madam. Bella told me how she had fallen out with Ms X after she sent her on a booking to see one of her clients at a swish London hotel. According to Bella, Ms X went to see the multi-millionaire Italian client but had broken the cardinal rule of any escort agency, by handing over her mobile number directly to the punter. In effect it meant that Bella would not know if and when the celebrity prostitute met the client again and would lose out on her hefty commission on any future bookings. Furious at the betrayal, Bella rang me urging me to expose her secret double-life. 'She is a greedy cow; she is perfect for the Fake Sheik. She will fall for it straight away,' assured Bella.

I realized that exposing the star model would not be a cheap operation. We couldn't simply get her to a hotel room, get her to offer sex for cash and sling her out with a few quid for her cab fare. She would probably want money up front as well as first-class air flights. With the full Fake Sheik entourage including luxury hotel suites and limos, there wouldn't be much change out of £50k to stand up the story.

I contemplated the possibility of paying a deposit to lure her to a hotel suite and not paying her the remainder; but short-changing Ms X simply wasn't an option. I remembered the time a hooker had dragged me to the High Court in London for breach of contract because I followed that time-honoured *News of the World* tradition, made my excuses and left without paying the full fee.

It was in January 1992 when vice queen Sara Dale came to see me at the Hilton hotel in Park Lane. Dale, who was known as Miss Whiplash, had recently been evicted from Conservative Chancellor Norman Lamont's flat. During the scandal, Dale had maintained that she was simply a 'sex therapist' and not a hooker. However, when I approached

her posing as an Arab, she readily offered to visit me at the hotel along with her pal Anne for a kinky threesome. She had agreed a fee of £3,000 for a night of anything-goes sex with the pair of them.

But once I'd got enough material to prove they were both on the game, which took less than an hour, I handed them their cab fares and sent them packing. Soon after the story was published court papers landed on my desk. I was being sued, not for libel but for loss of earnings. Dale wanted to be compensated for nine and a half hours worth of 'preparation and recovery', preparation which had included sorting out oil, condoms, vibrators, and dildos. Fortunately it was Miss Whiplash who got a spanking as I turned up at the High Court with the *News of the World* legal team. Judge Scott sternly dismissed the case within fifteen minutes, telling her that she had not satisfied him that she had entered into an undisputed contract with me or that it was enforceable.

But with Ms X, Bella had made it clear that if we wanted her to turn up if would mean paying her full whack. I casually mentioned the secret hooker's extortionate fee to Andy Coulson over dinner at Drones restaurant in Mayfair and he didn't bat an eyelid. He simply put down his knife and fork, picked up his glass to take another sip of red wine, before saying, 'It's a great story, let's do it. It's got to make her the world's most expensive hooker!' Andy was among the finest editors I worked with. He had great judgement and above all was fearless, with an in-built streak of mischief. He was always willing to take a punt and most times they came off. The fact that the supermodel had been linked to a string of celebrities, including Hollywood stars, added to the appeal of the story.

We were discussing the operation over dinner as I try to keep out of the office as much as possible, and Andy was happy to meet me outside regularly, perhaps for a meal, so that we could discuss stories and tips. I don't like being in the office when there are so many people coming in and out all the time, I was never sure who might be watching me.

With the money sanctioned, I asked my colleague Alex D'Souza to arrange a meeting between the Sheik and Ms X. Since Bella was no longer handling her extra-curricular activities, we had to meet her on the pretext of casting her for a new TV series. The meeting was fixed through her management company in the United States to take place in London where she was on a modelling assignment.

I recruited a stand-in Sheik for the job – with me posing as the Sheik's assistant, as this would enable me to discuss all the detail with Ms X before handing over any money. The freelance Sheik, Akbar Ali Malik, the editor of *Yoga* magazine, was a middle-aged man whose boyish looks and natural Asian accent belied his shrewdness. He had played both the Sheik and the Sheik's cousin in the past so was familiar with the script. With our two minders, Harry and Jaws, in tow, Malik, myself, and Alex were whisked to the Lanesborough hotel in London's Hyde Park.

Ms X, whose face has graced billboards across the globe, was already waiting for us in the meeting room at the hotel. As my entourage rolled up, she immediately stood up and approached my two suited and booted Asian minders, shook hands with them and gave them each a peck on the cheek. She'd clearly mistaken them for Sheik Mansour Al-Jamal and his sidekick, who made their grand entrance a few seconds later. The boys were thrilled with the kiss as it gave them something to brag about down their local.

Ms X was wearing a skimpy short brown dress with the buttons undone to reveal as much of her flesh as she dared; and with her black knee-length boots giving her height she made sure we all got a view of that expensive flesh. Over a glass of champagne, Ms X talked about her legitimate career, how she was in London for a calendar signing and to make an appearance on MTV. We laid our trail by talking about the Sheik's 'playboy' lifestyle, the yachts, casinos, and women that he enjoyed. After the Sheik raced off to attend 'an urgent meeting', I sat with her and came straight to the point. I told her that he was besotted with her and would like to invite her to spend the weekend with him. 'He said "how soon is she free?" Where would you like? Dubai? Maldives?', I asked her.

She loved the idea of Dubai, and didn't seem shocked at all that the Sheik wanted to pay her for sex. Although she claimed she had never sold sex before, she readily accepted my invitation and said the only thing that worried her was how much the Sheik understood what she said, as she found his thick accent tricky to understand. Well done Malik, I thought to myself. Ms X went on to make it clear that she didn't want her agent to know about the private arrangement and asked if she could contact me directly. She also insisted that we should be very discreet with our choice of venue, suggesting that a large hotel would be best. She said that she would slot the Sheik into her busy work schedule and asked me to call her back after she had checked her diary.

Eventually Ms X confirmed she would be available in a hotel in the US on a Wednesday evening – at a price. She asked me if the Sheik would be willing to spend 40,000; once satisfied our Arab could afford the fat fee, she suggested a venue. What she had in mind was perfect for us as well – a brand new, big, anonymous hotel, where they provided generous suites and where she herself had not stayed before. She explained that she wouldn't want a room in her name, but would simply come straight up to the Sheik's suite. And just to make absolutely sure that we could afford her, Ms X sent a text to point out the 40,000 fee was in Sterling not dollars – which almost doubled the price! Was this going to be a problem? Well, no, thanks to Andy, it wasn't a problem. I had the bundles of cash spread out on the bed in our £1,500-a-night suite on the 49th floor, to photograph before handing it over.

The supermodel arrived, wearing a stylish black fur coat, a figure-hugging jade silk dress, black stiletto heels, and fishnet stockings. Jaws stood guard outside the door. Despite the astronomical fee involved I knew that this was at the end of the day just another hooker story and accordingly I treated Ms X no differently to a more ordinary prostitute. It's best to be blunt so there is no chance of any misunderstanding about the deal later: 'When you fuck him [the Sheik] would you like him to wear condoms or without? What's best?' To my surprise she didn't seem at all offended by my brusque behaviour and said that she'd prefer him to use a condom because she was in a relationship with someone – who didn't know what she was up to. Like some sort of modern-day Cinderella, only with looser morals and a higher price tag, she explained that she had to get home to greet her unsuspecting partner and that the hefty fee only covered her company from 6pm to midnight.

Ms X had told her companion that she was having drinks with friends – which was my cue to provide her with the glass of champagne she ordered. As we sat waiting for the Sheik, she had the lights dimmed down and turned on the CD player, making herself comfortable in the spectacular suite. However the suite was soon shamed by the amazing outfit she then put on after heading to the bathroom to change; she emerged wearing nothing but a series of leather straps arranged around her naked breasts and bottom – a sort of gownless, frontless, backless black evening strap. It wouldn't even have counted as lingerie. We both agreed it was a little bit naughty.

But then Ms X was all business, wanting to know when she would be paid. I handed her a down payment of $38,000 in wads of US banknotes; the remainder was to be paid at the end of the evening. She casually examined the cash before throwing it into her designer bag, declaring that she trusted me and wouldn't bother to count it. Besides which she was a pretty good judge of the amount of money she could hold in her hands – or elsewhere; she told me that she would make appearances at clubs in Italy – between 10,000–15,000 Euros just to be looked at and sign some autographs – and that she would then carry the cash about stuffed into her bra. I struggled to imagine a bra encasing her almost totally naked figure as she gestured with her hands to indicate just how far her bra jutted out once she'd shoved in over a week's worth of Euros. Coming back through US Customs had her heart pounding because she was carrying $60,000, she confided to me, and the Customs officers could have insisted she reveal what was inside if they became suspicious.

With every hooker we expose our brief is to get admissions that they are selling sex for cash; and then to try and get sexy photographs to publish in the paper. One of the many ruses I have developed over the years to capture camera-shy girls is the 'birthday scam'. I would tell the hooker that I had booked her as a special treat for my friend who was celebrating his birthday. I could then ask her exactly what she would and would not do in bed to please him, before asking her to come into the room holding a birthday cake to surprise my pal. I would then whip out a camera and quickly take a few pictures as she helped him blow out the candles; while most prostitutes simply won't pose for photographs, it would be too rude for the girl to refuse a souvenir snap with the birthday boy.

On one occasion I asked the waiter in a hotel restaurant to bring out the cake and handed him the camera to take the photo with the hooker as she sidled up to Conrad. The unsuspecting waiter took a few snaps while Conrad blew out the candles. It worked a treat until we got the next hooker in an hour later and used the same scam, and the same bemused waiter delivered yet another cake. 'You guys certainly know how to celebrate your birthdays!' he commented, looking at the scantily clad girl.

I employed the birthday scam on Ms X, believing that she would be reluctant to pose for photographs as she was turning up so discreetly for an escorting job. With that much money being handed over, we simply had to get a photograph of her in the room, so I told her it was the Sheik's birthday. I ordered a $175 birthday cake from room service and asked her to present it to him. She was happy to oblige by hiding behind a pillar to surprise our Sheik.

As the Sheik entered the suite, Ms X tossed back her mane of hair, jumped out from behind a pillar and performed a Marilyn Monroe-style dance routine. She wished him many happy returns by singing a sexy version of Marilyn's famous rendition of 'Happy Birthday Mr President!' She happily posed for photographs, and sang seductively, before planting a kiss on his cheek. And then she offered him a birthday treat he'd never forget, asking him if he preferred to watch – or if he enjoyed blowjobs.

❝But in all my years I had never come across a hooker who had demanded $10,000 an hour with a minimum spend of $60,000.❞

This served to focus not just the Sheik's mind somewhat but also got the supermodel thinking. She wanted toys, she said; things to play with, as she liked to be spanked, she liked to use dildos, all manner of items were described. She recited the address of an all-night sex shop she just happened to know was not too far from the hotel, and suggested I make my way down there to buy a little something to spice up the evening, while she carried on.

I walked out but only as far as next door, to settle down with Conrad and watch the feed from the video cameras installed in the Sheik's rooms. Depending on which way you look at it, things went up – or down – from there.

Ms X continued to play with herself while she talked to the Sheik. She said she was very naughty, and had recently joined the Mile-High

Club on an airplane by bending over in the toilet and persuading her companion to enjoy a quickie with her. The Sheik couldn't resist asking her whether she'd ever enjoyed a threesome with another woman, which – surprise, surprise – she had. But the girl had to be really pretty, she insisted, and she preferred dark girls to blondes, saying that she had an Italian friend who was sexy and shapely, and that the two of them occasionally put on a lesbian show together. All this touching of herself was beginning to work and Ms X became more and more excited, asking the Sheik to join in; which he declined. She explained to the Sheik that she played with herself often and that this aroused her so much; she invited the Sheik to playfully smack her bottom, which he did. As things began to hot up he told her that he had a bad back and so would not be able to perform.

This caused the supermodel to pause and offer him instead a relaxing back massage. She took off his shirt, telling him all the while that

she was like a private masseuse for him, that she was good at European-style massages and that her hands were strong so he would have to tell her if her massage was too much for him. As she rubbed cream into his chest, she appeared solicitous, asking him if everything was okay all the time, before confessing she was impressed with his physical condition.

The Sheik – Malik – was of course a yoga expert in real life, but Ms X was not to know this. So when he mentioned that he was interested in meditation and tantric sex, she giggled with delight, calling him her guru, asking him to show her sometime what this meant – which prompted her to start touching herself again. Groaning with pleasure she asked him if he'd seen the Austin Powers films, and started quoting from them, telling the Sheik how much she liked the British word 'shag'.

The conversation then turned to one of her favourite hang-outs, New York. When the Sheik asked about the drugs scene in Manhattan,

Ms X even bragged that she could readily get hold of cocaine there, saying that if she'd known the Sheik wanted some she might have helped out. In Europe, she boasted, she always used cocaine. She reeled off a seductive sentence in French. The Sheik asked her what she'd just said; she told him that she'd said she liked to be fucked hard, really hard, right up against the window, and to be spanked.

The Sheik swiftly turned the conversation back to drugs, and to her experiences on Ecstasy. She told him that she found it to be a very sensual drug, that it made her just want to touch everyone around her; that she never took lots but enjoyed a little Ecstasy, some cocaine, and some cannabis, especially in the summer. She liked to party, she told him, and then went over to her coat and pulled a small vibrator out of her pocket. She started to masturbate with it in front of the Sheik, proclaiming its virtues to him. Once again she asked what she could do for the Sheik, to make him feel as excited as she was.

Having secured enough evidence it was time for the traditional excuse to leave; the regular one about how the Sheik was staying in town because his uncle was very ill in hospital. Often it would set us all off in gales of laughter; with Ms X, though, we all managed to keep our composure as I walked back into the suite from the adjoining room. The Sheik quickly left the room escorted by Jaws, and I made sure I didn't look at either of them in case it triggered the usual hysteria.

Before leaving, Ms X agreed to meet the Sheik again. She also offered to arrange twenty models for a sex party in Dubai, declaring she could provide the Sheik with a couple of numbers, and that she would have to be discreet. Later she gave me a number for a Mr Fix-it in Los Angeles who she said would organize as many girls as we wanted. As she was about to leave, I asked her if she would like a lift home in our limo with blacked-out windows; she declined, again telling me that she would take a cab as it would be more discreet.

Unfortunately for her, she hadn't been discreet enough and her sordid sideline had been rumbled.

WANTED!

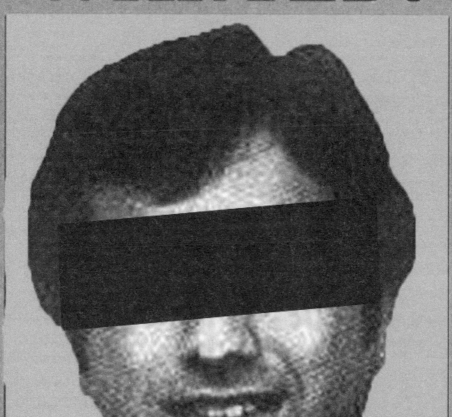

CHAPTER 21
SHEIK DOWN?

Threats are an occupational hazard for investigative journalists – villains don't like getting caught. And to be outsmarted by an undercover reporter who splashes details of their crimes across the pages of Britain's biggest-selling paper – often followed by a knock on the door by police – is hard to take. They invariably articulate their anger by making threats against the reporter who is only doing his job.

I regularly receive abusive phone calls, death threats, and from time to time have a price put on my head; but one threat I really didn't take seriously came from a man who I'd seen on Channel Four's *Celebrity Big Brother* dressed in a red leotard, crawling on the floor pretending to be a cat, purring and licking imaginary milk from actress Rula Lenska's hands. Rula rubbed the 'cream' from his greying 'whiskers' and stroked his head. The feline impersonator was no criminal but the Member of Parliament for Bethnal Green and Bow, George Galloway. He was threatening to circulate photographs of me because he felt that he had been unfairly targeted in one of my stings, which he had rumbled.

This was frustrating because Galloway was wrong, as he was not the subject of my investigation at all. I didn't think that he would carry out his threats – including putting up 'Wanted' posters with my photo around the House of Commons – but I should have taken him more seriously. This was a man whose judgement I knew to be suspect. In 1994 he stood in a Baghdad palace before Saddam Hussein and said: 'Sir, we salute your courage, your strength, your indefatigability.'

News International's legal manager Tom Crone rang me to tell me that he thought Galloway meant business, and that I should take legal action to prevent publication of the photo, which could have serious implications for my safety. A picture of me on the Internet would obviously affect my undercover work, but more importantly it would pose a serious risk to my life. With hundreds of people convicted as a result of my investigations, my photo would be a godsend to those who had vowed to kill me.

Tom instructed the Queen's solicitors Farrer & Co to act for me. At the High Court Justice Mitting granted a temporary order preventing publication of the old stolen passport photograph Galloway had got his hands on, probably from some Albanian website where it had popped up.

But I was disappointed when the judge indicated that my claim was 'more likely than not to fail' at a full trial. It would have cost a small fortune to argue the case in the High Court. I accepted defeat and waited for Galloway to rejoice in what he described as a 'very significant victory'.

The publicity-hungry MP organized a press conference at Portcullis House where he handed out two photographs of me – the old black-and-white passport photo and a picture taken from a video of me in my Sheik's robes. Galloway published them both on his Respect Party website, as well as circulating them to MPs and posting them to the Royal family. Galloway announced: 'I think people in public life should know what this man looks like. I call on the *News of the World* to announce his retirement. It's no longer acceptable for this man to be flying under the flag of the freedom of the press when he is in fact abusing the whole concept of freedom of the press.'

I wasn't going to mothball my Sheik's robes because of Galloway.

The background to my fateful dinner with Galloway at the Dorchester hotel was never made public. Once he'd gone public with his attack on me, we felt that for the paper to go ahead and print my investigation would look as if we were reacting to his mud-slinging, so we dropped it; which was a shame, as the original target deserved to be exposed.

It stemmed from an investigation into a prominent Muslim activist who rubbed shoulders with senior government figures – he had organized the televised 'Global Peace and Unity Event' in east London, at which guest speakers included the Lord Chancellor Lord Falconer, Mike O'Brien MP, the Solicitor General, and Met Police Assistant Commissioner Tarique Ghaffour – but was wanted for alleged acts of terrorism. Mohamed Ali Harrath, the CEO of the Islam Channel broadcast on Sky TV, is on Interpol's wanted list. His mugshots are accompanied by a list of alleged offences including 'terrorism, firearms, ammunitions, and forgery'. He was put on the list by the Tunisian government which Harrath and others have labelled an oppressive dictatorship. Harrath says the only reason he's on the list is his opposition to the Tunisian regime.

Harrath counted Abu Hamza, the cleric jailed for terrorism offences, as his close friend. The Tunisian, who lives in London, was sentenced to 56 years' imprisonment in his absence by a Tunis court on 16 June 2005, for his alleged involvement with an organization called the FIT (Tunisian Islamic Front). FIT has been branded a terrorist group, was said to have links with Al-Qaeda, and was co-founded by Harrath. Harrath was described by Tunis police as 'an intelligent, ruthless manipulator who is absolutely committed to terrorist acts'. Police spokesman Mohammed Abu-Said added: 'He is a very dangerous man who has continually evaded justice for his crimes.' Again, Harrath says the accusation is baseless and politically motivated.

I met Harrath posing as a wealthy Muslim businessman interested in setting up an Islamic TV channel in the subcontinent. Over a halal dinner at the Shezan restaurant in Knightsbridge, Harrath – who hid his surname by only using his first two names – laid bare his extremist views. 'There are 60, 70 Jewish MPs. After they get elected, they forget they are Labour, Conservative. They are Jewish. And nobody will dare to question them,' said Harrath, a slim man with a long beard. 'Lord Levy, he is a Zionist Jew, and he owns lots of property inside Palestine. Blair is a Zionist. He loves Zionists, he said it many times.'

Within minutes of meeting me and my colleague Alex, Harrath, in his forties, denied the Holocaust, claiming that only 200,000 Jews were massacred. 'Some people, they say 3,000. Because, before David Irving, Roget Garodet, the French philosopher, one of the founders of the Communist Party in France, [a] big thinker and one of the most respected philosophers of France; and he researched, and he went through the archives and he said the whole number of Jews in Europe in 1936, were 3 million. The entire population in Europe. How come, out of 3 million, 6 million were killed?' claimed Harrath. Asked how many people he thought were murdered in the Holocaust, Harrath replied: 'Maybe 200,000 or less.'

Harrath stressed the need to set up a monitoring group in Britain to target figures he perceived to be anti-Muslim. 'We need to have an institute to monitor Islamophobia. We need to know who our enemies are. We can start with just three people, we need an office,' he said. 'In the John Major government the Home Secretary and Foreign Secretary both of them were Jews, Michael Howard and Malcolm Rifkind. Howard is not his real name. He wasn't even born in Britain. Romania. And he was the Home Secretary.' He also claimed that the current Tory leader, David Cameron, was also anti-Islam. 'He is anti-Muslim, proper anti-Muslim and he has a big chance if the Labour Party don't sort out themselves.' Harrath even lashed out at the chairman of the Commission for Racial Equality, Trevor Phillips. 'He said Muslims who want to implement Sharia (Islamic way of life), they can leave. And this is a black coming from Jamaica. So if you want to become British, you must attack Muslims. So we must make it nightmare for them. So we have to make it hell. Nightmare.'

Harrath condemned the 7/7 atrocity but claimed that suicide bombings in the right circumstances were justified in Islam. 'The Palestinian population and the Jews are at war. And officially all Arabs are at war with Israel,' said Harrath. 'I don't want to give a *fatwah* on it, but that is what is happening. I have seen the scholars. Many scholars, they sanction it, they said "fine". And I don't see anyone with credibility who opposed that. They call it self-sacrifice, in jurisprudence, it is not suicide. Suicide is when you kill yourself to get rid of your problems. But someone who kills himself in order to kill another is not.'

Harrath lives in west London but says that he would not want to be a British citizen. 'I am not British citizen, and I don't want to be. I have five kids here. I have indefinite leave to remain, and they told me many times, why don't you apply?'

Amid all the politics, Harrath tried to interest me in investing in various schemes in Bosnia. Harrath told how he had lived in Bosnia as a charity worker and had been granted Bosnian nationality. 'In Bosnia there are a few projects which you can invest today and get the revenue tomorrow basically, but there are other projects which can be long term.' He wanted me to invest in MOT garages in Bosnia, claiming he personally owned two in Tuzla. He also suggested I buy electricity plants, shopping malls, hotels, and a telecommunications network in Bosnia and offered to put me in touch with his contacts.

When I eventually confronted Harrath, he vehemently denied any involvement with extremists. Although he admitted he had co-founded the FIT he claimed it was a peaceful organization. 'I may be sentenced to 300 years, maybe 500 years, I don't care. The charges are false coming from a dictatorship regime. What do you define terrorist, back in these terrorist regimes, if you oppose them you are a terrorist.' He confirmed that an extradition request had been made for him but had been disregarded. 'Of course I was a co-founder of FIT when I was back home. It has nothing to do with terrorism. There is a dictatorship regime, it is well known. I have no allegations against me other than the Tunisian regime. 100 per cent I oppose the Tunisian regime.'

He continued: 'FIT is a peaceful organization which doesn't exist anymore. I have never been involved in any terrorist activities. All I know the Zionist lobby in this country, since I started defending the rights of Muslims here, they have been frustrated and unfortunately are using someone like you.'

Harrath, who later ran a live phone-in on his Islam Channel asking callers whether my photo should be shown on TV, also felt a little bit guilty for introducing me to his friend George Galloway. A few days earlier, when he was hoping that I would invest millions in his various projects, Harrath was keen for me to meet Galloway to help boost his credentials.

A dinner meeting was lined up for 25 March 2006 at the Dorchester hotel in Park Lane, where Galloway breezed in wearing a long grey overcoat, grey suit, and puffing on a fat Cuban cigar. He'd just finished presenting his radio show on talkSPORT radio. I was wearing a blue silk *shalwar kameez* and a black jacket. Alex and Harrath were also at the dinner table. Galloway ordered walnut and raisin bread, and turbot for his main course. Later he said that he had almost immediately become suspicious of his host: 'It was so heavy-handed that I immediately smelled a rat.'

The MP and I have different memories of the dinner conversation that followed – but my memory is refreshed by virtue of the covert tape recording I made.

If he felt that I was a fake, why then did he go on to attack our war heroes, comparing them to suicide bombers? He claimed that British soldiers awarded the VC posthumously are no different from Palestinians who sacrifice their lives in suicide attacks. 'A heroic soldier who is posthumously awarded the Victoria Cross could be described as a suicide operation because he knew that he was sacrificing his life when he took the military action that he did. We call him a hero and we give him posthumous awards,' said Galloway. 'Many soldiers don't run away when they know that if they stay they are going to die, they think that it's their duty to sacrifice themselves. Palestinians have few alternatives but to fight violently with whatever weapons they can.'

The Respect Party MP continued to suggest that the suicide bombers were the same as soldiers: 'They are also armed combatants. So there is a lot of hypocrisy talked about this question. A suicide bomber and stealth bomber both deliver the same death. One is ordered by men in suits, and the other is ordered by men without suits, the only difference.'

Galloway continued: 'Palestinians are entitled to take up arms to fight for the liberation of their country. This is a legal right. Their country is illegally occupied. They're entitled to do it. The issue of what kind of military struggle they wage is, first of all, essentially a matter for them, and secondly, the only moral question that comes in is what the target is. Not the form of the attack, but who the target of the attack is. In other words, a suicide operation against Israeli occupation soldiers is, within the terms of the laws of the war, entirely legitimate. A suicide bomb attack on a small group of small children from kindergarten is entirely immoral.'

Reg Keys – whose son Lance Corporal Thomas Keys died with five other Red Caps of 156 Provost Company Royal Military Police in June 2003 in Al-Majar Al-Kabir in Iraq – was angered by Galloway's words. 'I find George Galloway's remarks very offensive,' said Mr Keys. 'Suicide bombers have a choice. They choose to go out and kill innocent people but my son didn't have a choice, he was following orders and he had no intention of killing innocent people.'

Galloway said he believed I was a wealthy businessman interested in helping Islam. He claimed that the best way to further his message was through the media and suggested I invest in a new radio channel so he could air his fanatical views. Galloway told how he had tried to persuade an Arab Prince to buy the Express newspaper group, but his advice had been ignored and it was now in the hands of a 'Jewish pornographer'.

'I spoke to a Prince in Qatar who had just donated a Boeing 747 to Saddam Hussein. Now I don't know the cost of a Boeing 747, but I guessed, it was a second-hand one, I guessed that maybe £100 million would do it. At that time the *Daily Express*, the *Sunday Express*, and the *Daily Star*, three mass-circulation English newspapers, were for sale for £100 million, exactly the same price as this airplane,' said Galloway.

'At the moment there are two people in for it. One was the Hinduja brothers who were the crooked Hindus who were on trial in India for the Bofors scandal, and the other was the Jewish pornographer Richard Desmond.'

'I said to the Prince, instead of giving this airplane to Saddam Hussein who can't fly anywhere, if you had bought these three newspapers – and they're still for sale, you can still buy them – you would have transformed the landscape of British media ownership. He didn't buy it, Richard Desmond bought it and now the Express group is the most anti-Muslim, anti-Arab, anti-liberty newspaper group in the land.'

As Galloway carried on talking, I couldn't help but feel as if he had out-Sheiked me. He repeatedly used Islamic terms and waved a *tasbee* – the Muslim prayer beads – while I'd not thought to bring mine to a dinner meeting. I used my *shalwar kameez* as a disguise, a distraction; I wondered what Galloway was doing with his Muslim accessories?

Meanwhile the MP was still holding forth. 'If somebody came along to me now and said we could provide financial backing, what do you think the best thing to do, I would say we should set up a radio station. We don't have money for a TV station.' Galloway claimed to have 2.2 million listeners to his radio show on talkSPORT. 'In the last three weeks, I've only been doing it for three weeks, [I've added] a new audience to the traditional Saturday night talk radio audience which is generally right wing, generally white, generally blue collar. Working class. Bit xenophobic. Bit Islamophobic. Now I'm attracting Internet users and *Guardian* readers and Muslims and so on, and I am trying to build these two audiences, trying to persuade the existing audience but also attract a more sympathetic one. Touch wood it's going well. Like the station I'm working for, talkSPORT, we need a talkSPORT for progressive people. A talkSPORT that's an anti-war talkSPORT, that's an anti-Islamophobia talkSPORT.'

However, to his credit, when the issue of sponsoring MPs was raised, Galloway pointed out that foreign funding is forbidden. 'Not from foreign sources, no, it's not allowed. Any foreign money is completely forbidden, and rightly so. It was massively abused by the existing parties.' He then went on to speculate that a senior figure in British political life was supported by Chinese billionaires.

Galloway later claimed that by the time the issue of party funding was raised he was convinced that he was talking to the Fake Sheik: 'I knew by this time really, that this was some kind of set-up, probably the

News of the World, probably the Fake Sheik. Robustly, leaning forward as it were, speaking into his hidden microphone, which I knew would be somewhere about his presence, I made it clear that this was completely illegal, and should be completely illegal and had corrupted the political process in Britain, and that it was completely out of the question,' he claimed. However, if he knew by then that the Fake Sheik was recording him it was odd that the lengthy conversation carried on.

Galloway claimed Zionists in Britain posed a threat to the Muslim world. 'Don't forget that you don't have to be a Jew to be a Zionist. In fact most Zionists are not Jews. George Bush is a big Zionist but he's not a Jew and he probably doesn't even like Jews as most right-wing people don't,' he said. 'Tony Blair announced himself that he was Israel's best friend, he said that on 20 March 2005. Now Gordon Brown who will be the next Prime Minister, he's even more Zionist than Blair. His father was one of the pioneers of Zionism.'

But it wasn't only 'Zionists' who felt the force of Galloway's scorn that evening, it was the very people who regarded themselves as his fellow travellers, even his supporters. Muslims who loyally stood by Galloway and helped him win his seat came under attack. 'Some of these mosque committees will sell their soul for a few extra car parking places in the mosque and they say "we have to back Labour, we know that they killed 100,000 Iraqis, we know they killed 30,000 Afghanis, but they've promised to give us planning permission for an extra four car parking places at the mosque," it's as cheap as that,' said Galloway. And then it was the Muslim MPs who didn't support his views that he had a go at: 'The presence of these so-called Muslim MPs is a good example that colour, ethnicity, professed religion is not the important thing. What's the point in electing a quote unquote Muslim MP if his job is to vote for the slaughter of other Muslims? To apologize for it and to justify it? One of them in particular in Birmingham, Khalid Mahmood, he even allowed non-Muslim government ministers to write articles defending the war in Afghanistan and Iraq in his name for the English newspapers. The *Observer* ran two pieces from him supporting both these wars in his name and it turned out it was Dennis

McShane, the Foreign Office minister, who had in fact written the articles.'

He claimed that the Labour MP for Perry Bar had been rewarded for
his loyalty. 'And it's worked in the sense that he has the smallest
foothill of government. He's an unpaid parliamentary private secretary. So he's not a minister, he doesn't get a salary, but he gets a badge
to wear as a small petty official.'

After chocolate dessert Galloway – who was described as 'a C-list
MP with an A-list ego' by Post Office Minister and MP for Poplar and
Canning Town, Jim Fitzpatrick – confided how he was considering
standing as an MEP when he stands down as an MP. 'I might stand for
the European parliament this time for a London constituency or I
might [for] another parliamentary constituency, but I won't stand
again in Bethnal Green.'

After dessert Galloway enjoyed a coffee and posed for a picture
with myself and my minder Jaws – clearly he wasn't troubled that he
was with the Fake Sheik, as he then went on to embrace me before he
left, parting with *Salaam Aleikum*, an Islamic farewell.

Within a couple of days Galloway contacted the Commissioner of
the Metropolitan Police, Sir Ian Blair, bleating that he had been the victim of a 'blatant and outrageous attempt to suborn a Member of Parliament'. He also asked Parliament to investigate my methods arguing
that my conduct was 'surely illegal' and amounted to an 'abuse of press
freedom'. It wasn't. Thankfully Media Minister Dick Caborn leapt to
my defence. Caborn reminded Galloway that investigative journalists
had 'uncovered a great deal of crime and impropriety'. And he said that
although he understood 'the anger and concern of those who find
themselves on the receiving end of this sort of behaviour, and who
have committed no crime or impropriety, that is part of the price that
we pay for our independent press'.

EPILOGUE

 It's as an investigative journalist that I shall continue to work. The Sheik's outfit has served me well, but it's not the only disguise I've used in the past and it won't be the only one I use in the future. As I did after each case, I had my robes dry-cleaned and pressed, ready for my next investigation; but the smugglers, and drug-dealers, and baby-sellers, and paedophiles, and hypocrites, and crooks, and all those whose conduct I examine should be wary. It may not be a Sheik that they sit next to in a restaurant, or in a hotel suite, it may not be the Sheik that they expose themselves to, but it could well still be me. The Fake Sheik is still in business.

PICTURE CREDITS

In order from top to bottom of page:

PLATES

Page 1 – From Afghanistan ... To Albania (Conrad Brown)

Page 2 – Kidnap Rescue (Mazher Mahmood)

Page 3 – Galloway on the warpath (Conrad Brown)

Page 4 – Paul Burrell & Sven (Conrad Brown)

Page 5 – Toon on Fire (Conrad Brown and *News of the World*)

Page 6 – 'Go Jerry! Spring Loaded!' (Conrad Brown)

Page 7 – Sophie and Jodie: Wild Things (Conrad Brown)

Page 8 – Faria – Caught Offside! (Conrad Brown and Paul Ashton, courtesy of *News of the World*)

Page 9 – Princess and the Cats (Conrad Brown)

Page 10 – Michelle Collins and the Sheik (Bradley Page, courtesy of *News of the World*)

Page 11 – Kidnap Attempt on Beckhams (Bradley Page, courtesy of *News of the World*)

Page 12 – Working Undercover (Geoff Thompson, and Conrad Brown)

Page 13 – Honest James (Paul Ashton, courtesy of *News of the World*, and Conrad Brown)

Page 14 – Harry's Man: The Cunning Doctor (Jamie Jones and Conrad Brown)

Page 15 – The Faces of Evil (Courtesy of *News of the World*, and Conrad Brown)

Page 16 – Marriage Scams (Conrad Brown)

CHAPTER OPENERS

Page 1 – Ready to Sheik the World (Conrad Brown)

Page 11 – Toes and the Toon (Steve Burton, courtesy of *News of the World*)

Page 29 – The Porn Stars, the TV Host, and the Hitman (Conrad Brown)

Page 49 – Dishing up the Evidence (PA Photos)

PAGE FILLERS

Champagne bottle (PA Photos)

Cash dollars (Conrad Brown)

Cash sterling (PA Photos)

Guns (PA Photos)

British Passport (Conrad Brown)

ENDPAPERS

All pictures Conrad Brown. *Except: EastEnders* Pub: Bradley Page, courtesy of *News of the World*; Sophie Anderton: Brian Roberts, courtesy of *News of the World*; Maz with helicopter: Kerry Davis, courtesy of *News of the World*; Asian Wedding Fixer being Arrested: Rob Todd, courtesy of *News of the World*; Beckham Kidnap Arrest: Bradley Page, courtesy of *News of the World*; Faria Alam: Paul Ashton, courtesy of *News of the World*; Conrad in woman's veil: Mazher Mahmood

INDEX